IELTS *Masterclass*

Student's Book

Simon Haines

Peter May

OXFORD
UNIVERSITY PRESS

Unit and Theme	Reading	Listening	Speaking
1 **Cultural differences** pages 9–20	*The pursuit of happiness* Skills: reading for gist, unfamiliar vocabulary IELTS practice: short-answer questions, sentence and summary completion	*Applying to study abroad* Section 1 IELTS practice: note and form completion	*Meeting people* Skills: describing your origins IELTS practice: Part 1 familiar discussion
2 **Conflicting interests** pages 21–32	*The other population crisis* Skills: paragraph summaries IELTS practice: matching headings	*Congestion charging scheme* Section 2 IELTS practice: note and sentence completion	*Changing places* Skills: speaking from notes IELTS practice: Part 2 extended speaking
3 **Fitness and health** pages 33–44	*The power of nothing* Skills: text structure, finding evidence IELTS practice: Yes/No/Not given, True/False/Not given	*University sports centre* Section 3 IELTS practice: matching lists, classification	*What do you really know about food?* Skills: giving reasons IELTS practice: Part 3 topic discussion
4 **The arts** pages 45–56	*When is a room not a room?* Skills: style, text structure, using question stems IELTS practice: multiple-choice questions, short-answer questions, global multiple-choice	*Musical instruments* Section 4 IELTS practice: labelling a diagram, note completion	*Arts events* Skills: getting started IELTS practice: Part 2 extended speaking
5 **Work and business** pages 57–68	*The great work myth* Skills: reading for gist, key words IELTS practice: sentence completion, summary completion	*Job enquiry* Section 1 IELTS practice: multiple-choice questions, labelling a map	*Jobs* Skills: describing an occupation IELTS practice: Part 1 familiar discussion
6 **Education** pages 69–80	*The education gender gap* Skills: scanning, identifying opinions IELTS practice: matching, sentence completion	*University clubs and societies* Section 2 IELTS practice: short-answer questions, sentence completion	*Learning styles* Skills: personal reactions IELTS practice: Part 2 extended speaking
7 **Science** pages 81–92	*Stars in their eyes* Skills: description schemes, reading for gist IELTS practice: labelling a diagram, multiple-answer questions, True/False/Not given	*Ethics in science* Section 3 IELTS practice: multiple-choice questions, multiple-answer questions	*Moral dilemmas* Skills: advantages and disadvantages IELTS practice: Part 3 topic discussion

H.W — 137—139

Language for writing	Writing	Help yourself	Unit and Theme
Describing data Similarities	*Cultural data* Skills: accurate description, selecting main features IELTS practice: task 1	How to use the *Help yourself* pages	**1** **Cultural differences** pages 9–20
Consecutive noun phrases Avoiding repetition	*Environment issues* Skills: taking a view and developing it IELTS practice: task 2	Global issues	**2** **Conflicting interests** pages 21–32
Relative clauses	*Health issues* Skills: organizing ideas, using organizing expressions IELTS practice: task 2	Vocabulary	**3** **Fitness and health** pages 33–44 H.W
Choosing tenses	*Spending on the arts* Skills: describing trends, describing figures IELTS practice: task 1	Reading more widely H.W	**4** **The arts** pages 45–56
Comparative and superlative forms	*Advertising* Skills: comparing data IELTS practice: task 1	Word formation	**5** **Work and business** pages 57–68
-ing forms and infinitives	*Student finance* Skills: introductions IELTS practice: task 2	Thinking skills	**6** **Education** pages 69–80
Passive forms	*Scientific processes* Skills: sequencing IELTS practice: task 1	English spelling	**7** **Science** pages 81–92

3

A guide to the IELTS modules

IELTS is divided into four modules, taken in the order below.

Listening
(30 minutes)

In each section you will hear a recording. The four sections become progressively more difficult and each recording is played once only. There are pauses to divide the recording into smaller parts. For each part you need to answer a series of questions of one type. References to examples of each question type are given in the table.

Section	Number of items	Text type	Task types
1	10	social or transactional conversation (2 speakers)	completing notes, table, sentences, diagram, flow chart or summary (page 15)
2	10	talk or speech on social needs (1 speaker)	short-answer questions (page 75)
3	10	conversation in educational context (2–4 speakers)	various kinds of multiple-choice questions (page 62)
4	10	talk or lecture on topic of general interest (1 speaker)	labelling parts of a diagram (page 51) matching lists (page 39) sentence completion (page 27)

Academic Reading
(60 minutes)

The three passages contain 2000–2750 words in total and become progressively more difficult, but they are always suitable for non-specialist readers. If any technical terms are used, they will be explained in a glossary. References to examples of each question type are given in the table.

Passage	Number of items	Text type	Task types
1	11–15	topics of general interest	various kinds of multiple-choice questions (page 48)
2	11–15	non-specialist articles or extracts from books, journals, magazines and newspapers	short-answer questions (page 12) sentence completion (page 12) classification (page 142)
3	11–15	one, at least, has detailed logical argument	matching headings with paragraphs or sections of text (page 24) completing notes, sentences, tables, summary, diagram or flow chart (page 12) matching lists/phrases (page 72) locating information with paragraphs (page 144) true/false/not given (text information) (page 36) yes/no/not given (writer's views) (page 36)

Academic Writing
(60 minutes)

There is no choice of task, either in Part 1 or 2, so you must be prepared to write about any topic. However, the topics in the exam are of general interest and you do not need to be an expert to write about them. References to examples of each task type are given in the table.

Task	Time	Format	Task types
1	20 minutes	150-word report, describing or explaining a table or diagram (page 18)	presenting information based on: • data, e.g. bar charts, line graph, table • a process/procedure in various stages • an object, event or series of events
2	40 minutes	250-word essay, responding to written opinion/problem (page 30)	presenting and/or discussing: • your opinions • solutions to problems • evidence, opinions and implications • ideas or arguments

Speaking
(11–14 minutes)

You will be interviewed, on your own, by one Examiner, and the conversation will be recorded on audio cassette. The three-part structure of the interview is always the same, although the topics will vary from candidate to candidate. References to examples of each main part are given in the table.

Part	Time	Format	Task types
1	4–5 minutes	familiar discussion (page 16)	• Introduction, ID check • You answer questions about familiar topics: yourself, your home/family, job/studies, and interests.
2	3–4 minutes	extended speaking (page 28)	• You are given a topic verbally and on a card. You have a minute to prepare a talk. • You speak for 1–2 minutes on the topic, e.g. a person, place, object or event. • You answer one or two follow-up questions.
3	4–5 minutes	topic discussion (page 40)	• You answer verbal questions, discussing more abstract ideas linked to the topic of Part 2.

Twenty tips for IELTS success

1   In Listening, use the example at the beginning of the first section to familiarize yourself with the sound, the situation, and the speakers.

2   Keep listening until the recording stops, looking only at the questions that relate to the part being played.

3   There are often pauses in the recording between different sections. Use these to prepare for the next set of questions.

4   Answer Listening questions in the order they appear on the Question Paper. Remember that they normally follow the order of the information in the recording.

5   At the end of the recording you have some time to transfer your answers to the Answer Sheet. Check your grammar and spelling as you do so.

6   In Academic Reading, begin by going quickly through each passage to identify features such as the topic, the style, the likely source, the writer's purpose and the intended reader.

7   As you read, don't try to understand the precise meaning of every word or phrase. You don't have time, and those parts of the text might not be tested anyway.

8   Reading tasks sometimes have an example answer. If this is the case, study it and decide why it is correct.

9   Some tasks require you to use words from the text in the answer; in others you should use your own words. Check the instructions carefully.

10 The instructions may also include a word limit, e.g. Use no more than three words. Keep to this by avoiding unnecessary words in your answer.

11 In Academic Writing, you must always keep to the topic set. Never try to prepare sections of text before the exam.

12 Keep to the suggested timing: there are more marks possible for Task 2 than Task 1.

13 Organize and link your ideas and sentences appropriately, using a wide range of language and showing your ability (in Task 2) to discuss ideas and express opinions.

14 If you write less than 150 words in Task 1 or less than 250 in Task 2 you will lose marks, but there is no maximum number of words for either.

15 When you plan your essay, allow plenty of time at the end to check your work.

16 In Speaking, don't try to give a prepared speech, or talk about a different topic from the one you are asked to discuss.

17 Always speak directly to the Examiner, not to the recording equipment.

18 Whenever you reply 'Yes' or 'No' to the Examiner's questions, add more details to your answer. In each case, aim to explain at least one point.

19 Remember that you are not being tested on your general knowledge but on your ability to communicate effectively.

20 Organize and link your ideas and sentences appropriately, talking clearly at normal speed and using a wide range of structures and vocabulary.

1 Cultural differences

1 Discuss these questions with other students.

  a Who are the people in the photos and where do they live?
  b What clues about the people and their lifestyles can you see in the photos?

2 🎧 Listen to four quiz questions about these cultures and choose one of the answers A, B, C or D for each question. Compare your answers with other students.

3 🎧 Listen again and check your answers.

4 Discuss these questions with another student.

  a What does the word 'culture' mean to you?
  b Read the definition of culture on the right. How is it similar and how is it different from your definition?
  c What customs and beliefs have you inherited from previous generations?
  d Do you think your character and behaviour are typical of the culture you belong to? If so, how?

> The system of shared beliefs, values, customs, and behaviours that the members of society use to cope with their world and with one another, and that are transmitted from generation to generation through learning.

Reading

1 Discuss these questions with other students.

a   What information does the bar chart on page 11 contain?
b   Make true statements about these countries.

   Nigeria   Romania   USA/Mexico   Australia/Russia

2 Discuss these questions.

a   What factors could explain why the populations of some countries are happier than the populations of others?
b   If your country is listed in the bar chart, do you think it is a true reflection of the people of your country? If it is not shown, where would you place it on the chart?

Reading for gist

> **note**
>
> Read texts quickly to get a general idea of what they are about.

3 Read the text *The pursuit of happiness* and say which of these general topics it covers.

* the growth in the academic study of happiness
* reasons for being unhappy
* the distinction between happiness and overall 'satisfaction' with life
* links between wealth, consumerism and happiness
* how people's happiness affects the jobs they do
* cultural attitudes towards happiness

4 Which parts of the text deal with the four topics you have identified?

The pursuit of happiness

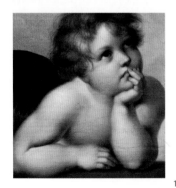

How are we supposed to find happiness? Through good works and helping people? By finding religion or discovering the joys of 5 downshifting? Whatever strategy you choose, where you live might make a difference. The latest global analysis of happiness and satisfaction levels shows that the most 'satisfied' people tend to live in 10 Latin America, Western Europe and North America, whereas Eastern Europeans are the least satisfied.

It is not the first time such international league tables have been drawn up. What is 15 new is how experts and politicians are taking such data increasingly seriously. Over the past decade, the study of happiness, formerly the preserve of philosophers, therapists and gurus, has become a bona fide discipline. It 20 even has its own journal, the *Journal of Happiness Studies*. As a result, government policy advisers are getting interested, and politicians are using the research as the basis for new strategies.

25 What above all else has made systematic study possible is data gathered from hundreds of surveys measuring happiness across different cultures, professions, religions, and socio-economic groups. 30 Researchers can investigate the impact of money and inequality; they could explore, for example, how much difference money makes to a person's happiness after their basic material needs have been met, and whether 35 inequality in wealth and status is as important a source of dissatisfaction as we might think. 'It is an exciting area,' says Ruut Veenhoven, editor-in-chief of the *Journal of Happiness Studies*. 'We can now show which 40 behaviours are risky as far as happiness goes,

'We should eventually be able to show
what kind of lifestyle suits what kind of person.'

in the same way medical research shows what is bad for our health. We should eventually be able to show what kind of lifestyle suits what kind of person.'

While it is tempting to hold up those nations that report the highest levels of happiness as a model for others to follow, this may be unwise. For one thing, the word 'happiness' has no precise equivalent in some languages. Another complication is that 'satisfaction' is not quite the same thing as 'happiness'. When asked how happy they are, people tend to consider first their current state. To get a better idea, researchers ask people to take a step back and consider how satisfied they are with their lives overall and how meaningful they judge their lives to be.

Comparisons between countries also need to be treated cautiously. Different cultures value happiness in very different ways. In individualistic western countries, happiness is often seen as a reflection of personal achievement. Being unhappy implies that you have not made the most of your life. Eunkook Mark Suh at Yonsei University in Seoul thinks this pressure to be happy could lead people to over-report how happy they feel. Meanwhile, in the more collectivist nations of Asia, people have a more fatalistic attitude towards happiness. According to Suh, 'One of the consequences of such an attitude is that you don't have to feel inferior or guilty about not being very happy.' Indeed, in Asian cultures the pursuit of happiness is often frowned on, which in turn could lead people to under-report.

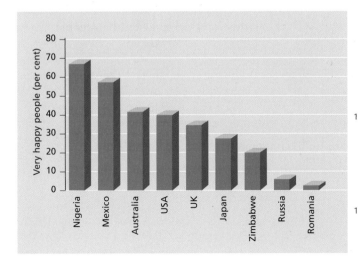

How satisfied a person is with their life also depends on how successfully they adhere to their particular cultural standard. In Japan, for instance, satisfaction may come from fulfilling family expectations and meeting social responsibilities. So, while in the US it is perfectly appropriate to pursue your own happiness, in Japan you are more likely to find happiness by not pursuing it directly.

One of the most significant observations to come from research findings is that in industrialised nations, happiness has not risen with average incomes. A growing number of researchers are putting this down to consumerism, claiming that the desire for material goods, which has increased with average income, is a 'happiness suppressant'. One study, by Tim Kasser at Knox College, Illinois, found that young adults who focus on money, image and fame tend to be more depressed and suffer more physical symptoms such as headaches. Kasser believes that since nothing about materialism can help you find happiness, governments should discourage it and instead promote things that can. For instance, they could support businesses that allow their employees plenty of time off to be with their families, whereas advertising could be classified as a form of pollution and could be taxed. 'Advertisements have become more sophisticated,' says Kasser. 'They try to tie their message to people's psychological needs. But it is a false link. It is toxic.'

These days even hard-headed economists tend to agree that the key to making people happier is to shift the emphasis from economic well-being to personal development, and to discourage the pursuit of social status. This last point is crucial, believes Richard Layard from the London School of Economics, since the pursuit of social status does not make society as a whole any happier. Motivating people through the quest for rank 'condemns as many to fail as to succeed – not a good formula for raising human happiness,' says Layard.

In view of these findings, it seems that governments would do well to worry about the happiness of their electorate. There could be dangers, however. Paradoxically, by striving too hard to climb the global happiness rankings, governments are in danger of turning the pursuit of happiness into yet another competitive quest for status – just what researchers have shown is a sure path to making people miserable. ●

Unfamiliar vocabulary

5 Read the first three paragraphs of the text again and underline any words that are unfamiliar to you. Compare ideas with another student. Can you understand the general meaning of these paragraphs, despite not understanding the words you have underlined?

IELTS practice

Questions 1–3: Short-answer questions
Answer these questions with words from the text, using no more than THREE words for each answer.

1 According to the text, what could influence your level of contentment? ~~line 6 pe~~
~~where you Wealth and status Good works and helpful~~

2 Which group of people is interested in the practical implications of the research into happiness? *Govt Policy advisor / Politician*

3 Which two factors are researchers able to study in their attempt to find reasons why some people are dissatisfied? *Inequality in wealth and status*

Questions 4–6: Sentence completion
Complete these sentences with words from the text, using no more than THREE words for each answer.

4 Happiness represents *Personal achievement* in the minds of people from western countries.

5 One of the implications of the Asian attitude is that being unhappy does not make individuals feel *guilty or inferior*.

6 An individual's level of satisfaction is partly determined by how closely they conform to their own *Cultural standard*

Questions 7–10: Summary completion
Complete the summary below. Choose no more than TWO words from the text for each answer.

Researchers have found that in developed countries happiness has not increased in line with (7) *average incomes*. In their opinion, the fact that people have more money feeds their obsession with buying things and this acts as a (8) *happiness suppresant*. Their theory is illustrated by the fact that there is a higher than average incidence of mental problems among (9) *young adults* who have materialistic concerns. There is also general agreement that people would be happier if they concentrated on (10) *personal development* rather than their financial or social status.

Exploration

6 Work with other students. Rank the following factors according to how much you think they contribute to people's happiness.

family life   wealth
social network   accommodation
job satisfaction   health

Are there any other factors you would add to this list?

7 What are the opposites of these adjectives? In some cases, you can add a prefix or a suffix; in other cases you may need to think of a completely different word.

*Un*satisfied (l.9)   collectivist (l.61) *individualist*
un risky (l.40)   inferior (l.64) *superior*
unwise (l.46)   significant (l.74)
im precise (l.47)   *Non* competitive (l.106)
n meaningful (l.52)   *Un* miserable (l.107)
less

8 Refer to the text to find answers to these questions.

a What do you understand by the verbs 'over-report' (l.60), and 'under-report' (l.66)? What other verbs do you know with these prefixes?
b What do you understand by the word 'consumerism' (l.77)? What other words do you know that end with *–ism*? What general meanings does this suffix have?
c Use a dictionary to check the difference in meaning between these compound adjectives: 'hard-headed' (l.92), 'hard-hearted', 'hard-pressed', 'hard-nosed'.

9 Match the words on the left with those on the right to form commonly occurring verb–noun combinations. Then check your answers by finding them in the text.

Example: *to meet someone's needs*

to draw up   data
to fulfil   expectations
to gather   league tables
to meet   someone's needs
to suffer   symptoms

10 Use the verb–noun combinations above to complete these sentences. You will need to change the form of the verbs.

a In their investigations, social scientists ...... from many different sources.
b Even businesses which make substantial profits can fail to ...... the ...... of the financial markets.
c Increasing numbers of people in the developed world are ...... the ...... of hay fever and other allergies.
d Education authorities in Britain ...... annual ...... showing which are the best and worst schools in their area.
e Research is currently being undertaken to look at how universities could ...... the learning ...... of individual students.

Listening

Section 1

In Section 1, you will hear two people exchanging practical information of some kind.

Orientation

1 Discuss these questions with other students.

  a Which countries do you think the photos were taken in? Check your answer on p177.

  b Which of the countries shown in the photos would you
      find most interesting?
      feel most at home in?
      experience the greatest culture shock in?

  c Why do people move from their own country to live in other countries? Think of as many reasons as you can.

  d If you had a completely free choice, which other country would you choose to live in?

Predicting answer types

2 Look at the form on page 15 containing items 1–6 and answer these questions.

  a In general, what sort of information will the speakers be discussing?

  b Which answers will be in numbers? What kinds of numbers are required, e.g. a sum of money, or a distance?

  c Which answers will be in words? What kinds of words are required. e.g. nouns, adjectives?

IELTS Practice

Questions 1–6: Note completion

🎧 Complete the form below. Write no more than three words and/or a number for each answer.

note

Read questions carefully in advance, and think about the type of information required.

Notes on University 2
Subject: International Business
Qualification: MIB

Entry requirements
Educational qualifications   **1** ....
English language   **2** .... in IELTS or higher.

Course hours: **3** .... per week.
Extended stay: at the start of the **4** ....

Course dates

Semester 1:   27th September to 22nd January.
Semester 2:   7th February to **5** .... th May.

Course content

Study of **6** ...., in particular how they are managed and
    their changing external context.

Questions 7–10: Form completion

🎧 Complete the form below. Write no more than three words and/or a number for each answer.

Phone enquiries
Purpose of call: Information about MIB course

Caller details

Name: Javed Iqbal

Home address: Aga Khan Road, Shalimar **7** ...., Islamabad, Pakistan

First degree

Subject: **8** ....
Class: **9** ....

University: Islamabad University

First language/s: **10** ....

Exploration   **3** Discuss these statements with other students.

’With so many people moving to other countries to work or study, culture shock is becoming a thing of the past.’

’It is the social rather than the physical environment which disorientates people most when they move to another country.’

Speaking

Orientation

1 Discuss these questions with another student.

a   How do you generally feel when you meet people for the first time?

b   What are the things you want to know about people when you first meet them?

c   Are there topics you could not talk comfortably about with people you have just met? Are there taboo subjects in your culture?

Describing your origins

2 🎧 Listen to the speakers 1–5 talking about the places they come from. Match each recording with one of questions a–e.

a   How could your town or village be improved?

b   Is there anything you dislike about your home town or village?

c   What do you like most about your home town or village?

d   What is there in your town or village that visitors would find interesting?

e   What kind of place is your home town or village?

3 🎧 Listen to the speakers again. Make a note of the phrases they use to introduce their answers.

4 Work in pairs, if possible with someone who you don't know well. Ask and answer questions 2 a–e, starting with some of the phrases you heard the speakers use.

Everyday questions

5 Imagine you have joined a new course. Use these question beginnings to write some questions of your own about the topics listed below.

Can you tell me something about … ?
What's your favourite … ?
What do you (most) like / dislike about … ?
What sort of things do you do …?

spare time	family and / or friends
travel and / or holidays	learning English
food	your country

> **note**
>
> Expect questions on a range of everyday topics. Always answer the questions you are asked, not similar questions you may have prepared or learnt by heart.

IELTS practice

Part 1: Familiar discussion
In Speaking Part 1, you may be asked questions about topics like these. Work in pairs or groups to ask and answer questions. Add extra questions where appropriate.

Language for writing

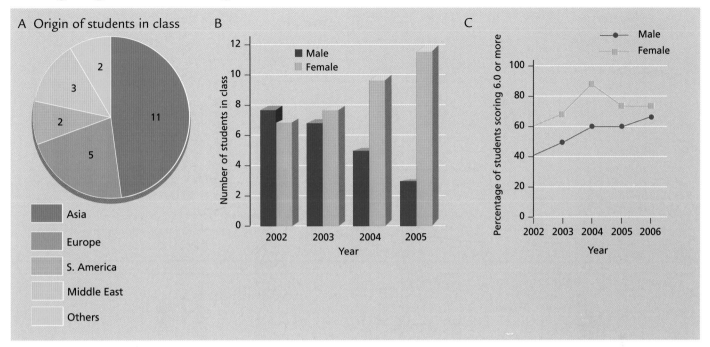

A Origin of students in class

Asia
Europe
S. America
Middle East
Others

B Number of students in class / Year / Male / Female

C Percentage of students scoring 6.0 or more / Year / Male / Female

Describing data

1 Look at the graph and charts based on an IELTS class in Britain and answer these questions.

  a What does chart A show?
  b What does each segment of this chart represent?
  c In chart B, how did the composition of this class change between 2002 and 2005?
  d In which years were there more or less equal numbers of male and female students?
  e In graph C, what do the male and female figures taken together indicate?
  f What conclusions can be drawn from graph C?

2 Collect information on your own class on one of these subjects or on another subject that interests you.

  How many students have been learning English for these lengths of time?
  0–2 years / 2–3 years / 3–4 years / 4–5 years / 5+ years.
  What type of holidays do students prefer? Examples: beach holidays / sightseeing holidays / working holidays
  What do you hope to do after this course? Examples: work / study / travel

3 Illustrate the data you have collected by means of a pie chart (A), a bar chart (B) or a graph (C). Then write one or two short statements describing your data.
  You could use some of these verbs: *demonstrate / draw conclusions from / indicate, represent / show*.

Similarities

4 Read statements a–d below. Using your own general knowledge, say which sentences are factually correct.

  a Neither Canada nor Australia has French as a main language.
  b Spanish is the main language in all the countries of South America.
  c India and Pakistan are neighbours. In each country, the rupee is the unit of currency.
  d Both Mexico and Norway are oil-producing countries.
  e In Britain you can spend either pounds or euros in all the shops.

5 Which words in sentences 4a–e express similarities?

6 Choose one of these tasks.

  a Work with a partner from a different country. Discuss and then write about similarities between your two countries.
  b Write about the similarities between your country and another country you know about.

Writing

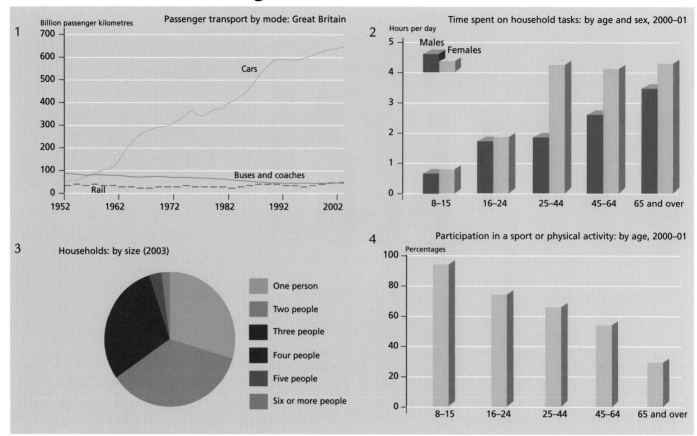

Accurate description

1 Illustrations 1–4 provide a snapshot of British life early in the twenty-first century. Answer questions a–d about the illustrations.

   a   Which aspects of life does each illustration relate to?
   b   What comparisons does each one make?
   c   Which are based on totals? proportions? percentages? averages? How do you know?
   d   What point in time or period does each illustration relate to?

2 Which illustration 1–4 does the following statement relate to?

The chart shows the average number of hours per day spent on househould tasks by both males and females of different age groups in the UK during the period 2000–2001.

What information has been included in the statement? For example, *during the period 2000–2001* = time frame the data refers to

3 Write similar statements for the other illustrations.

4 What do illustrations 1–4 tell you about British attitudes to these aspects of life?

   the home   the family   transport   leisure

Discuss your answers with other students. How would the graphs be different in your country?

note

Stating accurately, in your own words, what the data shows will clarify your thoughts and set the scene for the reader.

5 Which of the following statements give important information about illustration 2? Rank their importance from 1–8 (1 = most important, 8 = least important).

A In the youngest age group, both sexes spend under one hour on household tasks, but the amount is more similar than in later age groups.

B In general, the length of time both sexes spend on housework increases as they get older.

C Women between the ages of 25 and 44 spend over four hours per day on household tasks, slightly less between 45 and 64, and slightly more again when over 65.

D The columns in the chart are of different sizes. The ones relating to women are always larger than those relating to men.

E By the ages of 25–44, a clear pattern has emerged in which women spend approximately twice as much time on housework as men do, and this continues into middle age.

F The chart indicates that women spend more time on household tasks in each age group.

G Between the age groups 25–44 and 45–64, the amount of time men spend on housework increases by about half an hour.

H Men spend less time on housework because they do it more quickly.

6 Which of the statements in 5 above would you include in a description of illustration 2, and which would you omit?

7 Select two main points from each of the other illustrations and write a sentence expressing each.

Think, plan, write

note

Be selective in what you include in your answer. Include only statements which inform the reader of points which seem relevant to you. Omit irrelevant or insignificant details and personal opinions.

8 Read the Writing Task 1 below and discuss these questions with another student.
a What is the key feature of each graph below?
b What information will you include in your answer? What information will you omit?
c What similarities or differences are there between the trends illustrated in the graphs?

> The graphs below show some trends in visits to the UK by overseas residents and visits overseas by UK residents between 1982 and 2002.
>
> Summarize the information by selecting and reporting the main features, and make comparisons where relevant.
>
> Write at least 150 words.

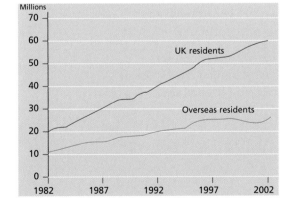

Visits to and from the UK

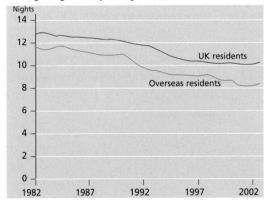

Average length of stay during visits to and from the UK

9 Write your answer to this task, using ideas you discussed with your partner.

Help yourself

How to use the Help yourself pages

1 Choose the most appropriate answers to this questionnaire about study habits.

> **I prefer to study ...**
> ☐ in a library
> ☐ in my own room
> ☐ in a cafe or public space
> ☐ outdoors
>
> **I find it easiest to concentrate ...**
> ☐ in the morning
> ☐ in the afternoon
> ☐ in the evening
> ☐ late at night
>
> **I get more done when ...**
> ☐ I study alone
> ☐ I have a study partner
> ☐ I share ideas with a group of friends
>
> **I prefer learning English from ...**
> ☐ TV, film, and radio
> ☐ books and newspapers
> ☐ the Internet
> ☐ exercises in grammar books
> ☐ talking to people who speak English

2 Compare your answers to the questionnaire with other students. In reality, do your study habits match your preferences? Why? / Why not? How could you plan your study to improve how effectively you use your study time?

3 *IELTS Masterclass* contains fourteen 'Help yourself' study pages which suggest ways in which you can use your study time more effectively. They can be used in any order. To familiarize youself with the pages and where they are located, find out which sections will help you

- solve your own problems in English
- improve how clearly you speak
- make fewer mistakes in writing
- develop your own ideas
- get information to support your study

4 Each Help yourself page contains the following features:

- 'IELTS to do list' like the one below, to help you plan projects for yourself outside the classroom
- 'Where to look' with references to websites and publications which you may find useful.

In addition, the *IELTS Masterclass* website, see below, contains additional reference pages and self-study exercises.

IELTS to do list

Choose one of the following to do outside class.

☐ Draw up an outline self-help study programme for the next fortnight or month. As you do this, remember your preferred study habits and how much free time you have for study.

☐ Make a checklist of any language resources you have regular access to. For example: the Internet; English-language newspapers and magazines; TV and radio; English-speaking friends or acquaintances.

Where to look

e www.oup.com/elt/ielts

2 Conflicting interests

1 Discuss photos 1–3 with another student.
  a What environmental issue does each photo illustrate?
  b What are currently the most important environmental issues in your country, city, or area?
  c What is being done to solve the problems related to these issues?
  d What is the general public attitude to environmental issues in your country?

2 Look at photo 4 and read this newspaper headline. In what way do you think public opinion is split?

> Public opinion split over plans to scrap hazardous ships in England

3 🎧 Listen to part of a radio broadcast in which people express their views on this story and answer these questions.
  a Whose viewpoints do we hear?
  b Are they for or against the plans?
  c Which view would you support if there were plans like this for your town?

4 Discuss these questions with other students.
  a Can you think of other examples where economic and environmental interests conflict?
  b Do you think these conflicts are occurring more often than they used to? If so, why?

Reading

Orientation **1** Compare the families shown in these photographs. What effects does family size have on society and on the families themselves?

2 Answer this population quiz.

1 What is the current population of the world?

  a 3.6 billion
  b 6.2 billion
  c 2.8 billion
  d 15 billion

2 How fast is the world's population changing?

  a increasing by 2.5 people per second
  b increasing by 5 people per second
  c increasing by 10 people per second
  d decreasing by 3 people per second

3 Which age range accounts for half of the world's population?

  a 0–25
  b 26–40
  c 41–60
  d 61 and over

4 What birth rate per couple does a country need to maintain its current population?

  a 2.5
  b 2.3
  c 2.1
  d 2.0

3 Compare ideas with another student, then turn to page 177 to find the answers.

Paragraph summaries **4** Read paragraphs A and B of *The other population crisis* and answer these questions.
  a   How would you summarize the main idea of paragraph A?
  b   What alternative view is expressed in paragraph B?

5 Read the other paragraphs quickly. As you read each paragraph, write a brief note to summarize the main idea.

THE OTHER POPULATION CRISIS

A IT IS AN UNQUESTIONED PRINCIPLE that has dominated international thinking for decades: we live in an overcrowded world teeming with billions of humans who are destined to suffocate our cities and
5 squeeze our planet of its precious resources. Our species is inexorably wrecking Earth: flooding valleys, cutting down forests and destroying the habitats of animals and plants faster than scientists can classify them. Our future is destined to be nasty, brutish, and cramped.

B Or is it? Now, it seems, population analysts have suddenly started to question the 'self-evident' truth that we are destined eventually to drown under our own weight. While accepting that populations will continue to rise, they point out that this rise will not
15 be nearly as steep or as long-lasting as was once feared. They even claim they can envisage the day when world population numbers will peak and begin to decline.

C As evidence, statisticians point to a simple,
20 stark fact: people are having fewer and fewer children. In the 1970s, global fertility rates stood at about six children per woman. Today the average is 2.9 and
25 falling. Such a rate will still see the world's population increase to nine billion by 2050, a rise of fifty per cent on today's figure. That is not good news for the planet, but it is far less
30 alarming than the projections of fifteen billion that were once being made. More to the point, statisticians predict that after 2050 the number of humans will go down. Such trends raise two key questions. Why has the rise in world populations
35 started to die out so dramatically? And what will be the consequences of this decline?

D Answers to the first question depend largely on locality. In Europe, for example, couples will have only one or two children when they might have had three or four in
40 the past. There are various reasons for this. Women now have their own career options, and are no longer considered failures if they do not marry and produce children in their twenties or thirties. This has taken a substantial number out of the pool of potential mothers.
45 In addition, parents have aspirations for their offspring, choices not available to past generations but which cost money, for example, higher education and travel. These and other pressures have reduced the average birth rate in European countries to 1.4 per couple. Given that a
50 country needs a birth rate of 2.1 to maintain its numbers, it is clear to see that in the long term there will be fewer Europeans.

E The causes of declining numbers in other countries are more varied and more alarming. Russia's population is
55 dropping by almost 750,000 people a year. The causes are alcoholism, breakdown of the public health service, and industrial pollution that has had a disastrous effect on men's fertility. In China, the state enforces quotas of offspring numbers, and it is expected that its population
60 will peak at 1.5 billion by 2019 then go into steep decline. Some analysts suggest the country could lose twenty to thirty per cent of its population every generation. There is also the exodus from the countryside, a trek happening across the globe. Soon
65 half the world's population will have urban homes. But in cities, children become a cost rather than an asset for helping to work the land, and again pressures mount for people to cut the size of their families.

F The impact of all this is
70 harder to gauge. In Europe, demographers forecast a major drop in the numbers who will work and earn money, while the population
75 of older people – who need support and help – will soar. So, the urging by a British politician that it is the patriotic duty of women to
80 have children makes sense. There will be no workforce if people do not have children. At present the median age of people is twenty-six; within a
85 hundred years, if current trends continue, that will have doubled. More and more old people will have to be supported by fewer and fewer young people. In China, the problem is worse. Most young Chinese adults have no brothers or sisters and face the prospect of having to
90 care for two parents and four grandparents on their own. Pensions and incomes are simply not able to rise fast enough to deal with the crisis.

G There are people who cling to the hope that it is possible to have a vibrant economy without a growing
95 population, but mainstream economists are pessimistic. On the other hand, it is clear that reduced human numbers can only be good for the planet in the long term. Until we halt the spread of our own species, the destruction of the last great wildernesses, such as the
100 Amazon, will continue. Just after the last Ice Age, there were only a few hundred thousand humans on Earth. Since then the population has grown ten thousandfold. Such a growth rate, and our imperfect attempts to control it, are bound to lead us into an uncertain future.

6 Read paragraph headings (i–x) below, only six of which you need to match with the paragraphs of the article.

    a The example shows that (i) is the most suitable heading for Paragraph A. Why is this?

    b Choose the most suitable heading for Paragraph B, based on your paragraph summary.

IELTS practice   **Questions 1–5:** Matching headings

From the list of headings below choose the most suitable heading (i–x) for each remaining paragraph C–G. Use your summary notes to help you.

    Example:

                                Answer

    Paragraph A   *i*

    Paragraph B
1 Paragraph C
2 Paragraph D
3 Paragraph E
4 Paragraph F
5 Paragraph G

Headings

i   The accepted view of the future
ii   The pros and cons of fluctuating birth rates
iii Falling birth rates: main facts and figures
iv Measures to reduce population growth
v   Population likely to grow indefinitely
vi A conscious decision to have fewer children
vii Experts challenge existing beliefs
viii Need to maintain ratio of workers to pensioners
ix Unintentional and engineered causes of falling birth rate
x   Medical breakthrough in birth control

note

Try to summarize for yourself what each whole paragraph is about. Each heading should correspond roughly with your own summaries.

Exploration

7 Refer to the text to find answers to these questions.

a *The other population crisis* describes future population movements. Find five verbs or phrases which refer to upward movement and five that refer to downward movement.

b Which verb means 'to reach its highest point'?

c What is the meaning of the word 'pool' in line 44?

d What is the more standard equivalent of the collective noun 'offspring' in line 45?

e At what age do students go into 'higher education' (line 47)?

f What do demographers 'study' (line 71)?

g What is the more informal way of saying 'ten thousandfold' (line 102)?

8 Match the words on the left with those on the right to form commonly occurring adjective–noun combinations. Then check your answers by finding them in the text.

Example: *key questions*

key	duty
patriotic	economy
precious	future
self-evident	questions
uncertain	resources
vibrant	truth

9 Use the adjective–noun combinations above to complete these sentences.

a We are using up the world's .... like oil and gas at an alarming rate.

b It is a .... that the fossil fuels will eventually run out.

c During wars, governments sometimes tell people that it is their .... to join the army.

d The fall in the value of our currency leaves us facing an ....

e High employment and increased consumer spending are signs of a ....

f When to have children and whether or not to go back to work immediately are .... facing many women.

10 Discuss these questions with other students.

a The article comes to no definite conclusions, but does it make you feel generally optimistic or pessimistic about the future? Give your reasons.

b Do you think we will be able to 'halt the spread of our own species', and prevent 'the destruction of the last great wildernesses, such as the Amazon'? If so, how will we do this? If not, why not?

Listening

Section 2

In Section 2, you will hear a talk or a speech by one main speaker on a subject related to social needs.

Orientation

1 Discuss these questions with another student.
  a What are the main differences between the photographs?
  b How could the differences between the two cities be explained?
  c What would it be like to live and work in these cities?
  d What measures do you know about or can you suggest for reducing traffic congestion in large cities? How effective are any of the measures you know about?

2 Read this brief description of the measures London has taken to reduce traffic congestion.
  a What is your reaction to the scheme?
  b If you were planning to drive through central London in the near future, what other information would you want to know?

Transport for LONDON

In 2003, London introduced congestion charging as a way of ensuring that those using valuable and congested road space make a financial contribution.

It encourages the use of other modes of transport and is also intended to ensure that, for those who have to use the roads, journey times are quicker and more reliable.

The London scheme requires drivers to pay £8 per day if they wish to continue driving in central London during the scheme's hours of operation. ●

3 You are going to hear a talk which gives more details about the congestion charging scheme. Read the notes you have to complete in Questions 1–10 below, and discuss these questions.
  a What clues tell you how the talk will be organized?
  b What do the notes tell you about the missing answers?

IELTS practice

Questions 1–5: Note completion

🎧 Complete the notes below. Write no more than three words and/or a number for each answer.

When it applies

Monday–Friday, from 7 a.m until (1).......... 6:30 .... p.m.

How much it costs

standard: £8

payment after 10 p.m.: (2) £.......... 10£ ....

after midnight: (3).......... Penalty charge ....

How to pay

by telephone

by (4).......... Text message ....

on the Internet

at one of (5).......... 2000 .... Pay Points in the zone

Questions 6–10: Sentence completion

🎧 Complete the sentences below. Write no more than three words and/or a number for each answer.

The congestion charging zone covers anywhere within London's inner

(6).......... ring road ....

The signs telling motorists when they are entering the zone show a white letter C on

a (7).......... red background ....

The congestion charging system recognizes British and European car

(8).......... registration change ....

Alternatives to driving include buses, trains, taxis, and (9).......... the underground ....

Public transport in London is now improving because there are fewer

(10).......... private vichles ....

Exploration

4 Discuss these questions with other students.
  a What conflicting interests do you think the authorities who introduced congestion charging had to take into consideration? Which groups of people would have been in favour of the scheme and which groups would have been against?
  b Which groups of people and vehicles should be exempt from paying the charge, for example, doctors and ambulances?
  c Would a similar scheme be effective in a congested city in your country? If not, why not?

Speaking

Orientation

1 Think about an area of your country that you know well, then discuss these questions with other students.

   a   What is attractive and unattractive about this area?

   b   How has the area changed in recent years? Have these changes improved or damaged the area?

   c   What other improvements could be made to the area?

Speaking from notes

2 Look at the two photos above. Write some key words and phrases about each photo using the categories in this list.

Examples: *in the city centre / on the side of a hill*

Location
Human activity
Atmosphere
Your opinion

3 Work with another student. Choose one photo and tell a colleague as much as possible about the photo based on the notes you have written.

IELTS practice

Part 2: Extended speaking

4 In Speaking Part 2, the examiner will give you a topic verbally and on a card. You then have one minute to prepare what you are going to say. During this time, you can make written notes on a separate piece of paper. Think about the task below and make a few notes. Write key words which you can refer to easily as you are talking and which will remind you what to say.

> **note**
>
> In the minute allowed, plan what you are going to say. Write brief clear notes, not a speech.

> Describe an area of countryside you know and like.
>
> You should say:
>   where it is
>   what its special features are
>   what you and other people do in this area
> and explain why you like it.

5 In Speaking Part 2 you must talk for one to two minutes. Take it in turns to talk uninterrupted about a place you know and like. Follow the instructions on the task card above, referring to any notes you have made and adding more details.

Language for writing

Consecutive noun phrases

1 Study these extracts from an article about the planned expansion of one of London's main airports and answer the questions.

> A campaign to help save Hatfield Forest, *a nature reserve and the home of several rare species of animals*, has been initiated by the National Trust.

> THE NATIONAL TRUST, *a long-established conservation organization*, is concerned that the expansion of the airport could have serious implications for the future of the forest.

    a   What is the purpose of the noun phrase in italic in each extract? What exactly do these phrases refer to?

    b   How are these phrases different from relative clauses? How are they similar?

2 Rewrite a–c below so that they include consecutive noun phrases, as in 1 above.

    a   Stansted Airport is in a largely agricultural area of Britain. It is London's third main airport.

    b   Hatfield Forest is very close to Stansted Airport. It is an ancient wooded area.

    c   Hatfield Forest is home to several thousand-year-old trees. It is an area frequently visited by naturalists.

Avoiding repetition

3 Study another extract about Hatfield Forest. What do the words in italic refer to?

> ENVIRONMENTALISTS ARE worried that the forest is already being damaged by aircraft and road traffic, *the former* by polluting the atmosphere, and *the latter* by causing traffic congestion. Without doubt, *such damage* will worsen if expansion plans, like *those* proposed recently, go ahead. *This area of woodland* currently allows visitors to step back into a medieval landscape and experience *its* special tranquillity. More air traffic could have a damaging effect on *this atmosphere*.

4 Rewrite this paragraph about Hatfield Forest, replacing the phrases in italic by paraphrasing or using reference words.

> HATFIELD FOREST IS a unique example of an ancient hunting forest. As a result, *Hatfield Forest* has a rich but fragile natural structure. *The fragile structure* will be damaged if noise and pollution increase. *The noise* will drive away rare species of animals, and *the pollution* will damage plant life. *The damage caused by noise and pollution* will be permanent.

Writing

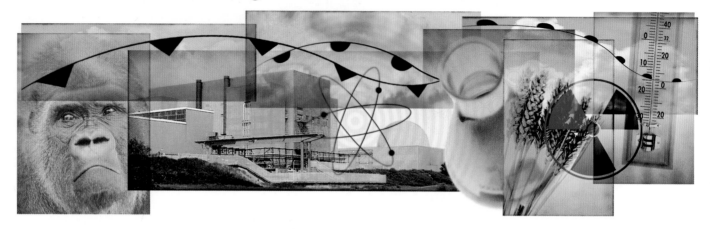

Orientation

1 What are your views on the statements a–d below? Choose one of these opinions for each of the statements:

    strongly agree   agree   disagree   strongly disagree

  a We shouldn't protect endangered species. Extinction is part of the evolutionary process.
  b Technology will solve our environmental problems.
  c Genetically modified crops are the future of food.
  d Nuclear power is the only clean and efficient fuel.

2 Discuss the statements with other students. Give reasons for your opinions.

Taking a view

3 Read Writing Task 2 below and answer these questions.
  a Which part of the task is a strong statement similar to 1a–d above?
  b Which of the opinion choices represents your view on this subject?

    strongly agree   agree   disagree   strongly disagree

> You should spend about 40 minutes on this task. Write about the following topic:
>
> Scientists and the news media are presenting ever more evidence of climate change. Governments cannot be expected to solve this problem. It is the responsibility of individuals to change their lifestyle to prevent further damage.
>
> What are your views?
>
> Give reasons for your answer and include any relevant examples from your own knowledge and experience.
>
> Write at least 250 words.

Developing your view

4 Which of the points below could you use to support your view on this subject?
  a Restrictions and incentives are required for industry.
  b People could take fewer long-distance holidays.
  c Greener modes of transport should be promoted.
  d International agreements are required.
  e Individuals should ensure that their houses or flats are energy-efficient.
  f Businesses need to take a broader view rather than just working for profit.
  g We should buy fewer electrical labour-saving devices.
  h People should get out of their cars.
  i The scientific evidence for climate change is unreliable and should not be believed.
  j There's no point in looking for a solution to this problem. It's already too late.

note

You are normally expected
to present your own views.
Develop your arguments by
giving appropriate
examples and reasons.

5 For each of the statements you chose in 4, note down answers to these questions.
   a   What specific examples could you use to support the statement?
   b   What would be the consequences of taking the action described in the statement?
   c   What would be the consequences of not taking the action?

6 Read the sample answer below and discuss these questions with another student.
   a   What is the writer's position on the statement?
   b   What are the writer's main arguments?
   c   What concrete examples and supporting reasons are given?

Recently, scientists worried about climate change have urged governments to introduce measures to reduce the greenhouse gas emissions that are seen as its main cause. Simultaneously, politicians and environmentalists have urged individuals to make changes to their lifestyle. I shall argue that governments and individuals should take joint responsibility for this problem.

Firstly, industry accounts for a large proportion of the greenhouse gas emissions, and this can only be controlled by government action. Measures could be taken to discourage pollution, such as limiting or taxing the use of fossil fuels. Alternatively, subsidies could be offered to industries to clean up their production processes. If these ideas were adopted, I believe that businesses would regard pollution as a financial issue.

Secondly, only discussion between governments can ensure that solutions are successful. The Kyoto agreement, for example, tried to reach global agreement on how to address the problem. Without such co-operation, it seems to me that efforts to reduce fuel consumption are unlikely to be effective.

However, national and international policies will only succeed if individuals also change their lifestyles. For example, people could think more carefully about how they use energy in their homes. By using less electricity, installing energy-efficient light bulbs and electrical appliances, or investing in solar panels, individuals can make a real difference.

In addition, I think individual attitudes to transport need to change. Instead of making short trips by car, people could choose to walk, cycle, or take a bus. Since cars are a major source of the problem, changing our behaviour in this area would have a major impact.

In conclusion, I would maintain that only a combination of international agreements, national policies, and changes in individual behaviour will succeed in preventing further damage to the environment.

Think, plan, write

7 Identify the key statement in the Writing Task 2 below. What is your opinion?

There is evidence that inhaling cigarette smoke causes health problems not only for smokers but for non-smokers who inhale other people's smoke. In view of this, smoking should be banned in all public places, even though this would restrict some people's freedom of action.

What are your views?

note

To plan effectively, analyse
the question, think up
ideas, and decide on your
opinion. Then bring these
three elements together to
form a coherent argument.

8 Think of some main arguments to include in your answer. Make a list in the left-hand column. Then make notes about how you will develop your ideas in the right-hand column.

Main arguments	Supporting ideas

9 Write your answer using your notes as a basic plan.

Help yourself

Global issues

1 Read the list of topics below. If you have an opinion about an issue in the list, write a tick next to the topic.

- ☐ fair trade
- ☐ climate change
- ☐ human rights
- ☐ politics in sport
- ☐ the international drugs trade
- ☐ increasing air travel
- ☐ multinational corporations
- ☐ genetic engineering
- ☐ epidemic diseases
- ☐ scarcity of fresh water

2 Compare your choices with another student. For topics you have both ticked, choose the corresponding statement below. Say whether you agree or disagree. Give reasons to back up your views.

Fair trade is the only way forward.
Global warming is not a reality.
Human rights are a principle worth defending.
Politics and sport should be kept completely separate.
The international drugs trade should be stopped by force.
Cheaper air travel is transforming the world for the better.
Multi-national corporations have too much power.
Genetic engineering will improve human health.
Epidemic diseases are the biggest threat to our world.
Fresh water will generate more conflict in the future than oil.

3 The topics in 1 represent subjects that often arise in the news. Which ones are in the news at the moment? Work with another student to think of any other topics that you could add to the list.

4 Which topics did you have no strong opinions about? Have you ever thought of these issues before? Which of the following sources would you choose to help you learn about them?

radio and television news
documentary programmes
newspaper editorials
current affairs magazines, such as *Time* or *The Economist*
other people's opinions
the Internet

IELTS to do list

Choose one of the following to do outside class.

☐ Choose topics from the list in 1 or your own list. Refer to a variety of information sources. For example, try putting a phrase like 'the case for/against X' into your favourite search engine.

☐ Build up a list of arguments from different perspectives on your chosen topics, even if you don't agree.

☐ Decide your own personal opinions on the issues you research. Make a note of these opinions as they develop over time. Add a note of any real-life events which you could use to back up your opinions on these issues.

Where to look

ⓔ www.oup.com/elt/ielts

3 Fitness and health

1 Discuss these questions with another student.

   a   What aspects of fitness and health does each picture relate to?
   b   What are its benefits or possible drawbacks?
   c   What are the best ways to get fit and stay healthy?
   d   Can attempts to improve fitness and health be dangerous?
   e   What are the biggest dangers to our health these days?
   f   What are the most significant recent breakthroughs in medicine?

2 Complete the headlines, using each word once.

explore	cloning	repair	cure
implants	vaccination	transplant	regrows

   a   **At last: a complete** ...... **for cancer**
   b   MALARIA ERADICATED BY NEW ...... AGAINST DISEASE
   c   **Artificial heart** ...... **'now as good as human hearts'**
   d   DOCTORS USE NANOTECHNOLOGY TO ...... INSIDE ORGANS
   e   Ageing film star 'looks 20 again' after face ...... from model
   f   STEM CELLS TO ...... DAMAGED BODY PARTS
   g   **IDENTICAL MILLIONS?** ...... **of humans 'now widespread'**
   h   MAN WHO LOST UPPER LIMBS ...... NEW ARMS

3 Discuss these questions about the headlines in 2.

   a   Which of these breakthroughs
       is possible now?
       will be possible soon?
       may never be possible?
   b   Which of them, do you think, should happen as soon as possible?
   c   Are there any that should never happen?

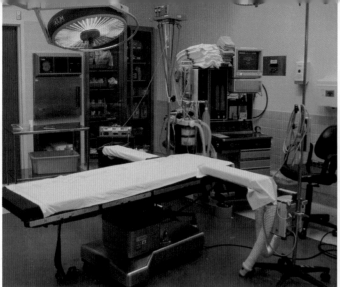

Reading

Orientation

1 Read the title of the text below and the first two sentences. Answer these questions.

 a What is the difference between conventional and alternative medicine?
 b Which do you think each of these people practises: conventional or alternative medicine? What do they actually do?

acupuncturist	complementary practitioner	physician
anaesthetist	doctor	rheumatologist
aromatherapist	herbalist	surgeon

Text structure

2 The passage entitled *The Power of Nothing* can be divided into three main sections A–C. Read the text and mark where each section starts.

note

In most cases you should read the passage quickly first to get an idea of how it is organized.

 A How to become a success in alternative medicine.
 B The placebo effect: what it is and how it works.
 C Integrating alternative and conventional medicine.

Be warm, sympathetic, reassuring and enthusiastic.

THE POWER OF
nothing

Want to devise a new form of alternative medicine? No problem. Here's the recipe. Be warm, sympathetic, reassuring and enthusiastic. Your treatment should involve physical contact, and each session
5 with your patients should last at least half an hour. Encourage your patients to take an active part in their treatment and understand how their disorders relate to the rest of their lives. Tell them that their own bodies possess the true power to heal. Make them pay you out of their own pockets. Describe your
10 treatment in familiar words, but embroidered with a hint of mysticism: energy fields, energy flows, energy blocks, meridians, forces, auras, rhythms and the like. Refer to the knowledge of an earlier age: wisdom carelessly swept aside by the rise and rise of blind, mechanistic science.

Oh, come off it, you're saying. Something invented off the top of your head couldn't possibly work, could it? Well yes, it could – and often well enough to earn you a living. A good living if you are sufficiently convincing, or, better still, really believe in your therapy. Many illnesses get better on their own, so if you are lucky and administer your treatment at just the right time you'll get the credit. But that's only part of it. Some of the improvement really would be down to you. Your healing power would be the outcome of a paradoxical force that conventional medicine recognizes but remains oddly ambivalent about: the placebo effect.

Placebos are treatments that have no direct effect on the body, yet still work because the patient has faith in their power to heal. Most often the term refers to a dummy pill, but it applies just as much to any device or procedure, from a sticking plaster to a crystal to an operation. The existence of the placebo effect implies that even quackery may confer real benefits, which is why any mention of placebo is a touchy subject for many practitioners of complementary and alternative medicine, who are likely to regard it as tantamount to a charge of charlatanism. In fact, the placebo effect is a powerful part of all medical care, orthodox or otherwise, though its role is often neglected and misunderstood.

At one level, it should come as no surprise that our state of mind can influence our physiology: anger opens the superficial blood vessels of the face; sadness pumps the tear glands. But exactly how placebos work their medical magic is still largely unknown. Most of the scant research done so far has focused on the control of pain, because it's one of the commonest complaints and lends itself to experimental study. Here, attention has turned to the endorphins, morphine-like neurochemicals known to help control pain.

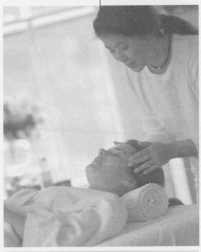

it should come as no surprise that our state of mind can influence our physiology

That case has been strengthened by the recent work of Fabrizio Benedetti of the University of Turin, who showed that the placebo effect can be abolished by a drug, naloxone, which blocks the effects of endorphins. Benedetti induced pain in human volunteers by inflating a blood-pressure cuff on the forearm. He did this several times a day for several days, using morphine each time to control the pain. On the final day, without saying anything, he replaced the morphine with a saline solution. This still relieved the subjects' pain: a placebo effect. But when he added naloxone to the saline the pain relief disappeared. Here was direct proof that placebo analgesia is mediated, at least in part, by these natural opiates. Still, no one knows how belief triggers endorphin release, or why most people can't achieve placebo pain relief simply by willing it.

Though scientists don't know exactly how placebos work, they have accumulated a fair bit of knowledge about how to trigger the effect. A London rheumatologist found, for example, that red dummy capsules made more effective painkillers than blue, green or yellow ones. Research on American students revealed that blue pills make better sedatives than pink, a colour more suitable for stimulants. Even branding can make a difference: if Aspro or Tylenol are what you like to take for a headache, their chemically identical generic equivalents may be less effective.

It matters, too, how the treatment is delivered. 'Physicians who adopt a warm, friendly and reassuring bedside manner', reports Edzard Ernst, professor of Complementary and Alternative Medicine at Exeter University, 'are more effective than those whose consultations are formal and do not offer reassurance.' Warm, friendly and reassuring are also alternative medicine's strong suits, of course. Many of the ingredients of that opening recipe – the physical contact, the generous swathes of time, the strong hints of supernormal healing power – are just the kind of thing likely to impress patients. It's hardly surprising, then, that aromatherapists, acupuncturists, herbalists, etc. seem to be good at mobilizing the placebo effect.

The question is whether alternative medicine could be integrated into conventional medicine, as some would like, without losing much of its power. But for much of alternative medicine – especially techniques in which the placebo effect accounts for most or perhaps all the benefit – integration might well be counterproductive. After all, the value of alternative medicine depends partly on its unorthodoxy. 'One intuitively feels that something exotic has a stronger placebo effect than something bog standard. And some complementary therapies are very exotic,' says Ernst.

Integration faces other obstacles, too. Doctors would face serious ethical dilemmas in recommending what they know to be placebo treatments to their patients. And complementary practitioners would likely be disparaged by their conventional counterparts, as they often are today. Integrated medicine 'would have about as much validity as a hybrid of astronomy and astrology', wrote anaesthetist Neville Goodman in the April newsletter of HealthWatch.

Some would also point out that a professor of surgery with a confident manner, an expensive suit and an international reputation who sees you privately and guarantees to solve your problem with a costly operation is still unrivalled as a source of placebo power. But most doctors are beaten hands down by countless alternative practitioners who might not know a lymphocyte from a lump of cheese. What they do know is how to make you feel better. And that's a big part of the battle.

Finding evidence

3 Read the following statements and answer the questions about each.

Alternative therapists should give free treatment.

a Does the writer mention anything in section A about free treatment, money, or payments?

b With reference to the text, do you think that the writer agrees or disagrees with the statement above?

Alternative therapy is particularly popular among young people.

c Can you find any evidence in section A that relates to this statement?

d Do you think that the writer disagrees with the statement above or that there is no information about this?

IELTS practice

Questions 1–5: Yes/No/Not given

Use the procedure in 3 to decide whether the following statements agree with the views of the writer in the Reading Passage. Write

YES	if the statement agrees with the views of the writer
NO	if the statement does not agree with the views of the writer
NOT GIVEN	if there is no information about this in the passage

1 Creating and practising a new alternative therapy can be a well-paid job.

2 It is dishonest to claim that alternative therapy can help cure patients.

3 Alternative practitioners always acknowledge the importance of the placebo effect.

4 Some surgical operations are now carried out by alternative practitioners.

5 We know that emotions sometimes have direct physical effects on the body.

Questions 6–10: True/False/Not given

Do the following statements agree with the information given in the Reading Passage? Write

TRUE	if the statement agrees with the information
FALSE	if the statement contradicts the information
NOT GIVEN	if there is no information on this

6 Benedetti found evidence of a link between endorphins and the placebo effect.

7 Anyone who understands the placebo effect can use it to stop their own pain.

8 The biggest-selling tablets in Britain and the United States are red or blue.

9 Practitioners of conventional medicine cannot bring about the placebo effect.

10 It would be very expensive to integrate the two kinds of medicine.

Exploration

4 Refer to the text to find answers to these questions.

a What has been omitted before 'Want to' at the beginning of the text? Why?

b What kind of things are 'energy fields, energy flows, energy blocks, meridians, forces, auras, rhythms'? Do you need their precise meanings to understand the text?

c Which common conjunction could replace 'yet' on line 27?

d Find a synonym of 'quackery' in the same sentence (lines 31–38). What do they imply?

e Where would you normally find 'a trigger'? What does it mean as a verb (line 65)?

f What is the usual meaning of 'recipe' (line 86)? Which other word in that sentence has the same associations?

g What part of speech is 'face/faces' on line 107? Which nouns collocate with it in each case?

5 Match the words on the left with those on the right to form collocations. Then check your answers by finding them in the text.

Example: *placebo effect*

placebo	vessels
pain	subject
touchy	manner
healing	hint
blood	relief
bedside	effect
strong	power

6 Use the collocations above to complete the sentences.

a Medical exams are a ...... with Tom at the moment: he's just failed all of them.

b The main ...... in the human body are the arteries and veins.

c Relaxing the body can bring ...... more quickly than analgesic drugs.

d A good ...... includes respect, politeness and listening to the patient.

e Although she said nothing definite, Jo gave a ..... that she's leaving nursing.

f Many people believe in the ...... of light, of music – or of religious faith.

g Clinical trials are used to detect whether a treament is a ...... or an effective cure.

7 Discuss these questions with other students.

a What other examples of placebos can you think of? Are there other ways in which 'our state of mind can influence our physiology'?

b Which kinds of alternative medicine are popular in your country? In your opinion, which work and which don't? Why?

c Do you think alternative medicine could be integrated with conventional medicine in your country? Why?/Why not?

Listening

Section 3

In Section 3, you will hear a discussion between two to four people in an academic context.

Orientation

1 Look at the photos and answer these questions.

    a Match these names with the photos.

        court   pitch   track   pool   rink

    b Which sports do you associate with the photos?
    c Which other sports do you associate with the places named in a?
    d Which of the sports you named in b and c have you taken part in? What sports facilities are there near your home?

2 Discuss these questions with other students.

    a You are designing a sports centre. Decide which three of the sports discussed in 1 you think should be available in the new centre.
    b Think of another sport you would like to see there. Try to persuade the rest of your group to include facilities for it.

Synonyms

3 Read options A–F in the box. What synonyms or words associated with each can you think of?

IELTS practice

note

Listen out for the key words in lists, for synonyms of them and for other words connected with the topic of each question.

Questions 1–6: Matching lists

Listen to the first part of the recording. Complete the notes below using letters A–F from the box. NB: You may use any letter more than once.

> A   first aid unit
> B   social areas
> C   teaching facilities
> D   sauna rooms
> E   fitness testing centre
> F   physiotherapy suite

Development proposals for the University Sports Centre

What Emma says the Sports Centre needs.
1   ....
2   ....
3   ....

What Adam has found useful in other sports centres.
4   ....
5   ....
6   ....

4 Read options A–C below. What synonyms for A–C might you hear? Which words associated with 7–10 might you hear?

Questions 7–10: Classification

Listen to the second part of the recording.
Where, at present, are there facilities for the following sports?

A   in the Sports Centre
B   elsewhere in the University
C   in the city

7   table tennis   ....
8   swimming   ....
9   squash   ....
10 basketball   ....

Exploration

5 Discuss these questions with other students.

a   Which of the words you expected to hear were actually on the recording?
b   Which other useful words do you remember hearing?

Speaking

Orientation **1** Answer the questions in this quiz on your own.

What do you really know about **Food**?

Confused about what foods you should be eating? Test your knowledge on which foods are important for a balanced diet.

1 Fresh fruit and vegetables are better for you than frozen fruit and vegetables.
True or False?

2 How many portions of fruit and vegetables should we try to eat each day?
- a five portions of fruit plus five portions of vegetables
- b five portions of fruit and vegetables excluding potatoes
- c five portions of either, including potatoes

3 If trying to lose weight, which of the following foods should be most strictly limited?
- a bread
- b biscuits
- c bananas
- d pastry
- e chips
- f potatoes

4 Semi-skimmed milk contains less calcium than full cream milk.
True or False?

5 Which of the following foods are good sources of calcium?
- a yoghurt
- b beef
- c fruit juice
- d cheese
- e pasta
- f sardines

6 Foods containing sugar are essential for energy.
True or False?

SOURCE: UNIVERSITY OF READING COUNSELLING SERVICE

Giving reasons **2** Compare your answers with a partner, giving reasons for your choices. Use some of the expressions under *Giving reasons*.

Giving reasons
I think, ... because ...
The reason is that ...
That's why ...

3 See page 177 to check your answers and find out what your score means.

IELTS Practice **Part 3:** Topic discussion

note

Give an extended reply to every question, giving reasons and adding more points connected with the topic to develop the discussion.

4 In Speaking Part 3, the examiner will ask you about more abstract aspects of a topic. Work in pairs. Take it in turns to ask your partner questions a–c below, allowing time for a full answer to each question.

a   What kinds of food do you think we should eat, and which should we avoid?
b   What role does food and drink play in your culture? Do you think people in your country eat better or worse nowadays than they did in the past?
c   Do you think science is improving the quality of the food we eat, or making some foods a danger to our health?

Language for writing

Relative clauses

1 Study the examples of defining and non-defining relative clauses and answer questions a–d.

Defining
Chocolate is something that nearly everyone likes.
People that smoke normally damage their health.

Non-defining
Tortilla, which is made from eggs and potatoes, is a
*   Spanish dish.*
Toby, whose job is difficult, spends his weekends relaxing.

a   What type of relative clause gives essential information?
b   What type of relative clause is separated by commas?
c   In which type can *that* be used?
d   In which type can the relative pronoun sometimes be left out?

2 Find and correct the errors in four of these sentences.

a   My mother who's a doctor works in the maternity hospital.
b   Ligaments, join bones in the human body, are made of strong tissue.
c   Do you know anyone I can ask about this?
d   The pharmacist gave me this medicine said it would help.
e   Distance running is a sport that requires no special equipment.
f   Dr James, that has written several books on the subject, is a dietician.

3 In academic English, prepositions such as *at*, *of*, *for*, *in*, *to*, *from* and *with* often go before the relative pronouns *which*, *whom* (not *who*) and *whose*.

Examples
It is a rare condition of which little is known.
Professor Harris, with whom the team worked, found a cure for the disease.

Rewrite a–f in a more academic style.

a   The study, which the Government had invested so much money in, proved nothing.
b   Darwin, whose findings the theory was based on, was the first to observe this.
c   The people who the researchers spoke at length to confirmed the earlier results.
d   Crick's work on DNA, which he received a Nobel Prize for, transformed biology.
e   Dr Fell is someone whose ideas few scientists would disagree with.
f   Orion is the star which light left hundreds of years ago from.

4 Quantifiers such as *many*, *both* or *none*, and numbers, can go before *of which* or *of whom* in a non-defining relative clause. Combine the sentences using a quantifier plus *of which* or *of whom*.

Example
Questionnaires were sent to 500 people, one third of whom completed them.

a   The team found two fossils. Neither of these was Triassic.
b   The disease was caught by sixty-four people. Most of them recovered quickly.
c   The examination was taken by 532 candidates. 43.4% of them passed.
d   We looked at many studies. Several of these indicated the same pattern.
e   The firm has appointed five new managers. All of them are men.

Writing

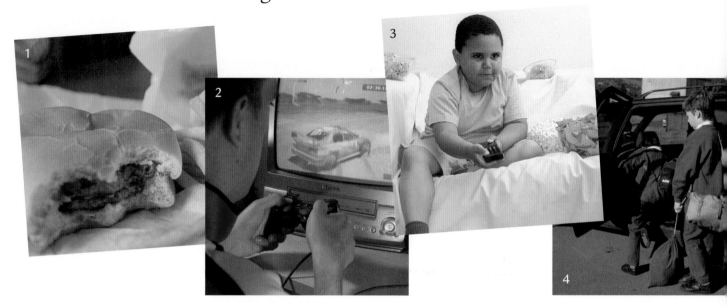

Orientation

1 Look at the photos and discuss these questions.

   a   In each case, what might children thirty years ago have been doing instead?

   b   Do you think the changes make present-day children less healthy?

Organizing ideas

2 Study the Writing Task 2 below and answer the questions.

   a   What overall topic do you have to write about?

   b   Which opinion do you have to respond to?

   c   How far do you agree or disagree with the opinion?

   d   Which of these would you include in your response to the task?

      Only arguments in favour
      Only arguments against
      Arguments both for and against

> In many countries today, the eating habits and lifestyles of children are different from those of previous generations. Some people say this has had a negative effect on their health.
>
> To what extent do you agree or disagree with this opinion?
>
> Give reasons for your answer and include any relevant examples from your own knowledge or experience.

3 Quickly read the sample essay and answer the questions.

   a   Which approach from 2d has the writer followed?

   b   Where does the writer state his/her position?

   c   Which aspects of the topic do each of the two main paragraphs deal with?

It has recently been suggested that the way children eat and live nowadays has led to a deterioration in their health. I entirely agree with this view, and believe that this alarming situation has come about for several reasons.

To begin with, there is the worrying increase in the amount of processed food that children are eating at home, with little or none of the fresh fruit and vegetables that earlier generations ate every day. Secondly, more and more young people are choosing to eat in fast-food restaurants, which may be harmless occasionally, but not every day. What they eat there is extremely high in fat, salt and sugar, all of which can be damaging to their health.

There is also a disturbing decline in the amount of exercise they get. Schools have become obsessed with exams, with the shocking result that some pupils now do no sports at all. To make matters worse, few even get any exercise on the way to and from school, as most of them go in their parents' cars rather than walk or cycle. Finally, children are spending far more time at home, playing computer games, watching TV or surfing the Internet. They no longer play outside with friends or take part in challenging outdoor activities.

To sum up, although none of these changes could, on its own, have caused widespread harm to children's health, there can be little doubt that all of them together have had a devastating effect. This, in my opinion, can only be reversed by encouraging children to return to more traditional ways of eating and living.

Using organizing expressions

4 What arguments does the writer use? What expression is used to introduce each point?

Example
children eating more processed food   'To begin with ...'

note

Use a range of organizing expressions to guide your reader through your arguments.

5 Which of the alternatives below could you use instead of the expressions in the text?

Lastly	Furthermore	First of all	Moreover
In conclusion	In the first place	As well as that	For another thing

Think, plan, write

6 Read the Writing Task 2 below. Decide your response to the opinion expressed. Note down your arguments and decide which aspects of the topic to cover in which paragraphs.

note

Decide your response to the question. Then, choose a clear paragraph structure in which to express your ideas.

> In some societies it is increasingly common to try to achieve good health and fitness through physically demanding sports, special diets, or preventative medicine – conventional or alternative. Some people, however, believe that the best way to stay fit and healthy is simply to lead a normal life.
>
> To what extent do you agree or disagree with this opinion?
>
> Give reasons for your answer and include any relevant examples from your own knowledge or experience.

7 Write your answer in at least 250 words, stating your position and then guiding your reader through your arguments with organizing expressions.

Help yourself

Vocabulary

1 A good English–English dictionary can give you a lot of useful information. Study the entry for *vocabulary* and answer the questions.

> **vo·cabu·lary** 0━ /vəˈkæbjələri; NAmE -leri/ *noun* [C, U] (*pl.* -ies)
> **1** all the words that a person knows or uses: *to have a wide/limited vocabulary* ◊ *your active vocabulary* (= the words that you use) ◊ *your passive vocabulary* (= the words that you understand but don't use) ◊ *Reading will increase your vocabulary.* ◊ *The word 'failure' is not in his vocabulary* (= for him, failure does not exist).—see also DEFINING VOCABULARY ⇨ note at LANGUAGE **2** all the words in a particular language: *When did the word 'bungalow' first enter the vocabulary?* ⇨ note at LANGUAGE **3** the words that people use when they are talking about a particular subject: *The word has become part of advertising vocabulary.*

from the *Oxford Advanced Learner's Dictionary* (seventh edition)

a   What *part of speech* is it?
b   How is it *spelled* in the plural?
c   Where is the *main stress* in the word?
d   How is it *pronounced* in Britain and the USA?
e   What *grammatical features* are given for each definition?
f   What *examples* of the word in context are given?

2 It is important to distinguish between *active* and *passive* vocabulary when you learn new words. Which of these are you likely to want to use (active), or understand but not use (passive)?

cool	voluminous	trendy
clockwise	anticyclonic	Cheers!

3 What are the advantages and disadvantages of each of these ways of organizing vocabulary notes?

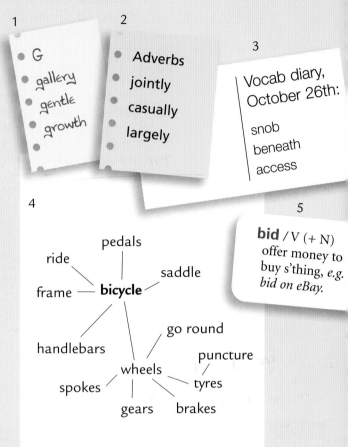

1
• G
• gallery
• gentle
• growth

2
• Adverbs
• jointly
• casually
• largely

3
Vocab diary,
October 26th:
snob
beneath
access

4
pedals
ride   saddle
frame — **bicycle**
handlebars   go round
                puncture
        wheels
spokes   tyres
    gears   brakes

5
bid / V (+ N)
offer money to buy s'thing, *e.g.*
bid on eBay.

IELTS to do list

Choose one of the following to do outside class.

☐ Decide which method of organizing new vocabulary would be best for you, and get the necessary materials.

☐ Choose three topic areas that interest you, for example, *travel*. For each one, note down some useful associated words, using your favourite method of organizing them.

☐ Read articles in an interesting magazine or journal, making a list of words that are new to you. Then check their dictionary entries for more information about them.

Where to look

ⓔ www.oup.com/elt/ielts

📖 *Oxford Advanced Learner's Dictionary*

Oxford Student's Dictionary of English

4 The arts

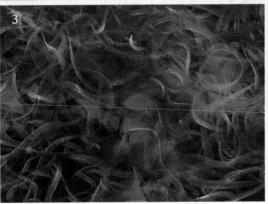

1 Discuss these questions with another student.

- a What does each of the images above show?
- b Which is the oldest, and which the most modern? Why do you think so?
- c What sort of person created each image?
- d Where would you expect to see each image?
- e Why do you think the images were created?
- f Which image do you like most? Which do you like least? Give reasons.

2 Read the text on the right and answer the questions.

- a How would you describe the writer's tone?
- b What does the writer think of more recent art?
- c Which kinds of art does the text mention? Do you understand what these are?
- d In your opinion is it necessary to understand the history of art to appreciate it?

3 Discuss these questions with another student.

- a When did you last look at a work of art? What was your reaction to it?
- b Who is your favourite artist and what is your favourite work? Why?
- c Have you ever created something artistic? If so, what was it and what was its purpose? If not, what would you like to create?

How to appreciate art

APPRECIATING ART is very easy once you understand art history. Art started with two-dimensional cave paintings. Then came two-dimensional church paintings. In the Renaissance, artists got perspective and started painting jugs. The Enlightenment brought us well-lit jugs with a side order of fruit. Romantic art depicted the landscape cave dwellers would have seen if they'd looked out, had perspective and understood lighting.

Art then became what artists saw inside them, rather than outside. Impressionism was the world seen through a couple of glasses of *vin rouge*. Expressionism was impressionism after the whole bottle. Vorticism was when the room started spinning, and modern conceptual art is the throwing-up stage.

Reading

H.W

Orientation

1 Look at the picture and answer the questions.

   a What does the picture show?
   b What do you think it means?

Style

2 Read the first paragraph of the passage on page 47.

   a What do you think is meant by 'installation art' and 'performance art'?
   b Why do you think the writer says 'yes' in line 6?
   c Do you think the necklace incident really happened?
   d How would you describe the writer's tone?

Text structure

3 In the second paragraph, the writer asks three questions. Read the rest of the passage and decide which parts of the passage answer each question.

Using question stems

4 Read the passage again. Answer the questions or complete the statements in a–f, using your own words.

   a The writer includes the story about the beads to show that …
   b Why aren't domestic lights considered installation art?
   c What important features do all installation works have in common?
   d Why was Duchamp's 1917 work so important?
   e Foster says there is now so much installation art because artists …
   f One reason why installations irritate us is that the artists …

When is a room not a room?

Answer: when it's an installation.

There was a bit of a fuss at a Tate Britain exhibition of modern art a few years ago. A woman was hurrying through the large room that housed an intriguing work entitled *Lights Going On and Off in a Gallery*, in which, yes, lights went on and off in a gallery. Suddenly the woman's necklace broke and the beads spilled over the floor. As we bent down to pick them up, one man said: 'Perhaps this is part of the installation.' Another replied: 'Surely that would make it performance art rather than an installation.' 'Or a happening,' said a third.

What is installation art? Why has it become so ubiquitous? And why is it so irritating?

These are confusing times for the visual arts audience, which is growing rapidly. More and more of London's gallery space is being devoted to installations, so what we need is the answer to three simple questions. What is installation art? Why has it become so ubiquitous? And why is it so irritating?

First question first. What are installations? 'Installations', answers the *Thames and Hudson Dictionary of Art and Artists* with misplaced self-confidence, 'only exist as long as they are installed.' Thanks for that. The dictionary continues more promisingly: installations are 'multi-media, multi-dimensional, and multi-form works which are created temporarily for a particular space or site either outdoors or indoors, in a museum or gallery'. As a first stab at a definition, this isn't bad. It rules out paintings, sculptures, frescoes and other intuitively non-installational artworks. It also says that anything can be an installation so long as it has art status conferred on it, so the flashing fluorescent tube in your kitchen is not art because it hasn't got the nod from the gallery.

The only problem is that this definition is incomplete. In some cases, installations have been bought and moved out of the gallery for which they were intended and re-installed in a different context. Also, unlike looking at paintings or sculptures, you often need to move through or around installations to appreciate the full impact of the work. What this suggests is that we are barking up the wrong tree by trying to define installations. They do not all share a set of essential characteristics. Some will demand audience participation, some will be site-specific, some will be conceptual jokes involving only a light bulb.

Which brings us to the second question: why are there so many of them around at the moment? There have been installations since Marcel Duchamp put a urinal in a New York gallery in 1917 and called it art. This was the most resonant gesture in twentieth-century art, discrediting notions of taste, skill, and craftsmanship, and suggesting that everyone could be an artist. But why has the number of installations been going up so quickly?

American critic Hal Foster thinks he knows why installations are everywhere in modern art. He reckons that the key transformation in Western art since the 1960s has been a shift from what he calls a 'vertical' conception to a 'horizontal' one. Before then, painters were interested in painting, exploring their medium to its limits. They were vertical. Artists are now less interested in pushing a form such as painting or sculpture as far as it will go, and more in using their work as a terrain on which to evoke feelings or provoke reactions. True, photography, painting, or sculpture can do the same, but installations have proved most fruitful – perhaps because with installations there is less pressure to conform to the demands of a formal tradition and the artist can more easily explore what concerns them.

Why are installations so irritating, then? Perhaps because in the many cases when craftsmanship is removed, art seems like the emperor's new clothes. Perhaps also because installation artists are frequently so bound up with the intellectual history of art and its various 'isms' that they forget that those who are not educated in this neither care nor understand.

But, ultimately, being irritating need not be a bad thing for a work of art since at least it compels engagement from the viewer. Take Martin Creed's *Lights Going On and Off* again. 'My work', says Martin Creed, 'is about fifty per cent what I make of it, and fifty per cent what people make of it. Meanings are made in people's heads – I can't control them.'

Another example is *Double Bind*, Juan Muñoz's huge work at the Tate Modern gallery in London. A false mezzanine floor in the massive main exhibition hall is full of holes, some real, some *trompe l'oeil*. A pair of lifts chillingly lit go up and down, heading nowhere. To get the full impact, and to go beyond mere illusionism, you need to go downstairs and look up through the holes. There are grey men living in rooms between the floorboards, installations within the installation. I don't necessarily understand or like all installation art, but I was moved by this. It's creepy and beautiful and strange, but ultimately you, the spectator, need to make an effort to get something out of it. ●

note

Writers sometimes start by indicating the structure of the passage to follow. You can use these clues to help you find where answers are located.

Questions 1–6: Multiple-choice questions

Choose the correct letter, A, B, C, or D. In each case, decide which option is most like your own answer in 4.

1 The writer includes the story about the beads to show that

   A installations are a relatively unsophisticated art form.
   B people get away from installation art as fast as they can.
   C the audience often actively participate in modern art.
   D the public are unsure what modern art forms consist of.

2 Why aren't domestic lights considered installation art?

   A They go on and off inside a building.
   B They are not created by painters or sculptors.
   C They are not officially recognized as art.
   D They only go on and off for a short time.

3 What important features do all installation works have in common?

   A immobility   *some intent*
   B viewer involvement
   C humour
   D none

4 Why was Duchamp's 1917 work so important?

   A It marked the beginning of installation art.
   B It made traditional artists extremely angry.
   C It was a particularly well-made object.
   D It was proof that installations were not art.

5 Foster says there is now so much installation art because artists

   A nowadays have a tradition of installation art to follow.
   B want to find their own new ways of involving audiences. *doesn't suggest*
   C find it easier than creating works within traditional art forms. *to find it easier*
   D cannot make audiences respond emotionally to paintings.

6 One reason why installations irritate us is that the artists

   A seem to be following fashion.
   B know nothing about art or its history.
   C are often too concerned with obscure issues.
   D try unsuccessfully to achieve technical perfection.

note

Watch out for misleading options which either say something which may be true but is not in the text, or which use words from the text in an untrue statement.

Questions 7–11: Short-answer questions

Answer the questions with words from the Reading Passage. Write NO MORE THAN THREE WORDS for each answer.

7 What is the writer's ironic response to the first part of the dictionary entry? ...... *thanks for that*

   It is incomplete

8 How much of the effect of *Lights Going On and Off* depends on the audience? ...... *compels viewer engagement*

   how much

9 Where is the best place to appreciate Muñoz's installation? ...... *through downstairs holes*

10 How did *Double Bind* make the writer feel? ...... *surprised,*

   moved

11 Who is responsible for ensuring the significance of the work is understood? ......

   The spectators.

Question 12: Global multiple-choice

12 Complete this statement about the text in your own words.
Overall, the writer believes that installation art is …

Choose the appropriate letter A–D. Decide which is most like your answer above.

Overall, the writer believes that installation art is

A only of interest to a small audience and the artists themselves.
B hard to define but challenging and sometimes worthwhile.
C impossible to appreciate without knowing the history of modern art.
D now of much higher quality than other visual art forms.

Exploration

5 Complete the expressions with the correct dependent prepositions. Then look back at the passage to check your answers.

a The exhibition is entirely devoted ...to... the works of Salvador Dali. (line 15)

b There is no simple answer ...to... the question 'What is art?'. (line 16)

c Some critics even conferred ...on... Warhol the title of 'Greatest Living Artist'. (line 34)

d To understand this piece, you need to see it ...in... context, not on its own. (line 40)

e The impact ...of... Picasso's work on twentieth-century art was enormous. (line 43)

f The public have become much more interested ...in... abstract art. (line 66)

g Certain artists seem to be conforming ...to... the current fashion for installation art. (line 75)

h The demands ...of... working full-time as a creative artist can be extremely stressful. (line 75)

i The tone of a painting is often closely bound ...up... with the colours used. (line 82)

j The Sunday street market is full ...of... works by local artists. (line 97)

6 Match the idioms (a–d) with their meanings (1–4).

a a first stab (line 29)
b got the nod from (line 35) *officially recognized*
c barking up the wrong tree (line 45)
d like the emperor's new clothes (line 80) *following fashion*

d — c — 1 following the wrong idea
      — 2 non-existent
b — 3 been officially accepted by
a — 4 an initial attempt

7 Discuss these questions with other students.

a How do you feel about the kind of art described in the text?
b Why do you think people visit art galleries and exhibitions? Why might other people prefer to stay away?
c How important is it that art is taught at school?
d Should governments support the arts with taxpayers' money?

H.W

Listening

Section 4

In Section 4, you will hear a talk or lecture by one speaker on a topic of general interest.

Orientation

1 Discuss these questions with another student.

a Can you describe the instruments shown in the photos above?

b How are the instruments being used in each of the photos?

c Are there similar instruments to these in your country? When are they used?

d How important is music in your culture?

e Which instruments can you play or would you like to be able to play?

f What is the instrument on the right called? What culture do you associate it with?

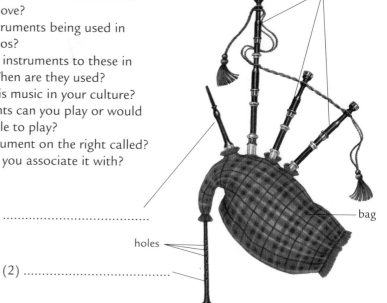

(3) ....

(1) ....

holes

(2) ....

bag

Diagrams and descriptions

2 The extracts below are a transcript from a description of how this instrument is played. Put the extracts in the correct order by writing 1–4 in the boxes.

☐ In addition, there are a number of other pipes or 'drones'. In the diagram you have, there are three of these. All drones play a constant note.

☐ In order to play the instrument, the musician begins by blowing air into the bag along a tube called the 'blowpipe'.

☐ Then, the air moves downwards along the main pipe which is known as the 'chanter'. This usually has nine holes in it. The musician plays the tune by covering these holes with his fingers.

☐ This causes the bag to inflate with air, which must be forced outwards by squeezing it lightly, in this case with the elbow.

3 Find expressions in 2 that indicate the following.

sequence, e.g. *begins by*
direction, e.g. *into*
naming, e.g. *called*
number, e.g. *nine holes in it*

4 Label the diagram in 1 with words from the text. Use one word for each answer.

5 Look at the diagram of a trumpet below. Describe the trumpet to yourself. Identify as many parts of it as you can and think about how it works.

IELTS practice

Questions 1–5: Labelling a diagram

🎧 Label the diagram below. Write NO MORE THAN THREE WORDS for each answer.

(1) ....

(3) ....

(4) ....

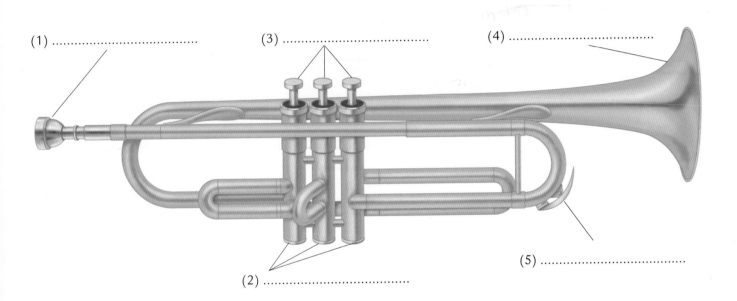

(5) ....

(2) ....

Questions 6–10: Note completion

Complete these sentences. Write NO MORE THAN THREE WORDS for each answer.

First evidence of trumpet in Ancient Egypt (6) .... ago.

Became orchestral instrument in early (7) .... century.

The trumpet often leads the brass section because of its (8) .... sound.

The trumpet is quite (9) .... compared with other instruments.

Some trumpeters now play the (10) .... instead.

Exploration

6 Discuss these questions with other students.

a Which musical instruments do you like most? Why? Can you think of some examples in particular songs or pieces of music?

b Which instruments do you *not* like the sound of? Give reasons.

Speaking

Orientation   **1** 🎧 Listen to the four speakers and answer the questions.

   a   Which of the events shown in the pictures is each speaker talking about?
   b   Which of the four events would appeal most to you? Why?

Getting started   **2** 🎧Listen to the speakers again. Which phrase (a–d) does each speaker use to introduce their experiences?

note

Introduce your chosen topic in Part 2 by saying exactly what the subject of your talk is.

   a   My favourite was …
   b   I've decided to talk about …
   c   I remember one …
   d   There are a lot that I've enjoyed, but the best one was …

3 Work in groups. Tell the others about events like those in the photos that you have attended. Use the phrases above.

IELTS practice   **Part 2:** Extended speaking

4 In Speaking Part 2, the examiner will give you a topic verbally and on a card. You have one minute to prepare what you are going to say. Read the card below and prepare to give an answer, making any notes to help you.

> Describe an artist or an entertainer you admire.
> You should say:
>   who they are and what they do
>   how they became successful
>   how you found out about them
> and explain why you admire them.

authentic — same

5 Work in pairs. In Speaking Part 2, you must talk for one or two minutes. Take it in turns to talk about an artist or an entertainer you admire. Follow the instructions on the card, using any notes you have made and adding more details.

Language for writing

Choosing tenses

1 Which of these verbs mean 'go up'? Which mean 'go down'? What are their past and past participle forms?

fall ~~(d)~~   rise ∪   drop ∩   increase ∪
decrease ∩   decline ∩   grow ∪

2 Which verb tense is used in each of these sentences?

a From 2000 to 2005, printing costs went up rapidly. *P-indefinit*
b Art values are going up quickly now. *continuse*
c This century, attendances have gone down. *Past Perfect*
d The number of performances will go up next year. *F*
e By the end of the decade, video recorders will have become obsolete. *F. Perfect*

3 Match the tenses in 2 with these uses.

b a trend happening now   a trend up to now
a predicted trend *d*   a trend in the past *c*
a trend happening before a future date *e*

4 Match these time expressions with the tenses in 2 which they are commonly used with.

since 1998	in five years' time *a*
last October	over the previous decade
at present *b*	nowadays *b*
before 2000	during the summer of 2003
at the moment	by 2025
up to now *e*	so far this century *c*
in the year after next *d*	between 2015 and 2020
currently	for the last six months

5 Complete the sentences below, using the verbs in 1.

Materials lent from public libraries 1995–2005 and 2010–2015 (projected)

	Percentage of total materials lent				
	1995	2000	2005	2010	2015
Adult fiction	53	48	45	42	39
Adult non-fiction	23	23	22	22	21
Children's	19	21	22	22	23
Audio-visual	5	8	11	14	17

a Adult fiction lending ....*increases* *rise*....... five per cent between 1995 and 2000.

b Audio-visual lending ....*is likely to rise*.... to seventeen per cent by 2015.

c The percentage of children's books being lent ....*grow*........ at present.

d The figures for adult non-fiction lending .....*fall decrease*.... a little since 2000.

e In the final years of the last century, children's books lending ...*the rise*... two per cent.

f Adult non-fiction lending neither .....*increases*..... nor ...*decreases*...from 1995 to 2000.

g Over the last decade, audio-visual lending ....*grows*.... a few per cent.

h In the five years between 2010 and 2015, adult fiction lending ...*is likely expected to decrease*.... by another three per cent.

6 To describe future projections, we often use the expressions below. Write three sentences about future trends in the table above, using these expressions.

is likely to
is forecast to
is set to
is expected to
is predicted to

Example

The total is likely to decline in the coming decade.
The figures are set to rise next month.

1 The adult fiction lending is expected to decrease for the projected years from (2010 – 2015)

2 Audio visual lending is expected to increase by three percent for the projected years (2010 – 2015)

3 Children lending is likely to remain the same for the projected years (2010 – 2015)

Writing

Orientation

1 Discuss these questions with other students.
  a Which of the items in the picture would you prefer to spend your money on? Why?
  b Which of them have become more/less popular in your lifetime?
  c Do you think these trends will change in the future?

Describing trends

2 Look at the graph below and answer these questions.

  a What does each axis relate to?
  b What do the lines represent?
  c Complete the opening statement below.
    The graph shows ...
  d Which verbs can you use to describe each line?
    Example
    Live music and theatre: *fall, recover, fluctuate,* etc.

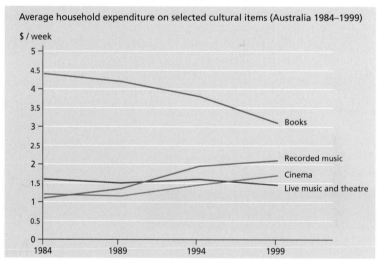

Average household expenditure on selected cultural items (Australia 1984–1999)

note

Use a wide range of vocabulary to describe trends in the data.

3 Complete the text below. Use suitable verbs, plus adverbs from the list where appropriate.

rapidly   gradually   sharply   steadily   slightly   initially

During that time the expenditure on books (a) ...... at first, (b) ...... over the next five years and then (c) ...... in the final period. Spending on live music and theatre (d) ...... between just above and below $1.5, whereas average spending on recorded music was the only amount to (e) ...... throughout the 15 years. This amount (f) ...... from 1989 to 1994 to nearly $2, almost double the 1984 figure. Expenditure on cinema tickets (g) ...... overall. It showed a downward trend at first, but (h) ...... from the end of the 1990s.

4 You can also use adjectives and nouns instead of verbs and adjectives to describe trends.

Example
The amount spent on cinema fell gradually from 1984 to 1989.
There was a gradual fall in the amount spent on cinema from 1984 to 1989.

Rewrite the first sentence in the text in 3 using adjectives and nouns.

5 Complete the summary statement below.

Overall the statistics show that ...

Describing figures

6 It was possible to describe the graph on page 54 without stating exact figures. You can also use approximate phrases and fractions. Rephrase sentences a–c using the expressions below.

just over/under	more/less than	almost	nearly
about	approximately		roughly

> **note**
>
> Avoid giving exact figures by using approximate phrases. This will make the main points clearer.

Examples
There was a 64% fall in cassette sales between 1995 and 2000.
There was a fall of almost two-thirds in cassette sales between 1995 and 2000.

In the last two months, sales of DVDs have risen by 97,487.
In the last two months, sales of DVDs have risen by just under 100,000.

a   There was a 9% decline in art values last year.
b   Since January, cinema audiences have gone up by 20,800.
c   Currently, the market for prints is growing by 32% per year.

Think, plan, write

7 Read the Writing Task 1 below. Use these questions to analyse the data.

a   What does each axis relate to?
b   What do the lines represent?
c   What are the main trends and important points?

The chart below shows the percentage of people attending the cinema once a month or more by age.

Summarize the information by selecting and reporting the main features, and make comparisons where relevant.

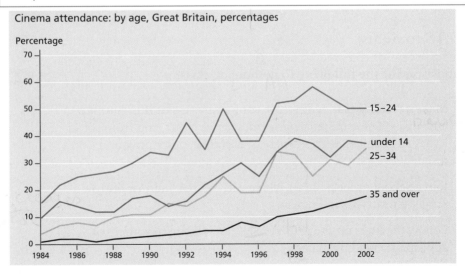

Cinema attendance: by age, Great Britain, percentages

8 Write your answer in at least 150 words.

Help yourself

Reading more widely

1 Extensive reading can greatly improve your reading skills, increase your knowledge of the language and help develop your writing skills. Look at what these students say about their reading habits. Which of these reading habits would suit you best?

a 'Whenever I can, I look at the more serious magazines like *National Geographic* and *New Scientist*. There are always some interesting articles, and they're well written.'

b 'I read an English newspaper every day. I like following news stories as they develop and that helps me learn because they often repeat the same expressions.'

c 'I love novels, particularly thrillers. You don't worry about difficult words; you just keep reading to find out what happens next!'

d 'I always buy text books for college in English rather than my own language. The more you read, the easier it gets.'

e 'There are three or four academic journals on the subject I want to study. They're a great way of finding out about the latest discoveries – and the controversies.'

f 'I don't read much – just magazines really. I like fashion stuff, or finding out about my favourite stars.'

2 Which of the reading sources in 1 are closest to what you find in IELTS? Which would probably never appear?

3 Think about ways you can practise reading the kinds of text used in IELTS. Which of the following have you tried? Which would you like to try?

a Visit local libraries that have reading materials in English, possibly in universities or schools.

b Look for free magazines on aeroplanes, in hotels or conference centres.

c Buy from English-language bookshops in your country, or books by mail-order from the UK, US, etc.

d Read online editions of newspapers and magazines.

e Buy English-language newspapers and magazines on sale in your country, or take out student-rate subscriptions.

f Ask relatives or friends travelling in English-speaking countries to bring or send you materials.

IELTS to do list

Choose one of the following to do outside class.

☐ Make a reading plan to improve your awareness of IELTS topics and styles. These might range from science to art, and from social issues to business, with a variety of narrative, descriptive and discursive texts.

☐ Join a school or local library where you can read and/or borrow a range of text types in English.

☐ Follow the links on the *IELTS Masterclass* website to sources of appropriate reading material.

Where to look

ⓔ www.oup.com/elt/ielts

5 Work and business

1 Look at the photos and discuss these questions with another student.

a   Which category does each job belong to?
    retail   manufacturing   creative
    business   service   technical
b   Which of these jobs are skilled/unskilled, manual/clerical?
c   Which of these job categories are important in your country now? Has this always been the case?
d   Which categories do you think will be more or less important in the future? Why?
e   Which of these categories do you intend to work in?

2 Answer these questions 'yes' or 'no'. Compare your answers with another student.

Are you willing to take risks?	
Do you have one or more goals to achieve?	
Are you an optimist?	
Do you make the most of opportunities?	
Are you motivated and willing to work long hours?	
Do you believe in yourself?	
Can you bounce back after a setback?	
Can you stand by your actions in spite of criticism?	
Can you take your own decisions?	
Do you have the potential to lead people?	

3 Read how to interpret your answers. Answer the questions with another student.

- If you answered 'yes' to six or more of the questions, then you probably have what it takes to run your own business.

- If you answered 'yes' to five or fewer, you may not yet have what's required to run a business. If you really want to go it alone, then you'll need to work on your weaknesses.

a   Do you think you could run your own business now? Why/Why not?
b   What type of business would you like to run one day?

Reading

Orientation

1 Which three of these do you think are most important in a job? Which three are least important? Give reasons.

short working week   interesting work   large salary
long maternity leave   home working   sabbaticals possible
friendly workmates   high-status job title   plenty of holidays
attractive colleagues   childcare facilities

Reading for gist

2 Do you think work is good or bad for you? In what ways? Quickly read the text. What is the writer's opinion?

The great **work myth**

Work gets a terrible press. Pick up any newspaper on almost any day and you'll read about how work is killing our marriages, generating stress, depriving children of 'quality time', hollowing out local communities, and depressing us.
5 Work has become the scapegoat for all our woes. The case against work is put in persuasive terms on an almost daily basis. There is only one problem with it: it's nonsense. For the truth is that, as far as work is concerned, we've never had it so good.

One survey shows that four out of ten British workers declare themselves 'very satisfied' with their jobs – more than in France, Germany, Italy, or Spain. Average earnings have increased, a lot of firms offer longer maternity leave, a third of firms now offer sabbaticals, and two-thirds allow their staff to work from home some of the time. The rhetoric about longer working hours also needs to be put in perspective. The average working day has increased in length over the last two decades, but by just one minute and forty-two seconds.

Despite all the improvements in work over recent decades, there is still an ingrained attitude that happiness lies outside work, that we are waiting for the weekend. This idea that work is essentially bad for us has a long history. Karl Marx described workers being 'alienated' from the product of their labour: 'What, then, constitutes the alienation of labour?' he asked. 'First, the fact that labour is external to the worker, i.e. it does not belong to his essential being; that in his work he does not affirm himself but denies himself; does not feel content but unhappy; does not develop his physical and mental energy but mortifies his body and ruins his mind.' However, relentless negativity about work condemns us to precisely the sort of work that Marx was trying to free us from 150 years ago. If we accept that work is dull and demeaning – a ransom paid for the hostage of our 'free time' – then we are allowing alienation to remain.

Work is becoming too important for it to be of dubious quality. Work is a community, the place where we meet friends and form relationships, a provider of our social as well as our work life. One in three of us meets most of our friends through work, two-thirds of us have dated someone at work, and, according to a poll by recruitment consultancy Sanders and Sidney, a quarter of us meet our life partners there. Work is also becoming a more important indicator of identity. Family, class, region, and religion are now less robust indicators, and work is filling the gap, making it the most important fact about ourselves we mention when we meet people. 'Work,' as Albert Einstein said, 'is the only thing that gives substance to life.'

In truth, they are simply made to feel as if they have a problem because of prevalent attitudes.

The shift of work towards the centre of our lives demonstrates the futility of much of the current debates about 'work/life balance'. It is true that some people are working longer hours. Yet the idea that it is being forced upon us without our choice just doesn't stack up. Take the people working the greatest number of hours – more than sixty a week. Surveys show that they are the ones who say they like their jobs the most. This may seem surprising, until you reflect that people who like something might do more of it than people who do not. People who love their jobs own up to having a 'work/life problem' because they put in more hours than they are strictly required to. In truth, they are simply made to feel as if they have a problem because of prevalent attitudes. Of course, this leaves open the question of who keeps the home fires burning and of the impact on children especially. It may be that people are choosing to invest less time and energy at home than others think they should, but, if these people get more out of their work than they do out of their home, then perhaps this is a clear and valid choice for people to be making.

Ultimately, our goal must be to begin seeing work as an intrinsic part of our life, rather than an adjunct to it. Theodore Zeldin, an Oxford don, has the right manifesto for the future of work: its abolition. But not in the way anti-work campaigners have in mind. 'We should abolish "work",' he says. 'By that I mean abolishing the distinction between work and leisure, one of the greatest mistakes of the last century, one that enables employers to keep workers in lousy jobs by granting them some leisure time. We should strive to be employed in such a way that we don't realize what we are doing is work.' Zeldin throws down the challenge for work in the twenty-first century. It is indeed time to abandon the notion of work as a downpayment on life, but, before we can do so, all the modern myths about work will have to be exposed: the ones that continue to stereotype work as intrinsically sapping, demeaning, and corrosive. It is time to give work a break. ■

Key words

3 Study these sentences. Which words establish the topic? Which other words carry the main content? What kinds of word are they, e.g. nouns, prepositions?

  a Nowadays, every problem we have is blamed on work.

  b In many companies, more time off can be taken after childbirth.

4 Find the parts of the text that express the same ideas as sentences a and b in 3. Which expressions have similar meanings to the key words you identified?

note

Use key words to identify the focus of the question and then look for similar ideas in the main text.

5 Before starting the IELTS task below, read the sentence stems 1–7. What are the key words or phrases in each of these?

IELTS practice

Questions 1–7: Sentence completion

Complete each sentence with the correct ending A–L from the box below.

  1 According to the press, work *K*

  2 A study in Britain indicates that job satisfaction *F*

  3 The workforce of most British companies *D*

  4 The current length of the working day *I*

  5 Marx said that work *G*

  6 The present-day cause of alienation from work *C*

  7 Romantic involvement with a colleague *B*

> A began a century and a half ago.
> B is usually followed by marriage.
> C is the belief that work is bad for us.
> D can do some of their work at home.
> E makes no sense at all.
> F happens to most people.
> G causes employees physical harm.
> H is better paid than in the past.
> I is little more than it was twenty years ago.
> J is higher than in other countries.
> K is much higher than it used to be.
> L destroys relationships.

Finding text

6 Read the summary of part of 'The great work myth' on page 61. Quickly identify which paragraphs of the text the summary relates to.

note

Summary tasks often relate to only a section of the text. Identify that section to save time when looking for answers.

Questions 8–12: Summary completion

Complete the summary with words (A–K) from the box below.

We should recognize that work provides a structure within which people build

(8) ......B......... , sometimes for a lifetime, and plays a growing role in establishing

our (9) ...F............ compared with other factors like social background. Most

people who spend longer at work do so by (10) .....K. SKILLS...... . There is some

debate about the damage this may cause to their (11) .....choice........ , but that is for

individuals to decide. One solution to the problem of work/life balance is to redefine

it, removing the view that our work should be a sacrifice we make for our

(12) .....leisure....... .

A	leisure	F	identity
B	relationships	G	partners
C	skills	H	children
D	health	I	income
E	choice	K	force

Exploration

7 To avoid repetition, part of a sentence can be left out without changing the meaning.

work is killing our marriages, ~~work is~~ generating stress, ~~work is~~ depriving children ...

What has the writer of the text left out of a–h?

a   more .... than in France (line 11)

b   two-thirds .... allow their staff (line 14)

c   but .... by just one minute (line 19)

d   .... a provider of our social (line 42)

e   they are strictly required to .... (line 67)

f   and .... of the impact (line 71)

g   others think they should .... (line 73)

h   rather than .... an adjunct (line 78)

8 Part of a sentence can be replaced with *do, so, not, one* or *ones*. What have the underlined words in italic in a–f replaced?

a   *the ones* who say they like their jobs (line 61)

b   people who do *not* (line 64)

c   than they *do* out of their home (line 75)

d   *one* that enables employers (line 84)

e   before we can *do so* (line 91)

f   the *ones* that continue (line 93)

9 Discuss these questions with another student.

a   Do you agree that the role of work in our lives is changing? In what ways?

b   How far do you agree with the writer's assertion that it is reasonable for people to put their work before their relationships and their families?

c   Do you think it is realistic to aim at making work as enjoyable as leisure? Why?/Why not?

Listening

Section 1

Orientation

1 Look at the photos and answer the questions.

a What job is this? What does the employee have to do?

b Which of the following are necessary for this job?
language skills   communication skills   IT and keyboard skills   organizational skills

c Which of these qualities are needed for each job?
intelligence   patience   experience   energy
creativity   punctuality   honesty
What are the adjectives formed from these words? Which adjectives describe you?

d Would you like to do this job while you study? Why?/Why not?

2 Study the questions and unfinished statements in 1–5 below. What answers do you think you might hear for each?

IELTS practice

note

As you listen, compare what you hear with what you expected for each question. Then choose the option closest in meaning to what the speaker actually says.

Questions 1–5: Multiple-choice questions

Choose the correct letter, A, B, or C.

1 Steve phones the agency to find out about
   A a permanent post at a call centre.
   B the nature of the job advertised.
   C the amount he would be paid.

2 Ellen says the problem with some students is that they
   A are not completely honest.
   B lack essential IT skills.
   C arrive late for work.

3 Steve would mainly take calls from customers
   A who want information about their credit card accounts.
   B whose credit cards have been stolen.
   C who have lost their credit cards.

4 Which chart shows the current proportion of female to male callers?

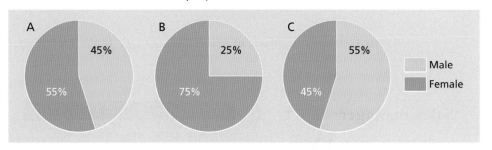

5 Ellen says that call centre operatives should be

   A experienced.
   B intelligent.
   C helpful.

Predicting

3 Study the map and the box, and answer the questions.

   a What information does the map give?
   b What do the answers in the box have in common?
   c What prepositions of place, e.g. *on, beside,* might you hear?

Questions 6–10: Labelling a map

🎧 Listen to the second part of the recording and label the map below with the correct letter.

note

Listen carefully to the beginning of the dialogue to find out where on the map to start. Then listen for prepositions of place to help you follow the directions.

A Insurance offices
B Shipping company
C Call centre
D Petrol station
E Hotel
F Railway station
G Shopping centre
H Local government offices

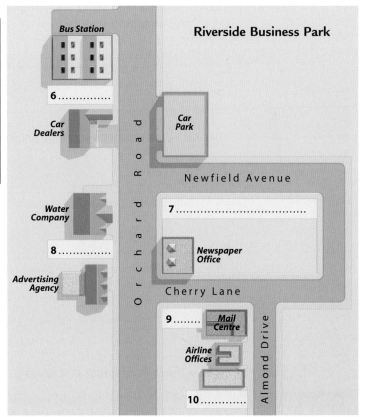

Exploration

4 Discuss these questions with other students.

   a What other qualities might also be required to do the job described by the speaker?
   b Would you like to do this job? Give reasons.

Speaking

1 Which of advertisements 1–3 would interest you? Which would you never apply for?

1

Sales manager

Local company wishes to appoint a
Sales Manager to lead a dynamic team
of sales personnel. A degree, preferably
in Business or Marketing, is required,
as is a proven record of success in
sales. Excellent communication and
presentation skills, both written and
verbal, are essential.

2

REPORTER

City radio station seeks reporter. The
successful candidate will be a graduate
with at least one year's experience of news
reporting. He or she will have the ability
to generate breaking news on a daily
basis, and will need to be on the spot for
the latest events wherever and whenever
they occur.

3

Researchers

An international survey group is recruiting
Researchers for a two-year inter-
disciplinary research and monitoring
programme at centres for global science.
They require biologists, chemists,
engineers, meteorologists,
oceanographers, physicists,
and technicians.

Applicants must be prepared to work in
remote parts of the world.

2 🎧 Listen to speakers a–c talking briefly about their work. Match each of them with one of the advertisements above.

Describing an occupation

3 🎧 Listen again and complete the table below with expressions they use to describe aspects of their jobs.

	a Mark	b Jennifer	c Chris
Their responsibilities			
What they like about the job			
What they dislike about it			
Their future career plans			

IELTS practice

Part 1: Familiar discussion

note

Don't just give short
answers. Try to explain or
give reasons.

4 In Part 1, you could be asked about your work or your studies. Work with another student to ask each other these questions.

a   Can you tell me about the job or course of study that you are doing?
b   What do you like or dislike about it?
c   What plans do you have for your career in the future?

Language for writing

Comparative and superlative forms

1 Correct the errors.

a Their marketing department is much bigger that ours.

b Williams is the better manager we've ever had.

c Prices have increased slowly this year than last year.

d These are the most bad figures in the firm's history.

e Family-run firms are sometimes the successful of all.

f Colin works least hard than anyone else in this office.

g Production didn't go up any fast last month than the month before.

2 Complete the sentences with the comparative or superlative.

a The competition is .... (intense) than it was five years ago.

b A global company's product range is .... (wide) than a small firm's.

c We all need to work .... (hard) than we did last year.

d In many companies, labour costs are .... (great) expense.

e Productivity is .... (bad) in this country than it is abroad.

f They are .... (efficient) firm in the industry.

3 Modifiers such as *much* can be used with comparatives and *by far* with superlatives.

Examples
Sales are usually much higher in summer than in winter.
These are by far the most popular goods we make.

Which of these modifiers indicate a small difference, and which a large difference? Which is used with superlatives only?

far	significantly	easily
slightly	a bit	
a great deal	marginally	

4 Study the graph. Complete the sentences with a modifier plus a comparative or superlative form.

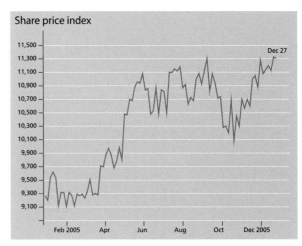

Share price index

a The figures for January to March were .... (low) in the whole year.

b Overall, the index rose .... (quick) in the spring than in the summer.

c By .... (big) increase was between March and June.

d The peak in September was .... (high) than that in July.

e Overall, it went up .... (slow) in the autumn than in the spring.

f The index fell .... (far) in October than in August.

Write three more sentences about the graph above. Use modifiers with comparatives or superlatives.

5 The form *as ... as* is used to express equality; the negative is *not as ... as* or *not so ... as*. Modifiers and quantifiers can be added.

Examples
Nokia is almost as valuable as McDonald's.
Microsoft is not quite as valuable as Coca Cola.
Nokia is worth less than half as much as IBM.
Coca Cola is worth just over three times as much as Marlboro.

Compare the following brands. In most cases more than one answer is possible.

a IBM / Microsoft
b Toyota / GE
c Disney / IBM
d Marlboro / Toyota
e GE / Marlboro
f McDonald's / IBM

The World's 10 Most Valuable Brands in 2005

Rank	Brand	Brand value ($ billions)	Rank	Brand	Brand value ($ billions)
1	Coca Cola	67	6	Disney	27
2	Microsoft	61	7	McDonald's	25
3	IBM	54	8	Nokia	24
4	GE	44	9	Toyota	22
5	Intel	34	10	Marlboro	22

Writing

1 Look at the six media forms in the charts below. In which would you expect to see or hear an advertisement for each of these products and services?

a cheap flights
b cut-price furniture
c a new model of car
d a bank
e a newly-released CD
f a hairdresser's

2 Look at the Writing Task 1 below.

a Can you explain why a pie chart and a bar chart have been used in each case?
b What is shown by each section of the pie chart? Which three dominate the market in the pie chart?
c What is shown by each bar in the chart? What is the overall trend?

> **note**
>
> If there is more than one chart, graph, or table, the information in them will be linked in some way. Find this link when you first study the diagrams.

> The charts below give information about the amount spent on different forms of advertising. Summarize the information by selecting and reporting the main features, making comparisons where relevant.

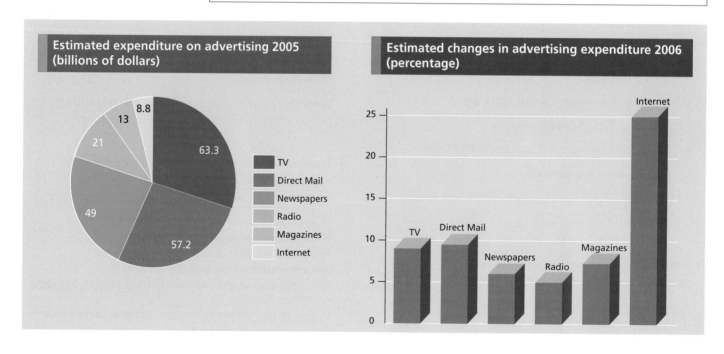

Estimated expenditure on advertising 2005 (billions of dollars)

- TV — 63.3
- Direct Mail — 57.2
- Newspapers — 49
- Radio — 21
- Magazines — 13
- Internet — 8.8

Estimated changes in advertising expenditure 2006 (percentage)

TV, Direct Mail, Newspapers, Radio, Magazines, Internet

3 Look at the data and answer these questions.

a Which categories of media match the following descriptions? Write a sentence expressing each.
   the smallest sum of money
   the largest proportion of total spending
   the next largest amount of total spending
   the lowest projected rise
   by far the highest expected growth
   increases in the region of 5–10%

b Which category is the lowest in one diagram but the highest in the other?

4 Rewrite the following sentences about the data, using the words given. You may need to change nouns to verbs or verbs to nouns.

a Slightly more money was spent on TV advertising than on direct mail.

Almost ....

b Newspaper advertising was predicted to grow relatively slowly in comparison with magazines.

Relatively ....

c Taken together, advertising in newspapers and magazines accounts for by far the highest spending.

Much ....

d Spending on most categories of advertising was forecast to rise by 5–10%, except for two.

Apart ....

e More was spent on TV, direct mail or newspapers than on radio, magazines and the Internet combined.

Not ....

f No other category was expected to increase even half as much as Internet advertising.

Internet ....

Think, plan, write

5 Plan your answer to the Writing Task 1 question in 2. Think about these questions before you begin.

a How will you begin your description of the data?
b Are there any important comparisons to make between the charts? Which ones?
c Which segments or bars from each chart will you focus on? Why?
d Which chart will you describe first?
e What other comparisons will you include?
f Which verb tenses will you mainly use?

6 Write at least 150 words in answer to the question in 2. Use comparatives, superlatives, and other expressions you have learnt. Where appropriate, adapt phrases and sentences you have written in this section.

7 Evaluate your partner's completed text, using these ten questions.

a Is it appropriate in length and style?
b Is there a suitable introduction to the topic?
c Are the points presented in a logical order?
d Are these points linked together correctly?
e Does it cover all the key points in both diagrams?
f Are relevant comparisons and contrasts made?
g Are there any unnecessary points?
h Is there any inaccurate information?
i Is there anything you don't understand?
j Are there any obvious language errors?

Help yourself

Word formation

1 In general, prefixes change the meaning of words. How do these prefixes change the meaning of the root words?

	Prefixes	Examples
a	anti-	*anti*social / *anti*climax
b	bio-	*bio*diversity / *bio*degradable
c	dis-	*dis*honest / *dis*obey
c	extra-	*extra*ordinary / *extra*terrestrial
d	mis-	*mis*behaviour / *mis*manage
e	re-	*re*wind / *re*fuel

2 How do these prefixes change the meaning of root words? Think of two or three examples of words starting with these prefixes.

auto-	post-
inter-	trans-
multi-	under-
over-	

3 Suffixes often change the part of speech of words as well as their meaning. What parts of speech are the root words below and what parts of speech result from the addition of the suffixes?

	Root	Examples
a	employ	employ*ee* / employ*ment*
b	create	creat*or* / creat*ive*
c	weak	weak*ness* / weak*en*
d	child	child*ish* / child*hood*
e	solid	solid*ify* / solid*ly*

4 To guess the meanings of words, start with the meaning of the root, then work out how prefixes and suffixes might change this. Work out the meanings of the words in italic in these sentences.

a A small *dehumidifier* is ideal for *enclosed* areas where excess moisture may have *undesired* effects.

b *Multidimensional* family therapy is an *outpatient* family-based drug abuse treatment for teenage substance *abusers*.

c He became *increasingly* aware of her tendency to point out his *imperfections*.

5 Adding two or more words together to make *compound words* is another way in which English words are formed. This is more common than using complex phrases. For example, 'a business meeting' is used in preference to 'a meeting to discuss business matters'. What combinations of parts of speech are used in these examples?

- right-handed · cold-hearted · quick-thinking
- a database · the generation gap · an eye witness account
- an outbreak · a breakout · a downpour
- a blackbird · grandparents
- writing paper · driving test · walking boots

Add other examples you know which follow the above patterns.

IELTS to do list

Choose one of the following to do outside class.

☐ Train yourself to work out or guess the meanings of words rather than always looking in a dictionary. Take account of prefixes and suffixes. This will help you to prepare for IELTS, in which you are not allowed to refer to a dictionary.

☐ When recording new vocabulary, note down related words: root words and words with different prefixes and suffixes.

☐ Make your own reference lists of words starting with particular prefixes and suffixes, especially less common ones, like *hyper-* (hyperactive), *omni-* (omnipresent), and *-dom* (officialdom).

Where to look

 www.oup.com/elt/ielts

Oxford Advanced Learner's Dictionary

Oxford Student's Dictionary of English

6 Education

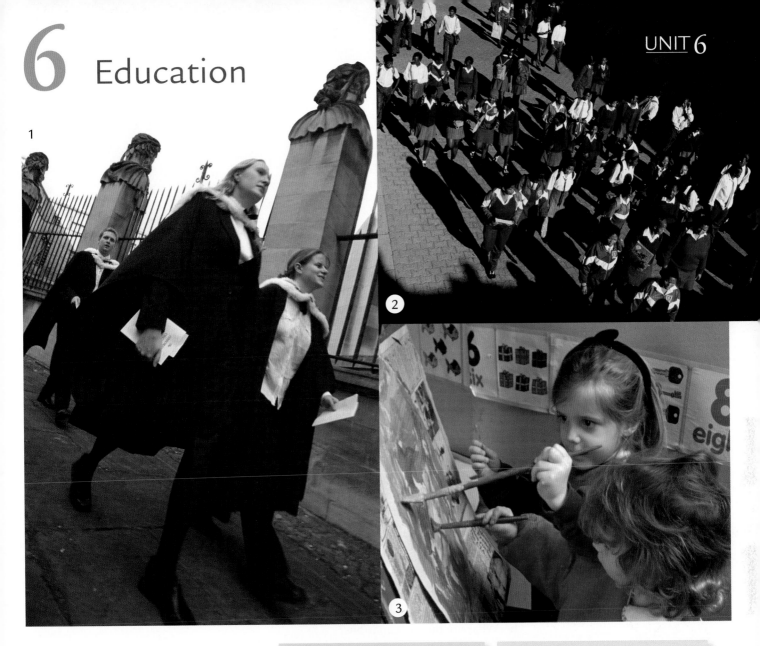

1

2

3

1 What are the distinct features of the kinds of education in the photos?

2 Read the newspaper headlines and then discuss these questions with another student.

a What educational issues are raised by the newspaper headlines?

b Which issues do you think are the most important?

c What educational issues are of current concern in your country?

Maths tests at 14 kill pupils' enthusiasm

University fees set to rise by 15% next year

Boys still lagging behind in reading and writing

Government plan for more faith schools

PARENTS CALL FOR ACTION ON BULLYING

SHARP RISE IN TEENAGE TRUANCY FIGURES

Demand for extra playgroups as more mothers choose to work

Hundreds on waiting list for popular school

All schools to have broadband Internet by end of the year

Reading

Orientation **1** Look at the photographs and discuss these questions with other students.

    a What do you notice about the activities the children are involved in?
    b In your experience, are there some school subjects in which boys do better than girls and vice versa?
    c How do you explain learning differences between boys and girls?

2 Read the title and first paragraph of the article and answer these questions.

    a What do you understand by these words and phrases?
       gender gap   literacy   an age-appropriate level
    b What aspects of education is the article going to deal with?
    c What conclusions do you think the article might come to? Make predictions.

Scanning **3** The article you are going to read includes the views of three people. Scan the text quickly to find the answers to these questions.

    a What are the people's names?
    b What are their occupations?

The education GENDER GAP

Research into gender differences in education has tended to focus on the poor performance of girls in science and maths, virtually ignoring the low achievement of boys in reading and writing. According to Cecilia Reynolds, from the Ontario Institute for Studies in Education, it has long been recognized that girls did well in literacy and that boys did not, but there was no great concern about this because in the real world, boys were still going on to get better jobs and salaries. However, a 2004 study by the Council of Ministers of Education, found that Canadian girls are outperforming boys in literacy skills by a wider margin than previously thought. Among thirteen-year-olds, about ten per cent more girls than boys meet expected targets for literacy, and among sixteen-year-olds, about seventeen per cent more girls write at an age-appropriate level.

As if that wasn't bad enough, recent testing has shown for the first time that the performance gap that once existed between boys and girls in science and maths has now almost disappeared too. Some experts even predict that at some time in the future, girls may actually move ahead of boys in science. According to Paul Cappon, Director General of the Council of Ministers of Education, one of the consequences of this will be to put girls in the lead in relation both to university entrance and to achievement in the labour market. Already, only forty-two per cent of university graduates in Canada are male, and that number is dropping each year.

While experts agree that now is the time to focus on the long-standing gender divide in literacy, their explanations for it, and their solutions, vary widely. In a culture that favours equal opportunity and advocates political correctness, some have found it difficult to discuss this troubling gender gap without entering into the touchy domain of sexism.

Some educators have put the blame directly on policy and its implementation by women teachers, saying that since educational practice has aimed at improving the performance of girls, boys have been forgotten. Cecilia Reynolds has warned that it is important to address any differences between boys and girls without assigning blame. Nevertheless, although she doesn't believe boys were forgotten, she does admit that insufficient attention may have been paid to their different learning needs.

Others have pointed to a more subtle cause, to what Paul Cappon has called the 'feminization' of education. Increasingly, teaching is becoming dominated by females as more young women enter the profession and more older men retire, he says. That leaves boys with few male role models in the classroom. 'It's women doing the teaching. Boys in the socialization process will tend to discount the importance of that particular subject area when it's only women teaching it,' he suggests.

Cappon also thinks the kinds of reading materials available in schools may be better suited to girls than boys. As he points out, the current wisdom is that boys' reading preferences include factual and instructional material that will help them understand particular areas of interest, whereas girls are attracted to stories that explore interpersonal relationships.

Since there is now concrete evidence of a significant gender divide, there is a growing body of opinion which argues that the only way to ensure equitable treatment of boys and girls is to segregate them. Some schools have used this tactic to improve girls' performance in science and maths, but with the latest emphasis on literacy and boys, some now say full separation is the only solution.

Leonard Sax, the founder of an organization promoting single-sex education, points to the success of an inner-city school in Montreal which introduced single-sex classrooms five years ago. Since then, absenteeism has dropped and the rate of students going on to college has nearly doubled. Sax, a family doctor and a psychologist, believes that many people in education are paralyzed by a feeling that it's politically incorrect to talk about innate differences in the ways girls and boys learn. He argues, however, that genetic differences between boys and girls mean that it's impossible for them both to learn successfully in the same classroom. According to Sax, every substantial choice made in schools benefits one gender and disadvantages another. As an example, he claims that girls hear better than boys and that part of the reason for boys falling behind is simply that they can't hear the teacher. He also points to research which shows that there are key differences in the way boys and girls respond to confrontation. Girls shrink away from a confrontational teaching style under which many boys would thrive.

What policy makers ultimately decide to do may depend on how far the results of the recent study are judged to be an accurate reflection of the general situation. Cecilia Reynolds emphasizes that gender differences are statistical, with significant numbers of individuals everywhere not following the general trend. Although she does not believe we should be seriously concerned, she does think that in future, parents and teachers will need to pay more attention to what is happening to boys both at home and in the classroom.

> Boys in the socialization process will tend to discount the importance of that particular subject area when it's only women teaching it

Identifying opinions

4 Work with another student to answer the questions below.

  a What are Cecilia Reynolds' views about blame? Which verbs and other phrases introduce her opinions?

  b What are Paul Cappon's views about reading materials? Which phrase suggests that other people share his views?

  c What are Leonard Sax's views about the differences between boys and girls? Which verbs and other phrases suggest he believes in the case he is making?

IELTS practice

Questions 1–5: Matching
Look at the following list of statements 1–5 relating to differences in performance between boys and girls. Match each statement with the correct person A–C.

  1 Not all boys and girls follow the general learning patterns.
  2 There are inborn differences in the way boys and girls learn.
  3 In the past, boys' poor literacy performance did not disadvantage them professionally.
  4 Boys and girls respond differently to different teaching styles.
  5 The high proportion of women in teaching is a disadvantage for boys.

  A Cecilia Reynolds
  B Paul Cappon
  C Leonard Sax

Questions 6–9: Sentence completion
Complete sentences 6–9 with words taken from the Reading Passage. Use no more than THREE words for each answer.

  6 Research suggests that the gender gap in maths and science has

     ....

  7 The proportion of male graduates in Canada is ....

  8 Whereas girls enjoy reading about ...., boys prefer non-fiction.

  9 The rate of .... in the Montreal school with segregated

     classrooms has fallen.

Exploration

5 Discuss these questions with other students.

  a The article puts the case for boys and girls being educated separately. What do you think about this idea?

  b In what sense do you think it might be 'politically incorrect to talk about innate differences in the ways girls and boys learn'?

6 What do you think the 'gap' phrases in italic mean in these sentences?

  a The 'dot com' companies filled *a gap in the market*.

  b The Prime Minister's popularity is due to his ability to bridge *the generation gap*.

  c The digital revolution is leading to *a credibility gap* between young people's lives and the educational processes they go through.

  d Many students spend *a gap year* travelling or doing voluntary work.

7 What meaning does the prefix *out-* add to the verb in 'outperform' (line 11)? What do you think the phrase 'to outstay your welcome' means? Make sentences using these verbs and the words in brackets.

a outgrow (family / house)
b outlive (old computer / usefulness)
c outmanoeuvre (president / political enemies)
d outnumber (female graduates)
e outweigh (disadvantages)

8 Refer to the text and answer these questions.

a 'Absenteeism' (line 81) means being absent from school or work when you should be there. What do you think the recently coined term 'presenteeism' means?
b 'Double' (line 83) means 'to increase by twice as much'. Which verbs mean 'to increase by three times', and 'to increase by four times'?

9 Match words on the left with those on the right to form collocations. Then check your answers by finding the pairs of words in the text.

academic   correctness
concrete   opportunity
equal   market
labour   graduate
political   background
university   evidence

10 Use the collocations you have made to complete these sentences.

a In schools these days, boys and girls have an .... to study all subjects.
b Recent research has provided .... that boys lag behind girls in many subjects.
c It is sometimes .... which stops people discussing subjects like race or gender.
d Even as a .... with a good degree, Sam is having difficulty finding work.
e The senator's .... in economics make him a strong candidate in the presidential election.
f These days more women are re-entering the .... after having children.

Listening

Section 2

Orientation

1 The photographs are taken from the websites of different clubs and societies at a university. Match each photo with one of these clubs or societies.

Ju-Jitsu   Gliding   DJ

2 Discuss these questions with another student. If you are at university now, or have been in the past, refer to your actual experience.

a What clubs or societies would you join at university?
b Would you like to help run one of these groups? Why? / Why not?
c What reasons do students have for joining clubs and societies?

Predicting answers

3 You are going to hear someone giving first-year students at the beginning of their university course information about activities they can do during their free time. Before you listen, answer these questions.

a What kinds of activities do you think the speaker will mention?
b Read the short answer questions and partial answers 1–10 opposite. What kinds of words are required? Can you predict an answer?
c Are there any answers that are impossible even to guess at?

IELTS practice

Questions 1–6: Short-answer questions

🎧 Listen to the recording and answer questions 1–6 using no more than THREE WORDS for each answer.

1 How many societies can students join at the university?

....

2 What is the Rock Society?

....

3 How often does the Mountaineering Club meet?

....

4 When does the Mountaineering Club visit actual mountains?

....

5 What kind of classes is the Dance Club putting on in the summer?

....

6 What does the Hellenic Society organize every month?

....

Questions 7–10: Sentence completion

🎧 Complete the sentences. Write NO MORE THAN THREE WORDS for each answer.

Most artistic events take place in or around the (7)... .

It is always possible to see Eastern European Art at the (8)... .

More unconventional plays can be seen at (9)... .

To get into the choir or jazz band, students have to have (10)................................... .

Exploration

4 Discuss these questions with other students.

a What facilities would you expect to find on a university campus?

b If an activity is described as 'thriving' or 'flourishing', what does this mean?

c To put on an activity means to organize it. What does 'put on' mean in these contexts?

He's not really surprised about passing the exam. He's just *putting* it *on*.

She had to *put* the brakes *on* sharply to stop in time.

He's an excellent student. I'd *put* money *on* him getting a first.

Speaking

1 The text below describes four learning styles. Read the text and choose which is most similar and which is least similar to your own habits. Note down examples of things you do which illustrate your choices.

Activist	Reflector	Theorist	Pragmatist
Activists like to be involved in new experiences. They are open minded and enthusiastic about new ideas but get bored with implementation. They enjoy doing things but tend to act first and consider the implications afterwards.	Reflectors like to stand back and look at a situation from different perspectives. They like to collect data and think about it carefully before coming to any conclusions. They enjoy observing others and will listen to their views before offering their own.	Theorists adapt and integrate observations into complex and logical theories. They think problems through in a step-by-step way. They tend to be perfectionists who like to fit things into a rational scheme. They tend to be detached and analytical rather than subjective or emotive in their thinking.	Pragmatists are keen to try things out. They want concepts that can be applied to the real world. They tend to be impatient with lengthy discussions, and are practical and down to earth.

2 Compare your choices with another student and then discuss these questions.

    a In what kinds of learning situations are you most and least comfortable?

    b As a learner at school or college, have you found yourself similar to or different from most other learners?

Personal reactions

3 Complete each of the following sentences with your own ideas. Explain your personal answers to 3a–c to other students. Use some of the expressions under *Personal reactions*.

    a My favourite teacher at school was ....

    b I never enjoyed .... classes.

    c The most useful thing I learnt at school was how to ....

Personal reactions

For me, this was interesting/horrible/fantastic/special because ...
My impression is that ...
My main reason for ...
The only explanation I can think of is ...

IELTS practice

Part 2: Extended speaking

4 In Speaking Part 2, the examiner will give you a topic verbally and on a card. You then have one minute to prepare what you are going to say. Think about the task below and make a few notes. The final instruction on the card will normally ask you to explain your personal reaction to an aspect of the topic.

> Describe a subject you enjoyed studying at school.
>
> You should say
>   when and where you started studying it
>   what the lessons were like
>   what made this subject different from other subjects
> and explain why you enjoyed the subject.

5 In Speaking Part 2 you must talk for one to two minutes. Take it in turns to talk uninterrupted about a subject you enjoyed studying at school. Follow the instructions on the task card above, referring to any notes you have made and adding more details.

Language for writing

-ing forms and infinitives

1 Identify all the *-ing* forms and infinitives in these sentences.

a Basing their findings on video recordings of children in infant schools, researchers found that boys were more active than girls.

b Computers allow us to store information, giving us time to study and analyse it.

c Evidence suggests that Dutch speakers have little difficulty understanding English.

d For most of the observation period, students were collaborating in groups.

e Researchers spent a year studying inner-city schools, gathering a range of data.

f The basic aim of our education system is to give children equal opportunities.

g The best schools can improve the attainment levels of most pupils.

h Many students go on to get well-paid jobs after graduating.

i The study shows that parents want their children to go to high-achieving schools.

2 When are the infinitive and the *-ing* form used?

a Write 'infinitive' and/or '*-ing*' after each of these uses.

after certain verbs
as nouns
to show a purpose for doing something
in participle clauses
as part of a continuous verb tense
as adjectives
after prepositions

b For each use, find an example in sentences a–i in 1 above.

3 Complete sentences a–i using the correct forms of the verbs in brackets and your own ideas.

Example
This research involved .... (measure)
This research involved measuring the increases in temperature between 1950 and 2000.

a Subjects were given opportunities .... (comment on)

b The survey showed that most people tend .... (respond)

c A sample of over a thousand people were asked .... (say)

d The questionnaire started by .... (ask)

e Without this research, it would be impossible .... (understand)

f There are many different ways of .... (interpret)

g The purpose of the project was .... (investigate)

h The report highlights the problem of boys' poor scores as well as .... (suggest)

i There are many issues to consider when .... (decide)

4 Complete this text using the correct form of the verbs in brackets. Remember, infinitives may or may not be preceded by *to*.

How does (a)... (learn) take place? (b)... (answer) this question has motivated psychologists (c)... (study) the (d)... (learn) process, (e)... (conduct) experiments and (f)... (develop) theories which should (g)... (help) us (h)... (understand) how we learn. (i)... (run) experiments on (j)... (learn) and (k)... (develop) a theory of (l)... (learn) is simply (m)... (try) (n)... (answer) that question. If you are curious about it, as many psychologists are, you could (o)... (carry out) your own experiments and develop a theory that might (p)... (improve) the current ones. You can (q)... (start) by (r)... (imagine) a simple theory that could (s)... (explain) basic observations of actual (t)... (learn).

Writing

Orientation

1 Discuss these questions.

  a   How do individuals benefit from a university education? Are there any disadvantages?
  b   How do countries benefit from the fact that a high proportion of their young people have a university education?

2 🎧 You are going to hear four speakers talking about university education. Answer these questions.

  a   Match the four speakers with one of these groups of people.
      Parents
      University students
      University authorities
      Politicians
  b   Which of the opinions expressed do you agree and disagree with?

Introductions

3 Study the Writing Task 2 below and discuss these questions with another student.

  a   Which parts of the question are fact and which parts are opinion?
  b   What is the viewpoint expressed in the question?
  c   Who do you think should pay for students to go to university? What are the main reasons for your opinion?

> In many countries today, increasing numbers of young people study at university.
>
> Students, who will probably earn higher than average salaries after graduating, should pay for their own higher education, rather than the state.
>
> What are your views?

4 What you write in your introduction to this type of essay will depend on your personal response to the question. Which of the sample introductions below is in favour of the statement, which is against, and which puts both sides of the argument with equal force?

1 The idea that students should entirely finance their own higher education seems at first glance a fair suggestion. Nevertheless, it makes the assumption that students are the principal or the only beneficiaries. As I shall argue, this is not the whole picture, and there are very good reasons why the state should fund university education from general taxation.

2 The view that students should contribute to the cost of their higher education is gaining popularity as more young people opt to go to university. Although I have some sympathy with this idea, I believe that state funding of higher education is a genuine investment in the future, not only for students themselves, but also for the country as a whole. I shall go on to suggest that students who can afford it should make some contribution to their university fees.

3 It is often assumed that education should be state-funded, especially in the early years. However, as the cost of university places increases, the assumption that the state should pay is being called into question. Since students themselves are likely to benefit so much, there are good arguments for expecting them to pay for their own education, allowing public money to be spent on other more important public services.

5 Read each sample introduction again carefully, and note down any phrases or expressions the writers use

a   to present an impersonal, commonly expressed view.
b   to suggest doubt about this view.
c   to indicate how the argument will continue.

6 Write introductions to the two tasks below. Refer to the samples above and use any appropriate phrases and expressions that you noted down. Write in favour of one of the statements and against the other.

1 In the context of today's competitive global economy, the main purpose of a country's education system is to prepare young people for particular types of work rather than to help them develop into independent-thinking individuals.

What are your views?

2 Many children are forced to stay at school and study subjects that will be of little value to them in the future. These children may disrupt the education of the majority and should be allowed to leave school early to find themselves a job.

What are your views?

Think, plan, write   **7** Choose one of the titles for which you have written an introduction and write the remaining paragraphs. Make sure that you follow up the points included in your introduction.

Help yourself

Thinking skills

1 The following puzzle has an easy solution, but it is not obvious. Work with another student. Think of at least one possible solution before you look at the answer.

The coffee drinker

A man in a restaurant complained to the waiter that there was a fly in his coffee. The waiter took the cup away and promised to bring a fresh cup of coffee. He returned a few moments later. The man tasted the coffee and complained that this was his original cup of coffee with the fly removed. He was correct.

How did the man know it was the same cup of coffee?

2 Check your answer on page 177. Did you find the correct solution? How did you reach your own conclusion?

3 Finding solutions can be easier if you use brainstorming. Work with a partner and answer the brainstorming tasks below.

Choose an everyday object, such as something that one of your group has in their pocket or bag. Place it on the desk. Think up as many uses for this object as you can in two minutes.
Example: a coin
Possible uses: jewellery, a paper-weight, put under an object to make it level, etc.

Think of a topic such as 'pollution'. Write down any ideas (such as examples or solutions) under four headings: personal, local, national, and international.

4 Discuss these questions in pairs.

a My brother likes carrots but not peas. He likes apples but not oranges. He likes lorries but not vans. He likes Joanna but not Julie. Does he like Sue or Sally?

b Is the following statement true or false?

THIS STATEMENT IS FALSE.

c Two babies born on the same day in the same year with the same father and mother are not twins. How can this be true?

d Read these statements. Are the parts in italic true or false?

* All dogs are animals. All cats are mammals. *Therefore, all dogs are mammals.*

* All criminals go to prison. Someone went to prison. *That person was a criminal.*

5 How might the thinking skills you have been practising on this page be relevant to tasks you may be faced with in the IELTS exam?

IELTS to do list

Choose one of the following to do outside class.

☐ Try lateral thinking or logic puzzles that you find in newspapers or magazines.

☐ When you hear about a social or economic problem in the news, think about how people with different opinions might deal with it.

☐ Collect different opinions with reasons on current issues. These could be personal, family or community issues (for example, ways of bringing up children; the building of a new road in your town, etc.), national issues, or international issues. Note down a definite personal opinion on each issue.

Where to look

ⓔ www.oup.com/elt/ielts

7 Science

1 Do this quiz with another student, explaining your answers where possible.

Check your answers and read the explanations on page 177.

Decide whether the following statements are **True** or **False**.

a The solar system's biggest volcano is on Earth.

b To put out a fire, we spray carbon dioxide onto the burning material in order to cut off its air supply.

c If you hold a small flame under a balloon filled with water, it will remain intact.

d Aeroplane tyres are normally filled with helium.

e On a hot day, switching on a refrigerator with its door open will make the room cooler.

f Per litre of water, there are more living organisms in the Arctic Ocean than in warmer seas and lakes.

g Compared to an earthquake of six on the Richter Scale, an earthquake of eight is thirty-two times stronger.

h In space, the yellow lights on a quickly-approaching space vehicle would look blue.

---

2 Look at this list of sciences and answer the questions.

biology	chemistry	physics
astronomy	geology	genetics

a Which science does each of the quiz questions relate to?
b Which science subjects did you enjoy most/least at school? Why?
c Which other sciences, or branches of science, would you like to have studied? Why?

Reading

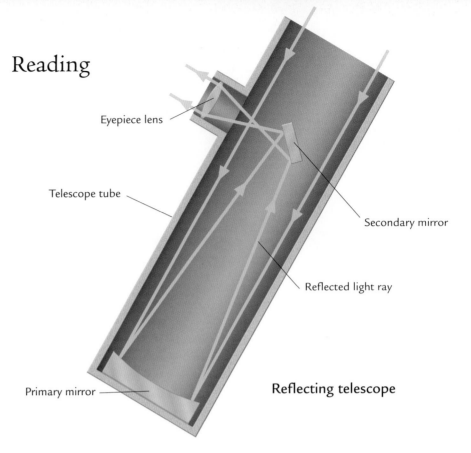

Eyepiece lens

Telescope tube

Secondary mirror

Reflected light ray

Primary mirror

Reflecting telescope

Orientation

1 With another student, study this diagram and follow the instructions.

a   Describe the telescope, explaining how it works.
b   Listen to the recording and note down any differences from your description.

Description schemes

2 Items a–e describe common schemes for organizing a description. Which of the expressions in the list do you associate with each scheme a–e?

a   Time: the order in which events occur or parts work
b   Spatial: the physical positions of parts and their relationships to each other
c   General to specific: from the main structure to individual parts
d   Importance: from the least to the most important
e   Topical: the order that comes naturally from the topic

a little further down	the third item	another part
overall	by far the biggest	from left to right
after that	going anti-clockwise	a few seconds later
even more difficult	taken as a whole	

3 Discuss these questions with another student.

a   How was the description you heard in 1b mainly organized?
b   How would you expect the following descriptions to be organized? Sometimes more than one type of organization may be used.

the contents of a library	an animal's appearance
a firm's management structure	a chemical process
a hurricane	a space rocket
a home cinema system	

Reading for gist

4 Read the text quickly and answer these questions.

a   What is Alma?   b   Where will it be?   c   What's it for?

High on a desolate plateau in the Chilean Andes, astronomers are constructing a series of telescopes so powerful they may provide the answer to the thirteen-billion-year-old question: what happened after the Big Bang?

Stars in their eyes

A It is dawn in the Andes. A grimy carpet of red dust stretches over rolling featureless hills towards a horizon dominated by the icy cone of Chile's Licancabur volcano. There are no trees, no bushes, not even a blade of grass in this lifeless landscape. Even the atmosphere
5 is alien. At 5,000 metres above the sea, oxygen levels are puny. Move suddenly, and bright spots blur your vision before you start to stagger and retch. This is Chajnantor, the most inhospitable portion of Chile's Atacama desert, and one of the world's most arid places. The annual rainfall here is negligible – a few drops of
10 moisture scattered yearly on desiccated, empty land. You wouldn't last a day unprotected in this dead zone. It is hostile, threatening, and in a few years is destined to provide astronomers with a new home.

B It sounds extraordinary. Nevertheless, the European Southern
15 Observatory has committed itself to begin building an array of giant microwave receivers on Chajnantor. When completed, these machines will allow the world's astronomers to view the birth of thousands of planetary systems in the deepest recesses of our galaxy and probe the early universe's 'Dark Ages', when dust
20 obscured the cosmos and the first stars flickered into existence. Unique knowledge is expected to flow from Alma, the Atacama Large Millimetre Array.

C Each Alma receiver will consist of a transportable structure supporting a dish measuring 10 metres in diameter. Extending
25 outwards from the smooth metal surface of the dish will be three support arms that hold a sub-reflector. This will direct the radio waves down into the heart of the receiver, where signals from deep space can be amplified, recorded and analysed. To compensate for the rotation of the Earth, the dish will need to be fully steerable. To
30 vary its angle it will be mounted on an elevation structure, beneath which will be a rotating structure. This will move smoothly around on the steel base, the cylindrical platform for the receiver.

D The construction of sixty-four such telescopes on a vast, adjustable grid of tracks covering 40 square kilometres is daunting. The
35 combined collecting surface of the receivers will measure 6,000 square metres, the size of a football pitch. Putting together such a mammoth piece of kit, with its £250 million price tag, in the thin air and red dust of the central Chilean Andes, seems outrageously ambitious.

E 40 But why bother? Given that the night sky is full of bright galaxies, why do astronomers build telescopes manufactured to a billionth of a metre accuracy, just to see faint ones? The answer is about looking back in time, says astronomer David Field of the University of Aarhus. 'The fainter the galaxy, the more distant it
45 is. And given that light travels at a finite speed, faint galaxies are also the oldest. In other words, telescopes are time machines. They have shown us what the universe was like ten billion years ago, how it evolved during its childhood.'

F Scientists are now satisfied they know about the universe's birth,
50 and about its childhood. But they still need to learn about its early infancy thirteen billion years ago, after the newly-born cosmos had exploded into existence and the heavens had filled with superheated particles, a thin gruel of matter that somehow coalesced to produce heavy solid objects. 'We want to know how a
55 hot, fluid universe turned into one with galaxies and stars and planets and continents and, eventually, people,' says UK astronomer Dr Paul Murdin. 'We want to know how the heavens got structure. In short, we want to understand how we got from the Big Bang to human beings.' One answer is to build even bigger
60 optical telescopes to gather photons from even more distant – and therefore older – objects. However, really distant galaxies recede from us so rapidly that much of their light is transformed – by an effect known as the Doppler shift – into microwave radiation.

G And that is why Chajnantor is so important. Its receivers will be
65 built specifically to collect this precious microwave radiation and help astronomers understand one of science's last major cosmological mysteries: the structured, solid nature of the cosmos. But collecting microwave radiation has one major drawback, as Esteban Illanes, of the European Southern Observatory, explains.
70 'It is absorbed by water. An observatory at sea level would pick up nothing. All the microwaves coming down from space would have been absorbed by clouds or water vapour in the atmosphere before they reached our instruments. That is why we picked Chajnantor. It is high and dry – perfect for picking up microwaves.'

H 75 This selection is also particularly appropriate, for mankind has been exploiting the aridity of the Atacama desert for millennia. This is the place where mummification – the process of drying corpses to preserve them – began. Now, the special conditions that made this possible are giving scientists a chance to explain how
80 the universe acquired the solidity that made life possible in the first place. It will be a key scientific milestone. □

5 Which paragraph A–H contains the description of the radio telescope illustrated below? How is this description organized? Which words tell you?

IELTS practice

note

Begin by looking at the diagram and any labels given, then find the part of the text that describes it.

Questions 1–4: Labelling a diagram

Complete the diagram below. Choose NO MORE THAN THREE WORDS from the passage for each answer.

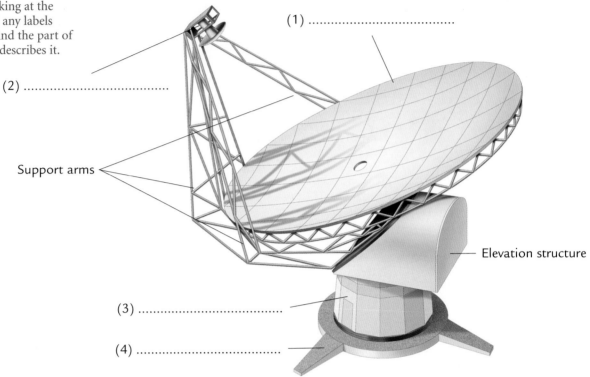

(1) ....

(2) ....

Support arms

Elevation structure

(3) ....

(4) ....

Questions 5–11: Multiple-answer questions

5–7 According to the information given in the Reading Passage, which THREE of these are features of Chajnantor?

    A completely flat land

    B a total lack of vegetation

    C extremely thin air

    D intense heat during the day

    E very little rain

    F unfriendly local people

8–9 According to the information given in the Reading Passage, which TWO of these will be features of Alma?

    A The telescopes will be moved from place to place.

    B The land area covered by the array will be 6,000 m².

    C There will be sports facilities on the site.

    D It will be difficult to assemble everything there.

    E The cost will be too high for any one government.

10–11 According to the information given in the Reading Passage, which TWO of these reasons are given by the writer for siting the telescope at Chajnantor?

    A to see how the universe was changing ten billion years ago

    B to discover how the universe began

    C to observe changes in the universe thirteen billion years ago

    D to minimize the effects of the Doppler shift

    E to avoid the limitations of optical telescopes

Questions 12–14: True/False/Not given

Do the following statements agree with the information given in the Reading Passage?
Write:

TRUE   if the statement agrees with the information
FALSE   if the statement contradicts the information
NOT GIVEN   if there is no information on this

12 Radio telescopes should be built as far away as possible from seas or oceans.
13 Alma will be sited in this part of the Andes because of the high levels of space
   radiation there.
14 The Atacama has long played a role in the history of human life and death.

Exploration   **6** Put these adjectives from paragraph A into pairs with similar meanings.

featureless	lifeless	puny	inhospitable
arid	negligible	desiccated	empty
dead	hostile		

7 Find words in the passage with the meanings indicated below.

a   three synonyms of 'very big' (paragraphs B and D)
b   the opposite of 'bright' (paragraph E)
c   the opposite of 'solid' (paragraph F)
d   two synonyms of 'universe' (paragraph F)
e   a synonym of 'people' (paragraph F)
f   two synonyms of 'receiving' (paragraph G)

8 Which adjectives in 6 and 7 would you use to describe each of the following?

a   the Sahara Desert
b   the planet Jupiter
c   the summit of Everest
d   deep space
e   the Pacific Ocean
f   a visible comet

9 Discuss these questions with other students.

a   Which space objects would you most like Alma to study? Why?
b   Do you think Alma is good value for money? Why?/Why not? Might these
    international funds be better spent on projects such as eradicating malaria,
    providing basic education in poor countries, or helping the victims of natural
    disasters?
c   Which of the following space projects do you find interesting? Give reasons.
    space telescopes
    manned moon flights
    space laboratories
    flights to other planets
    exploration of comets
    flights beyond the solar system

Listening

Section 3

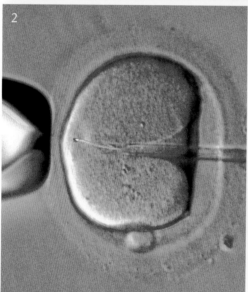

Orientation

1 Discuss these questions with another student.

   a Which issues are suggested by each photo?

   b How important are these issues in your country? Are other issues more important?

   c If you were working as a scientist, would you be comfortable doing research in these areas? Why?/Why not?

   d How important is it that scientists maintain ethical standards?

   e Should science courses train students to deal with ethical issues?

2 Look at multiple-choice questions 1 and 2 on page 87. What is the situation? What do you think the speakers will be talking about? When you hear the introduction, check whether you were right.

IELTS practice   **Questions 1 and 2:** Multiple-choice questions

🎧 Choose the correct letter, A, B, or C.

1 What, according to the tutor, happened to scientists in the twentieth century?

   A They lost contact with the rest of society.
   B They began to lose interest in ethical issues.
   C They did both good and harm to the world.

2 One of the students says that scientists should not

   A publish the results of certain kinds of research.
   B distinguish between pure and applied science.
   C feel responsible for the applications of science.

Questions 3–10: Multiple-answer questions

🎧 3–5 Which THREE of these things do the speakers suggest scientists should do?

   A improve science teaching
   B warn of future dangers
   C solve problems that arise
   D prevent discoveries going abroad
   E become politicians
   F improve their public image

6–8 Which THREE of these issues do the students mention?

   A genetically-modified crops
   B the cloning of human beings
   C using pesticides in agriculture
   D experiments on live animals
   E changing weather patterns
   F weapons of mass destruction

9–10 Which TWO of these does the tutor suggest the students should avoid?

   A making many car journeys
   B travelling frequently by air
   C communicating via computer
   D buying certain imported products
   E wasting energy at home

Exploration   **3** Discuss these questions with another student.

   a Which of the activities in the last question do you think are particularly important to avoid or at least reduce? Why?
   b In what other ways can we maintain ethical standards in our everyday lives?

5 In the IELTS Reading test you may have to complete a table with information from a text in note form. Study the table below and discuss these questions with a partner.

a   How is the table organized?

b   What kind of information do you need to find in the text?

c   What makes tables like this an effective approach to making notes?

IELTS practice   **Questions 1–7:** Table completion

Complete the table below. Write NO MORE THAN THREE WORDS AND/OR A NUMBER for each answer.

Technology	Range	Data transfer per second	Cost	Best for
Bluetooth	(1)..10..... meters	1 MB	(4)..£50........... for an adapter	secure short-range connections
WiFi	(2)..100.... meters	(3)..5.4MB........	(5)..£40 – £60.... for a network card	people who need to work while (6)..travelling.
GPRS	no limit		value-for-money packages	(7)..reliable communication and Internet browsing

Question 8: Multiple-choice question

Choose the correct letter, A, B, C, or D. Which of the following is the most suitable title for the text?

A   Technology companies determine future work patterns.

B   An introduction to wireless technology.

C   Wired and wireless technologies: a comparison.

D   The impact of wireless technology on productivity.

Exploration

6 Do you agree with the idea expressed in the last sentence of the text, that it is 'the users, not the developers of the technology, who will finally decide which ideas take off'?

7 It is not always obvious whether verbs should be singular or plural. Why are singular verbs used in these extracts from the article?
  a 'A new generation of portable devices is emerging.' (line 7)
  b 'A range of products and services is now available' (line 16)

8 Why are plural verbs used in these extracts? What other words do you know in the same category as 'workforce' and 'staff'?
  a 'The advantages for a workforce who adopt the new technologies are considerable.' (line 14)
  b 'Whereas staff on the move have traditionally had to wait,' (line 26)

9 Choose the correct verb forms in these sentences. Sometimes both are possible.
  a The government *is/are* introducing measures to make careers in teaching more attractive to graduates.
  b The introduction of online banking giving people instant access to their accounts *has/have been* generally welcomed by customers.
  c The committee *meets/meet* today to discuss the effects of digital technology on the company.
  d Having a choice of so many wireless technologies *presents/present* businesses with a number of dilemmas.
  e The number of people with mobile phones *has/have* doubled in the last year.
  f Early next year, one of the world's top IT companies *is/are* expected to announce an exciting new product.
  g Each of the main wireless technologies *has/have* strengths and weaknesses.

10 Complete each of the sentences with the correct form of the most appropriate verb from the list. The correct answers form common collocations with the nouns in italic.

access   place
provide   edit
transmit   update
download

  a Internet cafés ...Provide... *a service* for people who do not have their own computers.
  b They should have ...edited... this *document* more carefully. It's full of mistakes.
  c These days many employees can ...access... their work *database* from home.
  d Companies should ...update... their *records* regularly to ensure that information is always current.
  e You should be able to ...download... most of *the information* you need from the Internet.
  f To ...place... *an order* for a CD, all you do is give your name, address and credit card details.
  g Your laptop has to be WiFi enabled to ...transmit... and receive *data* to and from the hotspot.

Listening

Section 4

Orientation

1 Look at the photos showing different sources of information and discuss these questions with another student.

a What are the main advantages and disadvantages of searching for information on the Internet in comparison with other sources of information?

b If you use the Internet to look for information, do you have a favourite search engine or favourite websites?

c Where would you look for information about these?

recent research in a subject you are studying
yesterday's national news
information about your favourite rock band
historical information or the biography of a famous artist

Understanding flow charts

2 Part of the talk you will hear describes a procedure which is represented by the flow chart in Questions 3–6 on page 99. Study the words and phrases in the chart and answer these questions.

a How is the chart organized? What do the arrows between the boxes represent?

b What does the structure of the chart tell you about the information you are going to hear?

c What kind of language is used in the chart?

d During this part of the talk, the speaker will use a number of sequencing expressions. Predict where on the flow chart these expressions would be used.

| Finally ... | It is at this point that ... | When this has been done ... |
| Let's start by ... | The first step ... | |

Questions 1–2: Short-answer questions

🎧 Answer the questions below. Write NO MORE THAN THREE WORDS AND/OR A NUMBER for each answer.

1   What information source is Wikipedia similar to?

   ....

2   Who are the authors of Wikipedia?

   ....

Questions 3–6: Flow chart completion

note

Flow charts follow the organization of the recordings you hear. The answers required are in the same order as the information in the talk.

Complete the flow chart below. Write NO MORE THAN THREE WORDS AND/OR A NUMBER for each answer.

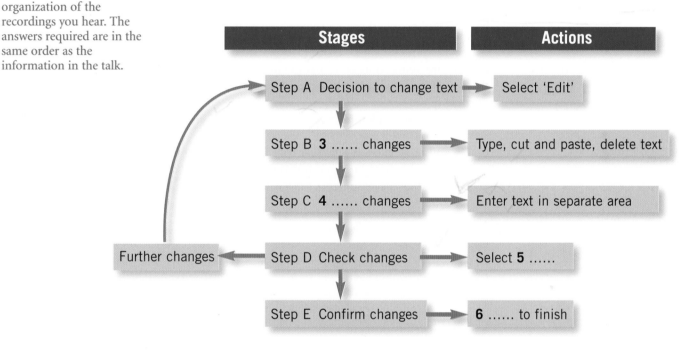

Stages	Actions
Step A Decision to change text	Select 'Edit'
Step B **3** ...... changes	Type, cut and paste, delete text
Step C **4** ...... changes	Enter text in separate area
Further changes ← Step D Check changes	Select **5** ......
Step E Confirm changes	**6** ...... to finish

Questions 7–10: Summary completion

note

In summary completion tasks you may be given a list of words to choose from. These will usually belong to the same word class, for example nouns.

Complete the summary below using words from the list.

accuracy   democracy   neutrality
vandalism   interest   originality
reputations   quality

Criticism of Wikipedia has focused on the question of (7)................. . Some contributors are registered with the site, and over time they are able to improve their (8)................. . There are also administrators who carry out checks on entries and prevent (9)................. . Other policies to maintain high standards include a rule that entries should aim at (10)................. in writing style.

Exploration

3 Discuss these ideas with other students.
   a   What subjects on Wikipedia could you make relevant contributions to?
   b   Who or what might feel threatened if democratic information sources, like Wikipedia, gain in popularity?

Speaking

1 Discuss these questions.

    a Which of the things shown in the photographs have you done?

    b How did people do these things before these modern devices became available?

2 🎧 You are going to listen to people answering more abstract questions about how they see IT developing in the future. Listen and match each speaker's answer with one of these questions.

    a How do you think information technology will change the way people work in the future?

    b Do you think there is a danger that future developments will encourage people to spend more time alone and less time with others?

    c Do you think developments in IT will lead to greater human happiness?

3 🎧 Listen again and tick which of these expressions the speakers use to speculate about the future.

☐ I can't see that happening.
☐ I think it's quite likely that …
☐ I'd say it's fairly unlikely that …
☐ If this continues, it could …
☐ It all depends on …

☐ My prediction is that …
☐ That doesn't seem very likely to me.
☐ This can only get worse.
☐ This will probably mean that …
☐ What I think will happen is that …

Part 3: Topic discussion

4 In Speaking Part 3, the examiner will ask you about more abstract aspects of a topic. Work with other students. Discuss some of these questions using speculating expressions from the list above.

Rights and wrongs
Do you believe that people's individual freedom and privacy will be in danger if IT continues to develop at the current rate?
Do you think that IT-related crime will become a more serious problem in the future? How well do you think society will deal with any increase in crime?

Money
How do you think developments in information technology will alter the way individuals deal with their money in the future?
How do you predict people's shopping habits will change in the future?

Creativity
In what ways does technology currently make it easier for individuals to be creative in music, writing and the visual arts?
Do you believe that future developments will make it easier for more people to realize their creative potential?

Language for writing

1 Which of the adverbs and adverb phrases given could be used to complete sentences a–f?

a The situation today is .... different from that of just a few years ago.
   completely   strongly   vastly

b Our investigations proved .... that improvements have occurred.
   conclusively   definitively   doubtlessly

c There is a .... significant association between achievement and social
   background.
   greatly   highly   statistically

d Computer ownership rose .... during the 1990s.
   distinctly   rapidly   sharply

e The price of petrol went up by ten per cent last year. ...., people used their
   cars less frequently.
   Amazingly   Not surprisingly   Probably

f Research has .... shown that exposure to loud noise can ....
   damage our hearing.
   clearly   evidently   consistently
   dangerously   seriously   severely

2 Adverbs and adverb phrases are often used at the beginning of sentences to indicate
the writer's attitude to the statement that follows.

Example
Interestingly, the number of women in the workforce has almost doubled in the last decade.

Group the attitude adverbs and adverb phrases below under the categories (1–3)
they most closely relate to.
1 Certainty / Expectation: *astonishingly*
2 Evaluation / Importance: *more importantly*
3 Generalization: *generally speaking*

apparently	as a general rule	as might be expected
astonishingly	by and large	(quite) clearly
disturbingly	fortunately	generally speaking
inevitably	interestingly	(even) more importantly
naturally	obviously	of course
predictably	quite rightly	significantly
(not) surprisingly	typically	undoubtedly
unfortunately	without a doubt	

3 Rephrase these sentences starting with appropriate adverbs or adverb phrases from the
list in 2.

a Crime rates have risen in line with unemployment figures. That doesn't surprise me.
b There is a very satisfactory solution to this problem. That's a good thing.
c Technology will cause more problems than it solves, so people say.
d Older people don't adapt so easily to new technology – at least that's usually true.
e Children often pick up new skills for themselves. That really interests me.

Writing

Orientation

1 Discuss these questions with other students.

  a How have people in your country adjusted to recent developments in technology?

  b What problems or difficulties have particular groups of people, for example the elderly, experienced in relation to technological change?

Supporting ideas

2 Study the Writing Task 2 below, then answer questions a–c.

> Rapid technological change has shaped the world we live in today. Far from having a positive influence, living in a high-tech world dependent on computers and mobile devices has distanced us from what is really important in life.
>
> How far do you agree?

  a What is your immediate response to the question?

  b What do you think is meant by 'what is really important in life'?

  c In what ways could our dependence on computers and mobile devices be said to have distanced us from this?

3 Which of the following arguments in favour of the statement in the writing task above do you agree with? Give reasons for your opinions.

  a Technology discourages people from really communicating with each other.

  b People want to own the latest gadgets out of concern for status rather than need.

  c Involvement with technology leaves people no time to appreciate life.

  d By making activities too easy, technology makes useful skills redundant.

4 Read this paragraph and answer questions a–c below.

> Another side-effect of technology is that by making activities too easy, technology makes us forget useful skills. 1 .... fewer people are able to do mental arithmetic than in the past. 2 *in addition to this* people can create images and music with less effort or artistic talent, so traditional skills are being undermined. 3 *Unfortunately,* many of these skills are in danger of dying out completely.

a   Which sentence states the main argument?

b   What is the purpose of the other three sentences?

c   Fill each gap with organizing phrases from the lists below.

Giving examples

For example,...
One example of this is (how/when/ etc.) ...
A good example of this is (how/when/ etc.) ...
For instance, ...
A case in point is ...

Additional points

In addition (to this), ...
What is more, ...
Not only ..., but also ...,

Adverbs see page 101

5 Choose one of the statements in 3. Write a paragraph giving your point of view and supporting it with appropriate arguments or evidence.

Think, plan, write

6 Read the Writing Task 2 below and answer the questions.

> Modern technology now allows rapid and uncontrolled access to, and exchange of, information. Far from being beneficial, this is a danger to our societies.
>
> What do you think?

a   What is the writer trying to convey with the phrase 'Far from being beneficial, ...'?

b   In what ways could 'uncontrolled access to, and exchange of, information' be considered 'a danger to our societies'?

c   What is your immediate response to the question?

7 Make a list of your main ideas. What supporting examples can you think of to back up these ideas? What additional points can you include?

8 Use your ideas in 7 above to decide on a paragraph plan and then write your answer. Include phrases to introduce supporting statements, examples, and additional points, and, where relevant, to indicate your attitude.

Help yourself

Using the Internet

1 Read these statements about the Internet. Which do you agree with? Compare your answers with your colleagues.

a The best thing about the Internet is shopping. I buy loads of things using my credit card.

b You can't believe most of what you find there. I don't trust it.

c It's great for people with hobbies. I'm interested in motorbikes, and there are lots of cool sites about them.

d It's the perfect source of information. I recently did a project for my course, and I found lots of up-to-date stuff.

e Unauthorized downloading of programs or music is really just theft.

f Just following links is the best thing. I normally surf from site to site, finding new things.

2 The list below contains things that you can easily find on the Internet, often for free. Which of these do you access in your own language?

　newspapers
　pop songs
　radio programmes (podcasts)
　online museums and galleries
　online libraries
　academic journals
　reference information (dictionaries, encyclopaedias)
　local information
　magazines

3 Think of ways in which English-language versions of the items in 2 would

a help improve your general English.
b prepare you for the IELTS exam.
c inform you about English-speaking countries and their cultures.
d interest you because of the content.

4 Email and other forms of electronic communication have completely changed the way we communicate. Look up the following terms using your favourite search engine. How could you use each of them to improve your English?

blog　　keypal　　chat　　discussion list

IELTS to do list

Choose one of the following to do outside class.

☐ Think of something you normally do on the Internet in your own language and do it in English instead.

☐ Compare the way a big story is covered on different news websites, e.g. 'serious' and 'popular', 'left' and 'right', UK and US.

☐ Choose a topic from this book, such as a writing task you have to do. Research the topic using key words. Ask yourself whether this helped you come up with new ideas.

☐ Follow the links on the OUP website (www.oup.com/elt/ielts) to sources of IELTS-style materials. Bookmark the most interesting websites, and go back to them frequently.

Where to look

ⓔ www.oup.com/elt/ielts

9 Social issues

2

3

4

1 Look at the photos.
   a What influences on our lives do they suggest?
   b Which of these influences are the most significant in your society?

2 Match each of the extracts 1–4 with the most appropriate headline a–d.

   a **How the rich exploit the poor**

   b **Racial discrimination persists**

   c **The family under threat**

   d **An end to class privilege?**

3 Refer to the extracts again and discuss these questions with another student.
   a If a society rewards the talented, what should happen to people who have fewer talents? (Extract 1)
   b Are the three main characteristics of the 'post-modern family' an accurate description of the current state of the typical family in your country? (Extract 2)
   c What should the wealthier nations of the world do to ensure that farmers and other workers in poor countries are not 'forced into a cycle of poverty and debt'? (Extract 3)
   d What can be done to improve the situation of ethnic groups like the Australian Aborigines? Are there similar groups in your country? (Extract 4)
   e What are the most pressing social problems in your country at the present time? What solutions are being tried or suggested to solve these problems?

1 Politicians often claim that their aim is to create a fairer society. The goal of achieving absolute equality has long been abandoned, but many claim that a meritocratic society is possible, by establishing institutions that ensure people get the opportunities to better themselves and are rewarded on the basis of their efforts and abilities. Thus, the factor that determines people's success in life is their own talent, not an accident of birth.

2 In the early 1970s, sociologists described what they called the 'post-modern family'. They noted three main characteristics: the indifference of adolescents to the family's identity; instability in the lives of couples, accompanied by increasing divorce rates; and the destruction of the 'nest' notion of nuclear family life. In the 1980s, there was a dramatic shift from mothers caring for young children in the home to the use of paid providers. This reflected women's increasing desire to return to work.

3 The United States consumes one-fifth of all the world's coffee, making it the largest consumer in the world. But few Americans realize that agricultural workers in the coffee industry often toil in what can be described as 'sweatshops in the fields'. Many small coffee farmers receive prices for their coffee that are less than the costs of production, forcing them into a cycle of poverty and debt.

4 It was not until 1967 that a referendum finally granted all indigenous people Australian citizenship. Since that time conditions for Aboriginal people have improved but remain significantly below those enjoyed by white Australians. There are still large differences in the state of health, education, housing, and employment between Aboriginal and non-Aboriginal peoples.

Reading

Orientation

1 Discuss these questions with other students.

   a How and where do you meet your friends?
   b What do you see as your responsibilities and obligations to your friends?
   c What, in your opinion, are the limits of friendship? Are there certain things you would not do, even if asked by a close friend?

Word formation

2 The following words are taken from the article opposite. What is the root word in each case? How do the endings change the grammar of the words?

Example
relationship   Root word = *relate*
relate > *relation* (changes a verb to a noun)
relation > *relationship* (changes a noun to another noun)

neighbourhood
inclusion
justification
usefulness
friendliness
virtuous
mobility

note

Endings help to identify the category of a word (noun, verb, etc.). Prefixes such as *over-* and *un-* also add to the meaning. When a word or phrase is unfamiliar, identifying the root word or words can help establish the meaning.

3 What is the meaning of the parts of these words in italic?

*inter*communication
*un*believable
*in*appropriate
*under*used
*counter*attack
*in*human

4 What is the meaning of each of these words taken from the article?

overstatement (paragraph B)
unevenly (paragraph F)
counter-productive (paragraph I)
intolerance (paragraph K)

5 Read paragraphs A and B of the article. Why does the author describe friendship as 'the invisible thread'?

The invisible thread

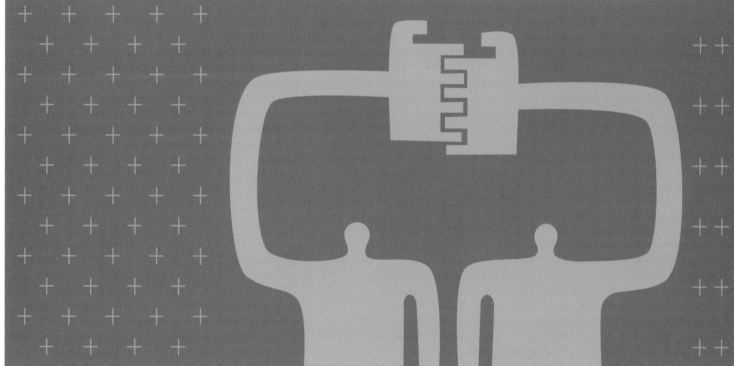

A It lifts hearts and lengthens lives. It has been hailed as the ultimate good by philosophers and promoted by major religions. The wondrous good in question is friendship. Aristotle's highest goal for men and the
5 third plank of the French revolution – liberty, equality, fraternity – friendship is as old as humanity and as important as love or justice. But while bookshop shelves groan with self-help books on finding the perfect partner and philosophical texts
10 on the nature of freedom, friendship barely gets a mention among academics or policy-makers.

B Friendship is the invisible thread running through society, yet its significance in our lives is, if anything, increasing. While the claim that 'friends are the new
15 family' is an overstatement, it is certainly the case that friendships figure prominently in both the lives people actually lead and the ones to which they aspire. Television programmes such as *Friends* portray a world in which close friendships define the
20 contours of the participants' lives: parents and children are allowed, at best, walk-on parts.

C One of the reasons why thinkers struggle to recognize this trend may be one of definition. After all, I am a friend to someone I have known and
25 loved for twenty-five years, but I am also a 'Friend of The Earth'. Friendship is a slippery category. This, however, is where philosophers are supposed to help. Aristotle divided friendships into three types: friendships for usefulness, friendships for pleasure,
30 and friendships of virtue.

D The first kind of friend is the one who will get you a job or membership of an exclusive club; the second makes you laugh. But in both cases the point of the friendship is that they provide something of
35 separate value to you. True friendship, the third kind, is valued for itself. There are few numerical limits on the first two kinds – I can have a vast business network and hundreds of agreeable acquaintances – but true friendship is, by definition,
40 a limited field: if someone has many friends, they have none.

E Virtuous friendship is long-term and committed and brings great psychological benefits, and there is plentiful research evidence showing that having
45 at least one close friend is associated with a range of health benefits, from recovery times from cardiac illness to reduced incidence of mental health problems.

F However, friendship is not always an unalloyed
50 good. Its benefits are unevenly spread and its impact on traditional liberal values, such as equality, diversity and mobility, is mixed. The first problem is that men are worse at friendship than women. It is now widely acknowledged that
55 women do more of the 'social' work than men and have better-developed friendship skills, which leaves men at a disadvantage.

G Secondly, friendship has political downsides for governments committed to social inclusion: it is,
60 by definition, exclusive. People from a particular social class or educational background are highly likely to form friendships, or romantic relationships, with people from the same background. Given that friends help each other,
65 the danger is that the friendships of the affluent and successful hoard social advantage to the detriment of social mobility.

H Friendship is seen – with some justification – as a private matter, but the strong links between
70 friendship and other social goods – including better health, more effective careers, and higher life satisfaction – should be enough to merit greater attention from decision makers. So what are the political implications of these observations?
75 Perhaps the best politicians can aim for is not to make things worse for friendship. But political institutions can improve or worsen the conditions in which friendships are formed.

I First of all, the issue of time needs to be
80 considered. Friendship requires time to flourish: Aristotle reckoned one and a half bushels of salt needed to be consumed together before a friendship became solid. At the present time, many people regard non-working hours as family time,
85 but little allowance is made for the time needed to build friendships. Ironically, for politicians to discourage people from working long hours could be counter-productive, since a third of us make most of our friends through work. What the
90 decision-makers could do, however, is discourage the drive for commercial gain that squeezes conviviality out of the workplace.

J There is also a case for encouraging spaces in which people from different backgrounds meet
95 and interact in order to increase the chances of cross-class friendships. Given the increase in geographical inequality, with rich people increasingly living in neighbourhoods of rich people, only hospital wards and places of religious
100 worship are sites of genuine social mixing.

K Friendship is a virtue with some of the appearances of a social vice. It can promote or demote social mobility; underpin tolerance or bolster discrimination; erode or sustain hierarchies. Society
105 could be composed of strong friendships between people of identical social backgrounds who treat everyone else with contempt, intolerance or fear. The true test of the friendliness of a community is not simply the way its citizens treat their friends,
110 but whether they behave generously towards the broader social world. We need not only the care of friends, but the kindness of strangers. ■

IELTS practice **Questions 1–6:** Locating information

Which paragraphs A–K of the article contain the following information?

1 the effect of gender on people's ability to make friends *F*
2 friendship: a frequently disregarded influence for good *A*
3 the difficulty of defining friendship *G*
4 the distinction between a real friend and other kinds of friends *D*
5 the similarities between people who are close friends *G*
6 people's need for friends as well as family *F*

Questions 7–13: Yes / No / Not given

Do the following statements agree with the views of the writer of the article? Write
YES if the statement agrees with the views of the writer
NO if the statement contradicts the views of the writer
NOT GIVEN if it is impossible to say what the writer thinks about this.

7 Friendship has become less important in people's lives. *No*
8 It is impossible for anyone to have a large number of genuine friends. *Yes*
9 Having a genuine friend improves a person's life in a variety of ways. *Yes*
10 Wealthy people find it more difficult to form close friendships. *No*
11 Politicians cannot influence people's chances of making friends. *No*
12 Reducing the number of hours people spend at work would help people to form friendships. *Yes*
13 It is difficult for people who do not live close to each other to be good friends. *Not gn*

Exploration **6** Words are often combined in English, as in the examples in italic below.
Explain the following phrases from the passage.
self-help books (paragraph A)
policy-makers (paragraph A)
walk-on parts (paragraph B)
political *downsides* (paragraph G)
cross-class friendships (paragraph J)

7 Some words are used metaphorically to give colour and interest to a phrase. What do the words in italic in these extracts from the article mean? What are their more literal meanings?
a ... bookshop shelves *groan* with self-help books ... (paragraph A)
b ... the invisible *thread* running through society ... (paragraph B)
c Friendship is a *slippery* category. (paragraph C)
d ... the danger is that the friendships of the affluent and successful *hoard* social advantage ... (paragraph G)
e ... *erode* or sustain hierarchies. (paragraph K)

8 Discuss these questions with other students.
a Do you agree with the writer that 'men are worse at friendship than women'? If so, how can this be explained? What could men do to develop their 'friendship skills'?
b Is it your experience that people tend to form friendships with people from the same social background (class) as themselves? If so, why do you think this is? Do you think that cross-class friendships should be encouraged? If so, how could this be achieved? If not, why not?
c Do you think that politicians and other policy-makers should take the issue of friendship more seriously? What measures could be taken that might encourage the development of friendships?

Listening

Section 1

Orientation

1 The photographs show volunteers working in different situations. Discuss these questions with other students.

 a What motivates people of different ages to sign up for voluntary work projects, often in situations very different from those they know?

 b Is it right that poor and underprivileged people should have to depend on voluntary workers for help and support? What alternatives are there, or should there be?

IELTS practice

Questions 1–5: Note completion

🎧 Complete the notes below. Write NO MORE THAN THREE WORDS AND/OR A NUMBER for each answer.

Volunteer applicant details

Name of enquirer: Ben Oppermann

Age: **1** _____

Qualifications

BA in Social Studies

Postgraduate Certificate in **2** _____

Interested in a placement lasting **3** _____ years

Other skills and interests:

Experience of **4** _____ work

Member of a **5** _____ group

Questions 6–10: Short-answer questions

🎧 Answer the questions. Write NO MORE THAN THREE WORDS AND/OR A NUMBER for each answer.

6   How long can the selection procedure for applicants take?

....

7   When are short-listed applicants usually interviewed?

....

8   Approximately what proportion of the cost of their training and travel are applicants expected to contribute?

....

9   How long does each volunteer's training last?

....

10   When do placements generally begin?

....

Exploration

2   The following words are taken from the recording. What is the root word in each case? What do the endings tell you about the grammar of the words?

dependent   qualification
placement   applicant
contribution   option
sponsorship   responsibilities

3   What do the words in italic in these extracts from the recording mean? Pay particular attention to any prefixes or suffixes they contain.
a   Hello, Volunteers *Worldwide*
b   ... suitable for *underprivileged* teenagers
c   who attend school on an *irregular* basis

4   Discuss these questions with other students.
a   What do you think voluntary work in these areas mentioned in the recording involves?
education
health
social participation
employment
b   If you were going to work for the organization, which area would you choose? Why?
c   How do you explain the fact that the voluntary organization gets 'many more applicants than they have placements for'?

Speaking

Orientation

1 How do you think each of these factors influence a person's sense of cultural identity? For example, for the person in the diagram, 'family life' is seen as the most important. Would you add any other factors to this list?

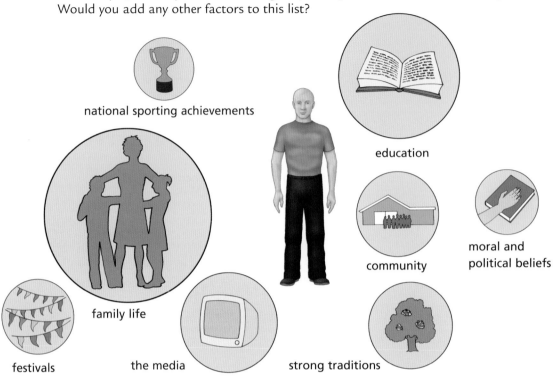

national sporting achievements

education

family life

community

moral and political beliefs

festivals

the media

strong traditions

2 Draw a diagram like the one above, showing the importance of these factors in shaping your own identity. The most important factors should appear in larger circles.

3 Discuss the factors that shape you with another student. Explain how you have ranked the factors and give examples.

Giving a presentation

4 Select one of the factors listed in 1 above and plan a presentation describing the importance of this factor in the context either of your own culture or the culture of an English-speaking country you know about.
a Think about the main ways in which this factor influences the people belonging to the culture you have chosen.
b Include interesting examples of ideas or behaviour resulting from this influence.

note

In IELTS Speaking Part 2, you will be expected to speak uninterrupted on a topic. This tests the presentation skills required to speak on a topic in an academic context.

5 Discuss these questions briefly with other students.
a Planning your presentation
Where could your ideas come from?
How can written notes help? What kind of notes will you find most helpful?
What sort of language is appropriate? Formal or informal?
b Delivering your talk
How should you begin?
How will you make use of written notes?
What can you do if you 'dry up'?

6 Work in small groups. Take turns to give your presentations.

Language for writing

Collocation

1 Choose the best word or phrase from the three options given in 1–4 below.

Different societies have often found their own idiosyncratic ways of
1 *treating / dealing with / sorting out* the problems of crime. In some cultures,
the 2 *prevailing / dominating / winning* view has been that criminals should
pay for their actions, and punishment has been seen as society's retribution
against the offenders. However, reformers normally 3 *give / make / raise* the
point that methods of rehabilitating criminals can be 4 *greatly / highly /
strongly* effective and are in society's interests in the long-run.

2 The correct answers in 1 are examples of collocation. Which of these definitions of
collocation is correct?
  a Some words fit together grammatically, such as nouns and verbs, adjectives and
     nouns, or verbs and adverbs. These word combinations are examples of collocation.
  b Some combinations of words which fit together grammatically occur more commonly
     than others. These common word combinations are examples of collocation.

3 Make a list of the collocations you can find in sentences a–f below. Look for
combinations similar to the examples.
Examples
make an assumption (verb + noun)
a key concept (adjective + noun)
fiercely independent (adverb + adjective)

  a The group presented the findings of a five-year survey carried out in three of the
     country's largest prisons.
  b We have made three fundamental assumptions in formulating our long-term strategy.
  c In a long, complicated article, the author raises serious questions about the basic
     rights of the individual.
  d By international standards, the organization of heavy industry in this country is
     highly efficient.
  e Many famous people have put forward convincing arguments against the
     introduction of identity cards. Others have made a strong case for having the cards.
  f The general public will have to accept the fact that there are two fundamentally
     distinct views on this subject.

4 Which of the verbs listed collocate with all the nouns in each of these groups?
give   raise   make   question
  a a decision, an argument, an assumption, someone's judgement
  b an effort, an assumption, a decision, a suggestion
  c a question, doubts, an issue, awareness
  d a reason, an explanation, a talk, an answer

5 Which of the adjectives listed collocate with all the nouns in each of these groups?
serious   simple   strong   possible
  a issue, problem, matter, concern
  b argument, influence, opinion, views
  c explanation, answer, idea, process
  d explanation, consequence, effect, outcome

Writing

Orientation **1** Answer these questions with another student.

a   What do you think the picture shows? Is the view it presents positive or negative?
b   In what ways can members of a family help each other at different stages in their lives?
c   In your view, should people put their families first and other people second? Why? Why not?

2 Read the Writing Task 2 below. Decide how you would do this task.
Think of some arguments to support your position, and compare your ideas with another student.

> The trend towards smaller family units and households is a positive development.
>
> To what extent do you agree with this statement?

Academic style **3** The sentences below are taken from a student's answer to the task above. For each of 1–6, choose which one you think is better for an academic text. The first one is done for you.

1 a   In loads of countries, families are getting smaller and kids move far away from their mum and dad when they leave home.
   b   <u>In many countries, family size is decreasing and young people move far away from their parents when they leave home.</u>

2 a   It is often argued that this is a positive development, leading to greater mobility and independence.
   b   You could argue that this is a good thing, leading to more mobility and independence.

3 a   But, being part of an extended family provides a useful support network to deal with difficult problems.
   b   However, being part of an extended family provides a useful support network to deal with difficult problems.

4 a Having lots of relatives around can be a source of experience and information for younger people.
   b Having lots of cousins, uncles, aunties, and grandparents around can be a source of experience and information for younger people.

5 a For example, it is often difficult to discuss problems with parents, whereas other family members might be able to listen more sympathetically and give advice.
   b For example, it is often difficult to discuss problems with parents. Other family members might be able to listen more sympathetically and give advice.

6 a Without this, individuals in small families have the hard prospect of having to work things out for themselves.
   b Without this, individuals in small families face the daunting prospect of having to work things out for themselves.

4 Match the sentences you chose with the following features of academic writing.

Impersonal style
Formal vocabulary
Choice of correct terms
Correct use of collocation
Correct use of linking words
Longer complex sentences

5 The paragraph below is taken from the rest of the essay and contains some errors of style in italic. What changes would you make to each one to improve the academic tone?

Large extended families are also *great for the oldies* as they become more dependent on others. *And,* having more helpers available means that the caring can be shared. In smaller families, *grandmothers, grandfathers, great aunties and uncles* may have to rely on a single carer or public resources.

Having a *near relative* in a particular career can also provide useful links and practical assistance for younger relatives who *fancy following* the same path. *The upshot is that* being part of a large family group provides a lot of benefits, *like* the support that other family members can offer.

Think, plan, write   **6** Read the Writing Task 2 below, then answer questions a and b.

> Society advances most when people break from the traditions of their predecessors.
>
> To what extent do you agree or disagree with this statement?

a What is your own opinion on this subject?
b What examples from your own experience or knowledge can you include to support your opinion?

7 Write your answer, remembering the following points:
   Illustrate your opinions with examples.
   Link your ideas both within and between sentences.
   Use appropriate features of academic language.
   Use common collocations where appropriate.

Help yourself

Giving presentations

1 Discuss these questions with other students.
   a In what situations do people give presentations?
   b In what situations, either at work or as part of your studies, might you need to give presentations?
   c In Part 2 of the IELTS Speaking test, candidates have to talk without interruption for 1–2 minutes. In what ways is this task similar and different to a 'normal' presentation?

2 🎧 Listen to the beginnings of two talks, then discuss these questions.
   a What are the situations and who are the speakers?
   b In what ways are the talks different?
   c Which talk do you personally find more effective? Give your reasons.

3 Read these tips on making presentations. Some of the advice is sensible, but not all. Write a tick next to advice which you think is worth following.

Tip 1: Equipment
☐ Impress your audience by using as many different aids as possible.
☐ Practise using any equipment or aparatus beforehand.

Tip 2: Planning
☐ Write headings and brief notes that you can understand at a glance.
☐ Write the full script of your presentation and underline key points.

Tip 3: Practising
☐ Practise referring to written notes while you speak.
☐ Practise using your voice effectively. Don't speak too quickly or too slowly. Vary the pitch and volume of your voice.

Tip 4: Starting
☐ Break the ice with a joke or anecdote related to your topic.
☐ Define all the difficult terms you are going to use.
☐ Involve your audience in some way, for example, by asking them a question.

Tip 5: Rounding off
☐ Summarize the key points you have made in your presentation.
☐ End with a provocative statement, or a question to the audience.

IELTS to do list

Choose one of the following to do outside class.

☐ Watch different kinds of presentations: speeches, lectures and talks, both live and on video and TV. Analyse the good and bad points of each.

☐ Choose three of the topics from the 'Global issues' page (page 32) and think of an attention-grabbing way of starting a presentation on those topics.

☐ Make a video or audio recording of yourself beginning a presentation. Note down your own strengths and weakenesses, or ask a friend to comment.

Where to look

ⓔ www.oup.com/elt/ielts

10 The natural world

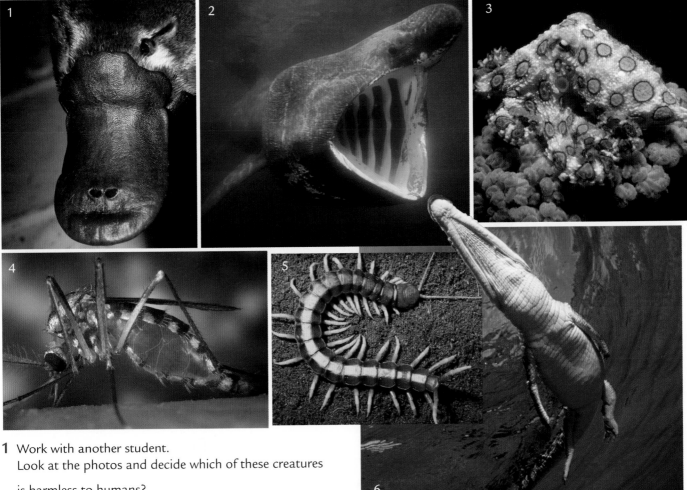

1 Work with another student.
Look at the photos and decide which of these creatures

is harmless to humans?
can injure people but not kill them?
sometimes kill people?
kills the most people?

2 Match the descriptions a–f to each of the photos.
Were your answers above correct?

3 Which of a–f do you think people find most alarming?
Why? What other creatures often scare people?

4 Discuss these questions with another student.

a Which are the most interesting wild creatures in your
country? Are any of them considered dangerous?
If so, how do people protect themselves?

b Which creatures – for instance, vampires or werewolves
– exist in the mythology or folklore of your country?
Why do you think these stories are told?

c How are animals often portrayed in cartoons and in
films for children? How do you think this affects
people's attitudes to real-life animals?

a Sometimes reaching eight metres in length, this aquatic
reptile will devour almost anything that moves, including
humans.

b An inhabitant of rock pools, its tentacles grow to ten
centimetres in length. A bite from its sharp beak can cause
death within minutes.

c Although it can measure up to twelve metres long and
weigh seven tonnes, it uses its huge jaws only to eat
microscopic sea plants and animals called plankton.

d It has forty-six legs, not 100. Up to twenty-five centimetres
long and fast-moving, it will catch and eat mice. Its
poisonous bite causes severe pain.

e Only about seven millimetres long, it has a thin body, long
legs and hairy wings. The diseases it can carry cause many
deaths, making it the deadliest creature on Earth.

f This egg-laying mammal lives in water or on land. It is
about sixty centimetres long and on each hind leg the
male has a poisonous spur. This can inflict painful wounds.

Reading

1 Look at the picture and answer these questions.

    a What sort of creature is this?
    b What do you think is unusual about it?
    c Which parts of its body can you identify?
    d What do you think they use them for?

Paragraph summaries

2 Read the text 'Armed and dangerous'. As you go through each paragraph, write a brief note next to each one to summarize the main idea.

IELTS practice

Questions 1–7: Matching headings

The reading passage has eight paragraphs A–H. Choose the most suitable headings for paragraphs B–H from headings i–x below. Use your notes from 2 to help you.

Example:

	Answer
Paragraph A	*iii*

1 Paragraph B ix
2 Paragraph C ii
3 Paragraph D vi
4 Paragraph E i
5 Paragraph F viii
6 Paragraph G vii
7 Paragraph H iv

Headings
i   Measuring mobility
ii   Deadly venom essential
iii Stung while swimming
iv Recovering from the stings
v   How to avoid being stung

vi   Unexpected discoveries
vii A serious lack of knowledge
viii All-round vision
ix   Very small but highly dangerous
x   Spiders that kill

Armed AND dangerous

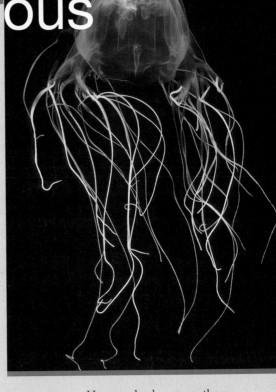

A The yacht was anchored 200 metres off the Queensland coast when Chris Slough dived into the water. That's when it got him. 'I felt a couple of little stings on my chest,' he says, 'but I thought nothing of it and carried on.' But as soon as he got back on the boat he realized he was in big trouble. 'I suddenly came over very nauseous,' he says. Within minutes he was in agonizing pain, vomiting and struggling to breathe. 'It felt like my organs were popping out.'

B Chris had been stung by an irukandji, a vicious creature named after an aboriginal tribe whose folklore tells of a terrible illness that struck people who went swimming in the sea. Irukandjis, a species of box jellyfish, grow no bigger than a peanut, yet relative to their size are probably the most toxic creatures on earth, putting many people in hospital each year with 'irukandji syndrome'. All but invisible in the water, their transparent bodies are covered from head to tentacle tip in stinger cells that discharge at the slightest touch, harpooning your skin with venomous barbs. The sting itself is often so mild that you barely notice it – until the powerful venom kicks in.

C When Chris arrived in hospital, he was given a massive dose of painkillers but no antivenin. Despite the severity and frequency of irukandji stings, no one has characterized its venom, or identified the properties of that of any other species of box jellyfish. In fact, almost everything about box jellyfish is a mystery. Chris was lucky not to have brushed up against *chironex fleckeri*, a brutish creature the size of a birthday cake with sixty sting-encrusted tentacles. Chironex has killed at least sixty-seven people in Australia since records began in 1883, more than the notorious red-back spider. It can kill a grown man in three minutes flat. Even so, no one knows what's in its venom.

D Rattled by bad publicity, the tourist industry has been pouring money into box jellyfish research. What the biologists are finding comes as a big surprise. It turns out that box jellyfish are not jellyfish at all. In fact, it looks as though they have been ploughing a separate evolutionary furrow since the Pre-Cambrian period, 543 million years ago. What's more, the sea is teeming with unknown species. Even a cursory survey has revealed more than a dozen undescribed ones, some probably even more dangerous than chironex and the irukandji.

E Jamie Seymour, a tropical biologist at James Cook University in Cairns, has developed a technique for tracking chironex's movements using tiny ultrasonic transmitters stuck on with surgical superglue. True jellyfish are dim-witted ocean drifters, but, the first time Seymour managed to tag a chironex with one of these, it immediately headed straight for the bottom, then suddenly swam off covering nearly half a kilometre in fifteen minutes. One simple fact underlies this behaviour: box jellies are voracious predators. 'You see whole chunks of fish inside them,' says Seymour. Drifting around aimlessly is not a good strategy for a fish eater, so they charge around in search of prey.

F Another remarkable feature of box jellyfish is their visual system. They have twenty-four eyes, arranged in clusters of six, one on each side of their cuboid body. Each cluster contains two types of eye – four simple light-sensing pits plus two sophisticated 'camera eyes'. The latter are anatomically similar to human eyes, with lenses, retinas, and corneas, and can form detailed colour images, but all this sophisticated equipment begs a question. How do box jellies deal with all the information their eyes gather when they don't have a brain? What happens, for example, when two different eyes are sending out contradictory information? No one knows. Why would a creature so apparently primitive need such sophisticated eyes, and so many of them? Some scientists have suggested that this is to do with finding optimum hunting grounds, but Seymour goes one further. He believes that box jellyfish actively seek out prey. He says he has seen them swim around obstacles and home in on individual fish.

G Their predatory eating habits also explain why they have such lethal toxins. It's one thing to stalk fish, but how do you catch them when all you have are flimsy, rubbery tentacles? The answer is to take them out with as much lethal force as possible. A chironex sting certainly does that – its venom can dispatch a fish in less than two minutes. It's just an evolutionary accident that the toxin works so well on us too. Seymour suspects there are more deaths than are officially recognised. He points out that *chironex fleckeri* was thought to be confined to northern Australian waters but has now been found in Papua New Guinea, Malaysia, Indonesia, the Philippines, Thailand, and Vietnam. The irukandjis too are probably widespread in the Indo-Pacific. 'People are getting stung and killed all over the tropics without anybody realizing the true cause,' he says.

H As for Chris, the painkillers worked well enough to let him lie down without it hurting. And he was lucky to have a short bout – it only took twenty hours for him to stop feeling like he was going to die.

Unfamiliar vocabulary

note

If you think you need to understand an unfamiliar word, identify its part of speech and then look for other clues in the text.

3 When you read a word that you don't know, ask yourself the questions below. Use these questions to decide the meaning of the words given.

a **Do I really need to understand it?** Can you ignore these words and still understand the text? 'agonizing' (paragraph A), 'notorious' (C), 'flimsy' (G)

b **What part of speech is it?** In the text, is each of these words a verb, adjective, noun, etc? 'discharge' (paragraph B), 'flat' (C), 'rattled' (D)

c **Is it formed from other words I know?** What are the meanings of the base words in each of these? 'anchored', 'nauseous' (paragraph A), 'light-sensing' (F)

d **Does it appear again in the text?** What do the different contexts tell you about these words? 'stings' (paragraph A), 'tentacle', 'species' (B)

e **Is there a clue, such as a synonym or opposite, near it in the text?** Which words have similar or opposite meanings to the following? 'toxic', 'invisible' (paragraph B), 'primitive' (F)

f **Are there other clues?** What clues are there to the meaning of these words? 'Pre-Cambrian', 'cursory' (paragraph D), 'corneas' (F)

4 With another student, decide what these words and phrases mean, using the ideas above.

mild, venom (paragraph B)
painkillers, characterized (paragraph C)
dim-witted, tag, underlies, voracious, predators, drifting around aimlessly (paragraph E)
confined to (paragraph G)

IELTS practice

Questions 8–11: Sentence completion

Complete sentences 8–11 with the correct ending A–G from the box below. Some combinations of sentences and endings are logically impossible: make a note of these when you start.

8 At first, box jellyfish stings may not hurt much D
9 Doctors could not give Chris antivenin at the hospital G
10 Box jellyfish have to be able to swim well
11 The number of human victims is probably underestimated

note

When all endings begin with 'because', search the relevant parts of the text for reasons.

A because they have extremely good eyesight.
B because these creatures live in more places than was realized.
C because they are not really a kind of jellyfish.
D because they cause much less pain than the venom.
E because we don't know how many kinds of box jellyfish there are.
F because they need to go after the fish they eat.
G because the exact nature of the venom is unknown.

Questions 12–14: Short-answer questions

Answer the questions with words from the Reading Passage. Write NO MORE THAN THREE WORDS for each answer.

12 How long, apparently, have box jellyfish differed from true jellyfish?
543 million years ago

13 What did Seymour fasten to the box jellyfish?
an ultrasonic transmitter

14 What do box jellyfish lack for processing visual data?
a brain

Exploration

5 Work out the meanings of these phrasal verbs. What are the clues in the text?

kick in (paragraph B)
brush up against (paragraph C)
stick on, head for, swim off (paragraph E)
deal with, send out, seek out, home in on (paragraph F)
take out (paragraph G)

6 Rewrite the sentences so that they begin with 'Although'.

Example
I felt a couple of little stings on my chest, but I thought nothing of it and carried on.
Although I felt a couple of little stings on my chest, I thought nothing of it and carried on.

a Irukandjis grow no bigger than a peanut yet are probably the most toxic creatures on Earth.
b Despite the severity and frequency of irukandji stings, no one has characterized its venom.
c It can kill a grown man in three minutes flat. Even so, no one knows what's in its venom.

7 Discuss these questions with other students.

a Has reading this text changed your ideas about swimming in the sea?
b Should measures be taken against animals that endanger humans, or should such creatures be left to live their own lives and play their part in the ecosystem?
c Which are more dangerous: animals to humans, or humans to animals?

Listening

Section 2

Saying figures

1 Practise reading these figures aloud with another student.

33 mg	455 BC.	5 ft 10 in	37°C
the 90s	8,850 m	100 mph	25^2
850 cc	£1500	2/3	
3,634 sq km	3.141	7 cm/day	

2 🎧 Listen and check your pronunciation. Then write the figures out in full.

Example
33 mg   *thirty-three milligrams*

3 Complete the notes on the Maasai Mara National Reserve with these figures:

12–30   83   450   1510   1500–2180

Compare your answers with another student, saying the figures in full. Check your answers on page 177.

Area: 1510 sq km
Altitude: 1500 2180 m
Rainfall: 9.3 mm/month
Temperature range: 12 ? °C
Species: 80 mammals, 450 birds

Maasai Mara
National Reserve

herds of animals wildebeast

4 Look at the map, notes, and pictures of the Maasai Mara. Answer these questions.

a Where is it?
b What's the climate like?
c What kinds of landscape and vegetation are there?
d What species of wildlife are found there? What's special about them?

5 Tell other students about a National Park or wildlife area in your country. Think about questions a–d above.

6 With another student, answer these questions on the pictures and IELTS questions below.

    a How does the place below differ from the Maasai Mara?
    b Which of answers 1–8 require numbers?
    c Which have abbreviations and how are they pronounced?
    d What do you think the numbers in the other questions refer to?

IELTS practice

Questions 1–8: Note completion

🎧 Complete the notes. Write NO MORE THAN THREE WORDS OR A NUMBER for each answer.

Scottish Highlands: travel facts

Total area (with islands): (1)............*39000*............ sq km

Getting there

By train
Glasgow to Fort William: 174 km. Journey time:
(2)........*4 hrs*..............
Glasgow to Inverness: (3)............*3 280*............ km.
Journey time: 3.5 hours

By car
Glasgow to Fort William: take the (4)........*A82*............ road.

Climate

Average maximum temperature (West Coast):
(5).................*18*............. °C
Average rainfall (West Coast): (6)...........*2 000*............ mm/year.

Accommodation costs

Fort William: (7)......*£25*............ per night
Inverness: £30 per night

Events (Inverness)

Highland Games (Date: (8).......*23rd July*.....)

Questions 9 and 10: Multiple-answer questions

🎧 Choose TWO letters A–E.

    What advice does Moira give visitors?
    A Wear bright clothes.
    B Get as close as you can to the animals.
    C Watch wildlife from your car.
    D Avoid making a noise.
    E Take your dog with you.

Exploration

7 Which would you rather visit, the Maasai Mara or the Scottish Highlands? Why?

Speaking

education

habitat

living conditions

freedom

entertainment

research

endangered species

Expressing opinions

1 Work with another student to answer these questions based on the photographs and the words above.

a What arguments can you think of for and against keeping animals in zoos? Make two lists.

b Which list reflects your personal point of view?

2 Work with a different student. Tell them your own opinion of zoos. Use phrases from the lists below to help you express the arguments for and against.

Your opinions	**Other views**
From my point of view, ...	Some people say ...
In my opinion, ...	I know some people think ...
Personally, I believe ...	I'm not convinced that ...
My own feeling is ...	As for the argument that ...

IELTS practice

Part 3: Topic discussion

3 In Speaking Part 3, the examiner will ask you about more abstract aspects of a topic. Work with another student. Take it in turns to ask your partner the questions below, allowing time for a full answer. Ask follow-up questions where necessary, for example, 'Can you tell me a bit more about that?', 'Why do you think that?'

Animals and humans
In what ways are humans different from other animals?
What are the main roles of animals in your country?
Conservation
Why is it important to conserve the world's animal and plant species?
Which species are endangered in your country? Why?
Animals and ethics
Do you think modern farming methods are cruel to animals?
Why do many people refuse to eat meat?

Language for writing

Concession

1 We use clauses of concession for contrasts in which something unexpected is stated or implied.

Example
Though the eel is a fish, it can live on land.

Complete the examples using each of these expressions once.

but, (and) yet
however, nevertheless
although, even though (+ subject + verb)
despite, in spite of (+ noun or -ing)

a It rained heavily in the autumn. ......*yet / nevertheless*......, there still was not enough water.

b ......*Even though*...... they hate to shoot animals, sometimes it is necessary.

c Every year thousands of zebras cross the river, *in spite / despite* the danger from crocodiles.

d Bears became a protected species, ...*But*...... their numbers continued to decline.

e The increase was slight in 1995–2000, ...*yet / but*...... much greater in 2000–2005.

f ......*Despite*...... the overall upward trend in sea mammal poulations, the number of blue whales showed a slight fall last year.

g The fish population has probably risen. ......*However*...... there are no data to confirm this.

h ......*Although*...... no nests had been seen in March, several young birds were spotted in June.

2 Use clauses of concession to complete the sentences with similar meanings.

a The young deer ran quickly, but it couldn't escape from the lion.

In spite ......*of running quickly The young deer could escape from the*......

b There was a minor dip in whale sightings in July. However, the figures for the year show substantial growth.

Even though ......*there was minor dip in july, the figure show substantial growth.*......

c The death adder is not a long snake. Nevertheless, it is extremely dangerous.

Though ....

....

d Tropical rainforests cover less than seven per cent of the land, and yet they contain around half the world's species.

Tropical rainforests contain half the world's species, despite ......*Covering the fact they covered*......

e Some plants survive in the Sahara, though it hardly ever rains there.

It hardly ever rains in the Sahara. ......*However*......

....

f Although global warming has made certain plants less common, sub-tropical varieties have largely replaced them. *Although*

Global warming has ....

....

g Despite the fact that it is a huge lake, nowadays there are few fish in it.

It is a huge lake, ...

....

h Five years ago the wolf population stood at just twenty-two. Since then, however, their numbers have risen to over a hundred.

Although ......*Five years ago*......

....

3 Combine the sentences using concession clauses. Use a different linking expression for each.

a The butterfly population is actually rising. It seems strange.

b Over a million hectares of wetlands have been lost. The destruction continues.

c The rate of extinctions has slowed a little. The total number is still rising.

d There was an initial fall in panda numbers. The overall trend is upwards.

e They are going to build the motorway. The protests are growing.

f Sixty per cent more money was spent. Agricultural production was twenty-five per cent lower.

Writing

1 Answer these questions with another student.

   a   What does the graph below show?

   b   What main comparison is being made?

   c   Are there any obvious trends and exceptions?

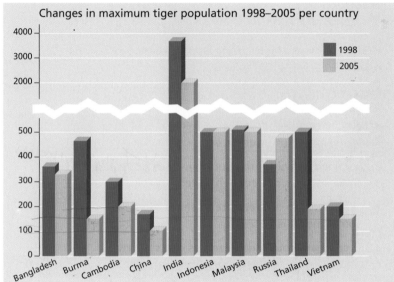

Changes in maximum tiger population 1998–2005 per country

Bangladesh Burma Cambodia China India Indonesia Malaysia Russia Thailand Vietnam

2 Read the description below. Complete the description with the correct information based on the graph.

> The graph shows the estimated maximum population of tigers in a range of Asian countries in both 1998 and 2005.
>
> In most of the countries included in the graph, the population fell. This was most noticeable in **1** Burma and **2** Cambodia, where the number of tigers was thought to be less than half the figure in 1998. In the former, the number of tigers dropped as low as 150. **3** India remained the country with by far the largest tiger population, but experienced a dramatic fall in numbers so that in 2005 there may have been as few as 2000. Despite its size, **4** China had a very small population of at most 100 tigers by 2005.
>
> Although the trend was downwards overall, tiger populations were thought to have remained stable in **5** India and **6** Malaysia at approximately 500. The only country where tigers showed signs of recovering was **7** Russia, where numbers may have risen by up to 100.

3 What examples of concession can you find in the description?

4 Which of the options below most closely describes how the description above is organized?

   a   Say what the graph shows. Describe each category in turn, comparing and contrasting the statistics across the period.

   b   Say what the graph shows. Describe the general trend, giving the most obvious examples. Contrast this with examples which do not follow the trend.

   c   Say what the graph shows. Point out the most extreme or exceptional data. Describe the general trend, giving the most obvious examples.

5 Look at each of the data sets a–c below, which relate to three species of animal. What are the key points in the data? What would be the best approach to describing these in order to emphasize the key points?

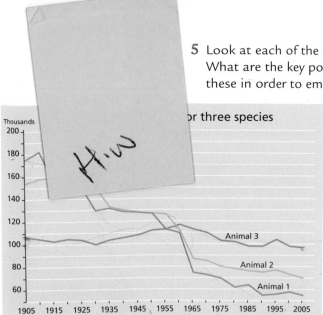

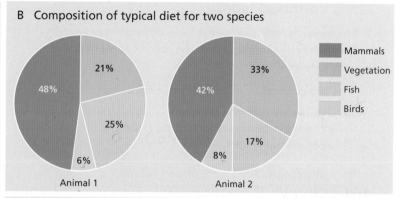

B Composition of typical diet for two species

C Distribution of three species across four habitats

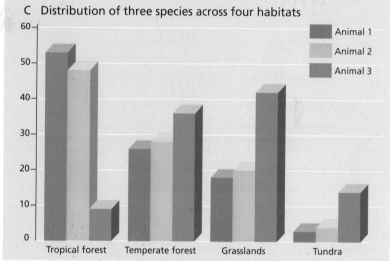

Think, plan, write

6 Read the Writing Task 1 below. What would be the best approach to describing this data set?

> The table below shows trends in captures of sea and ocean fish over a ten-year period.
>
> Summarize the information by selecting and reporting the main features, and make comparisons where relevant.

Marine fish: total capture (thousand metric tonnes)

	1989–1991	1999–2001
Asia, excluding Middle East	25,427	28,102
Europe	18,032	14,315
Middle East & North Africa	1,622	2,343
Sub-Saharan Africa	2,169	3,140
North America	5,069	3,995
Central America & Caribbean	1,445	1,377
South America	14,382	15,235
Oceania	602	944

Source: Food and Agriculture Organization of the United Nations

7 Write your answer to the writing task in at least 150 words. Use concession structures where appropriate.

Help yourself

Easily confused words

1 Some words look similar but have different meanings. Complete the sentences with the correct form of the words given.

  a 1 affect /ə'fekt/   2 effect /ɪ'fekt/

      The disease mainly ... the skin.
      A change in temperature had no ... on the experimental results.

  b 1 desert /'dezət/   2 dessert /dɪ'zɜːt/
      It can reach 55°C in the ... .
      Let's have ice-cream for ... .

  c 1 1definite   2 definitive
      The professor wrote the ... work on the subject.
      We now have a ... date for the confererence.

  d 1 accept /ək'sept/   2 except /ɪk'sept/
      People over 65 are ... from the new rules.
      Congratulations. Your application has been ... .

  e 1 continuous   2 continual
      There were ... warnings of the danger.
      Recycling waste forms part of a ... process.

2 Write sentences to show the difference in meaning of the following pairs.

- shade/shadow
- lose/loose
- economic/economical
- lie/lay

3 Other words sound the same but their meanings and spelling are different. For each sentence, choose the correct word and define the other word.

  a Town *councillors/counsellors* are elected every four years.
  b Motor vehicles are not *aloud/allowed* on the campus.
  c There is no need to dress *formally/formerly* for the dinner.
  d The *tale/tail* of the fish measures four centimetres in length.
  e We visited the *site/sight* of an ancient temple, of which little remains.

4 Explain the difference between these pairs.

  past/passed   break/brake   roll/role
  principle/principal   they're/their   its/it's
  who's/whose

5 Academic writing requires accurate expression, so care must be taken with words that are close in meaning, but not the same. Find the error in each sentence, and replace it with one of these words.

  between   earn   foreigners   number   means

  a The only way of transport is an infrequent bus service.
  b On average, industrial workers win less than $20,000 per year.
  c Last year there was little trade among the two countries.
  d A large amount of scientists took part in the study.
  e Strangers who wish to work in that country require visas.

IELTS to do list

Choose one of the following to do outside class.

☐ Look back at your written work for vocabulary mistakes of this kind, and make sure you know the correct words.

☐ Key 'commonly confused words' or 'easily confused words' into your Internet search engine. Download, copy, or note down any pairs that might cause you difficulty, then check them in your dictionary.

☐ Try out the words you have studied the next time you are writing or speaking. If possible, check with the reader or listener that you are using them correctly.

Where to look

Ⓔ www.oup.com/elt/ielts

11 Psychology

1 Look at the photos and discuss these questions.

    a   What differences do you notice about people's behaviour?

    b   How would you behave on an occasion like this?
        Which person in the photos do you identify most closely with?

    c   What determines how sociable an individual is?

2 Look at the people in the photos again and discuss these questions.

    a   What can you say about the personalities of the individuals from their body language, for example, from the way they are standing or using gestures?

    b   Choose one or two of these adjectives that you think could describe each person.

ambitious	nervous
anti-social	obsessive
big-headed	self-centred
confident	sociable
easy-going	timid

3 Think about your own personality and answer these questions.

    a   Where would you put yourself on these scales?

altruistic |___|___|___|___| self-centred   balanced |___|___|___|___| obsessive

sociable |___|___|___|___| anti-social   easy-going |___|___|___|___| highly-strung

courageous |___|___|___|___| timid

    b   Compare yourself with other students, explaining your choices and giving examples.

Reading

Orientation

1 Discuss these questions with another student.

  a What are the five senses?

  b Which senses are associated with these words? Think of other words associated with each sense.

acidic	beauty	deafening	gas	whisper
perfume	rough	salty	sticky	yellow

  c Have two of your senses ever contradicted each other? For example, have you ever seen food which looks delicious but tastes terrible?

  d Which of the senses do you personally most appreciate? Which one could you most easily survive without?

  e Which of the five senses do you think is the most essential for human survival?

Finding specific information

2 Read the 'The Phantom Hand' to answer this question: 'What are the practical applications of the experiments described in the article?' Time yourself to find out how long it takes you to find the answer. When you have found the answer, stop reading.

3 Compare reading strategies with a partner.

  a How long did it take you to find the answer?

  b Did you start reading the article at the beginning?

  c Did you glance briefly at each paragraph to identify the relevant topic?

  d Did you look for specific words?

Text organization

4 Read the whole article and label this diagram with the relevant topics from the list of headings below. There are two headings you do not need to use.

- A historical perspective
- Philosophical implications
- Practical application
- Sociological implications
- The experiments and the explanation

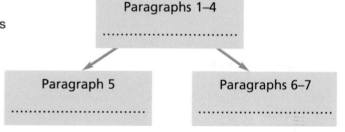

The **Phantom** Hand

This illusion is extraordinarily compelling the first time you encounter it.

1 There is a very striking illusion in which you can feel a rubber hand being touched as if it were your own. To find out for yourself, ask a friend to sit across from you at a small table. Set up a vertical partition
5 on the table, rest your right hand behind it where you cannot see it, and place a plastic right hand in view. Ask your assistant to repeatedly tap and stroke your concealed right hand in a random sequence. Tap, tap, tap, stroke, tap, stroke, stroke. At the same time, while
10 you watch, they must also tap and stroke the visible plastic dummy at exactly the same time in the same way. If your friend continues the procedure for about twenty or thirty seconds, something quite strange will happen: you will have an uncanny feeling that you are actually being
15 stroked on the fake hand. The sensations you feel will seem to emerge directly from the plastic.

2 Why does this happen? Matthew Botvinick and Jonathan Cohen, at the University of Pittsburgh and Carnegie Mellon University, who reported the so-called rubber-
20 hand illusion in 1998, have suggested that the similarity in appearance fools the brain into mistaking the false hand for your real hand. They believe this illusion is strong enough to overcome the discrepancy between the position of your real hand that you can feel and the
25 site of the plastic hand you can see.

3 But that is not the whole story. William Hirstein and Kathleen Carrie Armel of the University of California discovered a further twist: the object your helper touches does not even need to resemble your hand. The same
30 effect is produced if they tap and stroke the table. Try the same experiment, but this time get your acquaintance to rub and tap the surface in front of you while making matching movements on your real, concealed hand. You will eventually start feeling touch sensations emerge
35 from the wood surface.

4 This illusion is extraordinarily compelling the first time you encounter it. But how can scientists be certain that the subject really believes that they are feeling sensations through the table? Kathleen Carrie Armel again and
40 Vilayanur S Ramachandran learned that, once the illusion has developed, if you 'threaten' the table by aiming a blow at it, the person winces and even starts sweating. This reaction was demonstrated objectively by measuring a sudden decrease in electrical skin resistance caused by
45 perspiration. It is as if the table becomes incorporated into a person's own body image so that it is linked to emotional centres in the brain; the subject perceives a threat to the table as a threat to themselves.

5 This may all sound like a magic trick, but it does have
50 practical applications. In fact, the experiments were inspired by work with patients who had phantom limbs. After a person loses an arm from injury, they may continue to sense its presence vividly. Often, the phantom seems to be frozen in a painfully awkward
55 position. To overcome this, a patient was asked to imagine putting their phantom arm behind a mirror. By then putting their intact arm on the reflective side, they created the visual illusion of having restored the missing arm. If the patient now moved the intact arm, its
60 reflection – and thus the phantom – was seen to move. Remarkably, it was felt to move as well, sometimes relieving the painful cramp.

> Beyond a practical application, these illusions also demonstrate some important principles underlying perception.

---

6 Beyond a practical application, these illusions also demonstrate some important principles underlying
65 perception. Firstly, perception is based largely on matching up sensory inputs. As you feel your hand being tapped and stroked and see the table or dummy hand being touched in the same way, your brain asks itself, 'What is the likelihood that what I see and what I feel
70 could be identical simply by chance? Nil. Therefore, the other person must be touching me.' Secondly, this mechanism seems to be based on automatic processes that our intellect cannot override. The brain makes these judgments about the senses automatically; they do not
75 involve conscious thought. Even a lifetime of experience that an inanimate object is not part of your body is abandoned in light of the perception that it is.

7 All of us go through life making certain assumptions about our existence. 'My name has always been Joe,'
80 someone might think. 'I was born in San Diego,' and so on. All such beliefs can be called into question at one time or another for various reasons. One premise that seems to be beyond question is that you are anchored in your body. Yet given a few seconds of the right kind
85 of stimulation, even this obvious fact is temporarily forsaken, as a table or a plastic hand seem to become part of you. ∎

IELTS practice

Questions 1–4: Classifying statements

The text reports the findings of three teams of researchers. Match statements 1–4 with the correct team A, B or C.

  A   Botvinick and Cohen
  B   Hirstein and Armel
  C   Armel and Ramachandran

  1   The illusion does not depend on the 'phantom' looking like a real hand. *A*
  2   The brain can disregard spatial information. *C*
  3   If the fake hand is threatened, the subject will show signs of fear. *C*
  4   A hand-shaped object is required for the illusion. *B*

Questions 5–7: Multiple-choice questions

Choose the correct letters A, B, C or D in answer to these questions.

  5   How do researchers explain the fact that subjects respond physically when someone threatens to hit the table in front of them?
      A   The table becomes an integral part of the image subjects have of themselves.
      B   It is a reflex action triggered by the movement of the other person's hand.
      C   An electrical connection is established between the subject and the table.
      D   Over time, the subject comes to believe that the table is one of his possessions. *(D circled)*

  6   What does the phantom hand experiment show us about the nature of human perception?
      A   It is based on conscious thought processes.
      B   It is primarily an unconscious process. *(B circled)*
      C   It is closely related to intellectual ability.
      D   It relies only on sensory information.

  7   Which of these statements best summarizes the wider implications of the experiments described in the text?
      A   The experiments are valuable in treating patients who have lost limbs. *(A circled)*
      B   The experiments cast doubt on a fundamental human assumption.
      C   The experiments show humans to be less intelligent than was once thought.
      D   Human beings arrive at the truth by analysing the evidence of their senses.

Questions 8–13: Summary completion

Complete the summary below. Choose ONE WORD FROM THE TEXT AND/OR A NUMBER for each answer.

It is a recognized phenomenon that patients who have been injured and lost (8) *arm* sometimes continue to have feelings, like pain or (9) *movement*, in these parts of their body. In order to assist patients like this, doctors can use a (10) *phantom* placed vertically on a flat surface. The patient imagines that he is putting his phantom arm behind the mirror and his (11) *intact* arm in front. When the patient moves the latter, the (12) *reflection* also moves, giving the patient the illusion that his non-existent arm is moving. In some cases, this illusory movement may succeed in (13) *relieving* the patient's discomfort.

5 'Dummy' can be used as an adjective or a noun to refer to something which is not real. (lines 67 and 11). What do you think the 'dummy' expressions in these sentences mean?

    a   A small group of directors transferred some of the company's profits into a *dummy corporation* they had set up.

    b   Before carrying out the first experiment, researchers did a *dummy run* on animals.

    c   The condition of patients given the *dummy pills* improved slightly.

    d   Some shops install *dummy security cameras* to deter would-be shoplifters.

6 Refer to the text to find answers to these questions.

    a   What is the difference in meaning between the verbs 'tap' and 'stroke'(line 7)? What other verbs with similar meanings to these do you know? Make a list starting with the gentlest.

    b   What other word in the first paragraph means the same as 'strange'?

    c   What do you understand by 'phantom limbs'? What is the more common meaning of the noun 'phantom'?

    d   In what situations or for what reasons do people 'wince' and 'sweat' (line 42)?

7 The article is about an illusion of feeling something that does not exist. What other sensory illusions have you experienced, or do you know about?

8 Follow the instructions related to these two optical illusions, and discuss possible theories to explain what is happening.

Stare at the eye of the red parrot while you count slowly to twenty, then look immediately at one spot in the empty bird cage. A faint image of a bluegreen bird will appear in the cage. Try the same thing with the green cardinal. A faint mauve bird will appear in the cage.

Stare at the bluish dot for a while without moving your eyes or head. The dot will gradually fade into the field of green. As soon as you move your head or eyes, notice that the blue dot reappears.

Check your explanations by turning to page 177.

Listening

Section 4

Orientation

1 Psychometric tests are commonly used to assess people's aptitudes, abilities, and personal characteristics. Work with another student you know well. Read these sample questions taken from an online test. Answer the questions for yourself and for your partner.

Step 1: For each question pick which statement is most like you.
Step 2: Pick the one least like you.
Step 3: Prioritize the remaining two, one of which is more like you than the other.
Note: You cannot tick two boxes in the same vertical column.

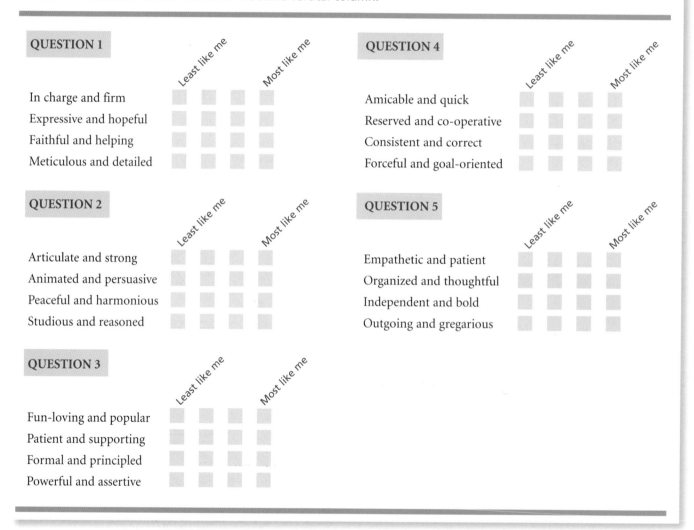

QUESTION 1

Least like me   Most like me

In charge and firm
Expressive and hopeful
Faithful and helping
Meticulous and detailed

QUESTION 2

Least like me   Most like me

Articulate and strong
Animated and persuasive
Peaceful and harmonious
Studious and reasoned

QUESTION 3

Least like me   Most like me

Fun-loving and popular
Patient and supporting
Formal and principled
Powerful and assertive

QUESTION 4

Least like me   Most like me

Amicable and quick
Reserved and co-operative
Consistent and correct
Forceful and goal-oriented

QUESTION 5

Least like me   Most like me

Empathetic and patient
Organized and thoughtful
Independent and bold
Outgoing and gregarious

2 Make sure you can see your own answers and your partner's answers. Discuss these questions.

a   Do you think your partner has answered the questions about themselves accurately?
b   Has your partner answered the questions about you in the same way as you have?
c   Why do you think people take tests like these? What do you think they reveal about their character?
d   How might your answers to these questions help a prospective employer or university admissions officer?

Questions 1–5: Sentence completion

🎧 Listen to the recording and complete statements 1–5 in no more than THREE words.

1 Some employers use a psychometric test as one element of their

....

2 A better name for psychometric tests would be ....

3 One reason why questionnaires are popular is that they are straightforward to

....

4 In the .... test format, someone else answers questions about you.

5 In the .... type of test, subjects have to do something practical.

Questions 6–7: Multiple-choice questions

Choose the correct letter A, B, or C.

6 Psychometric testing aims to assess
A permanent personality features
B personality tendencies
C personality deficiencies

7 How effective a questionnaire is depends on
A the standard of questions
B the subject's attitude
C the subject's ability

Questions 8–10: Short-answer questions

Answer the questions below. Write NO MORE THAN TWO WORDS for each answer.

8 How many areas of a person's character does the Myers–Briggs test assess?

....

9 In the Myers–Briggs test, what is the third area concerned with?

....

10 What are the two ways in which people may prefer to organize their lives?

.... and ....

3 According to the speaker, a test sometimes requires a subject to do something. How they do it will tell the tester something about their personality. For example, the subject might be asked to blow up a balloon until it bursts.

a How would you do this?
b What would this tell someone about your personality?

Collecting things   Playing an instrument   Restoring old objects

Speaking

Orientation

1 Look at the photos and discuss these questions.

  a What do a person's free-time activities tell you about their personality? What kinds of people might have the hobbies shown in the photographs?

  b How do the free-time activities people choose help them to combat stress and remain well-balanced, stable human beings?

Describing interests

2 🎧 Listen to three people talking about their free-time activities and saying how they benefit from them.

  a Match each speaker with one of the categories shown in the photos.

  b What benefits does each person mention?

3 🎧 Listen again and tick which of these expressions the speakers use to talk about their hobbies and how they benefit from them.

What I do	**How I benefit**
I do various things in my spare time.	For me, it's just good fun.
I spend nearly all my free time …	I like it because it's so different from what I normally do.
I'm into … in a big way.	I've made loads of new friends through my hobby.
I've got lots of hobbies but my favourite is …	It makes a change.
My passion is …	It's a chance to be with my mates.
What I like doing in my free time is …	It's a real change from …
	It's a very relaxing way to spend time.
	It's quite a lucrative hobby.

IELTS practice

Part 1: Familiar discussion

4 In Speaking Part 1, you may be asked questions about topics like these. Work with other students to ask and answer questions. Add extra questions where appropriate.

What do you do in your spare time?
How long have you been interested in this?
Do you do this alone or with other people?
How much time do you spend doing this in an average week?
Where do you do it?
Do you need any special equipment to do it?
What is it about this particular activity that suits your personality?
Why is it generally beneficial for people to have hobbies?
How do you benefit from yours?
Is it an expensive hobby?
What are the disadvantages of your hobby?

Language for writing

Articles

[handwritten: abstract noun = violence / courage]

1 What part of speech is the word in italic in each of sentences a–e?

a Despite fears, people with mental health problems rarely use the *violence*. *[handwritten: noun]*

b Not everyone has *courage* to admit when they have made a mistake. *[handwritten: noun, the]*

c We are currently carrying out the *investigation* into anti-depressants. An *investigation* is likely to last at least a year. *[handwritten: an, the]*

d The team were doing a *research* into how well crows can solve problems. *[handwritten: noun]*

e Online journals are mostly read by the *academics*. *[handwritten: plural, honor]*

2 In each of sentences a–e above, articles have been used incorrectly. Correct each sentence.

3 Answer each of the following questions about the sentences a–e in 1.

a Why can't an article be used with the abstract noun in (a)?

b In contrast with (a), why *can* an article be used with the abstract noun in (b)?

c Can you explain the correct use of 'an' and 'the' in (c)?

d Is 'research' in (d) normally countable or uncountable in English?

e What could you add to (e) to make it unnecessary to correct it?

Abstract nouns

4 Complete each of the following sentences with a noun from the list. Use an appropriate article if necessary.

intelligence
honesty
behaviour
information

a *[handwritten: Honesty]* ...... is an essential quality for anyone considering a job in crime prevention.

b *[handwritten: behaviour]* ...... like that is not considered acceptable in most societies.

c The committee did not have *[handwritten: information... the honesty]* ...... to admit that the findings of their report were wrong.

d The researchers were studying how *[handwritten: the ... st]* ...... of *behaviour* mammals changed in captivity.

e Not everyone has ...... to understand theoretical physics. *[handwritten: the intelligence]*

f *[handwritten: Information]* ...... on famous people is widely available on the Internet.

g Doubts have been raised about how effectively IQ tests measure *[handwritten: intelligence]* ......

h Some candidates at interviews cannot remember *[handwritten: information]* ...... they included on their application form.

Uncountable nouns

5 Each of the following nouns is normally uncountable in English. Is this the same in your language? How can you make them countable?

advice
help
work
news
knowledge
money
rubbish
luck

Articles and adjectives

6 Articles can be used with adjectives to name classes of people or abstract qualities.

Examples
Studies have found that people donate more money to charities that help the young.
As religion has declined, belief in the supernatural has increased.

Replace the phrases in italic in these sentences with a phrase like those above.

a Animals kept in zoos develop serious mental problems that never develop *in their natural habitats*. *[handwritten: the wild]*

b Depression affects all kinds of people. *People with lots of money* are no exception. *[handwritten: the wealthy]*

c *People who are out of work* can suffer from stress and illness. *[handwritten: the unemployed]*

d Our ability to make decisions about the future can be affected by a fear of *things we do not know*. *[handwritten: the unknown]*

e *People who cannot see* often have a very well-developed sense of hearing. *[handwritten: the blind]*

Writing

Common errors
1 Each of the extracts a–d contains examples of a specific category of error. Answer these questions. Which type of error from the list does the extract contain? How could you correct each of the errors?

spelling
word order
articles
singular/plural agreement

singular/plural (handwritten)

a More choice are not always better than less. The more alternatives there is when we make a selection the less satisfaction we derive from our ultimate decision.

b Many members of the animal kingdom will help readily immediate family, but humans alone extend altruism beyond this, helping regularly strangers for no personal gain.

c Psichiatrists label someone as delusional when they have a false view of reality, believeing falsehoods with total conviction. Evidence against the delusion will not shake they're view.

d People with the synaesthesia have their senses mixed or overlapping. For example, a visual stimulus will also cause them to hear the sound. It is not normally thought to be an indication of the poor health, and some synaesthetes say they enjoy the experience.

Punctuation
2 Match each of the descriptions a–f with an item of punctuation.
   a ... indicates that a letter or letters are missing, especially in informal style.
   b ... separates a non-defining relative clause.
   c ... separates items in a list. *a com.* (handwritten)
   d ... indicates the end of a sentence.
   e ... can be used to introduce an explanation or an example.
   f ... indicates possession.

   a colon — *b*
   c — a comma
   d — a full stop
   f — an apostrophe — *a*

3 Add the correct punctuation and capital letters to this paragraph.

its a classic philosophers conundrum how does my perception of the world which only I can experience differ from yours take a red rose for example we can probably agree its red rather than blue but what exactly is red do I see the same red as you philosophers have been wrestling with this question for centuries and sensory scientists too have long been interested in why people report such different experiences of the same colours odours or flavours the question is whether it is purely subjective or based on some objective difference in their sensory experiences

Think, plan, write

4 Read the Writing Task 2 below, then discuss these questions with another student.

a Can you think of any examples in favour of the statement? Consider these ideas.

celebrities and politicians
ordinary people in your country
yourself and your acquaintances

b Can you think of any clear examples of people about whom the statement is not true? What other kinds of motivation are there?

c Overall, what is your opinion in response to the question?

> The desire for higher status or greater wealth than others is what motivates most people to succeed in the world. To what extent do you agree or disagree with this statement?
>
> Give reasons for your answer and include any relevant examples from your own knowledge and experience.

5 Write your answer to the writing task in at least 250 words. When you have finished, either review your own work or exchange essays with another student. Check the essay for errors in each of the following categories.

singular / plural agreement
articles
word order
spelling
punctuation

Help yourself

Planning remedial work

1 Read these students' comments about their difficulties. Which of these problems and others have you had? How have you dealt with them?

a   'I miss a lot of words in the Listening – they speak really fast.'

b   'Some of the texts are nearly 1,000 words long, and it takes me an awfully long time to read through them.'

c   'When I'm speaking I'm worried all the time about making mistakes, so I don't speak very fluently.'

d   'I'm OK talking about practical things like how to send a text message, but answering questions about complex ideas is much harder.'

e   'My essays alway looks a mess because when I'm writing I keep on thinking of more points and I don't know where to put them.'

f   'Talking non-stop about something for two minutes is very difficult – even in my own language!'

Find other students in the class who have had the same problems as you. Ask them what solutions they have found.

2 Which of the IELTS modules (Listening, Reading, Writing, or Speaking) causes you most problems? Within each module, which task(s) do you find most difficult? Why?

3 Make a list of your 'Top 5' mistakes, e.g. prepositions or when to use articles. Consider these ideas.

a   Look back at your corrected written work.
b   Think about speaking errors that you often make.
c   Ask students you have worked with to tell you your most common mistakes.

4 Draw up a plan to work on each problem area. Add your own ideas to the suggestions below, and decide how much time you can spend on each.

• Increase the time you spend working on a particular module.

• Listening extensively to a range of accents, for example, radio, songs, satellite TV or the English soundtracks on DVDs.

• Read more widely. (see page 56)

• Check for your top five mistakes whenever you finish written work.

• Listen to exam materials for models of pronunciation.

• Work through a book of IELTS Practice Tests, referring to the explanatory key.

• Practise academic skills such as giving short talks or taking notes in your first language, too.

IELTS to do list

Choose one of the following to do outside class.

☐ On the *IELTS Masterclass* website find more practice material for specific exam tasks.

☐ Exchange letters, emails or audio cassettes with someone wanting to learn your language, or who has about the same level in English as you. Correct each other's mistakes and point out anything that isn't clear.

☐ Keep an IELTS Diary. After every lesson, note down details under headings such as 'What I learnt', 'Things I enjoyed', 'Problems' and 'Marks'. At the end of term, write a report on yourself.

Where to look

e www.oup.com/elt/ielts

📖 *IELTS Practice Tests*, Peter May (Oxford University Press)

Oxford Practice Grammar Advanced, George Yule (Oxford University Press)

12 Engineering and innovation

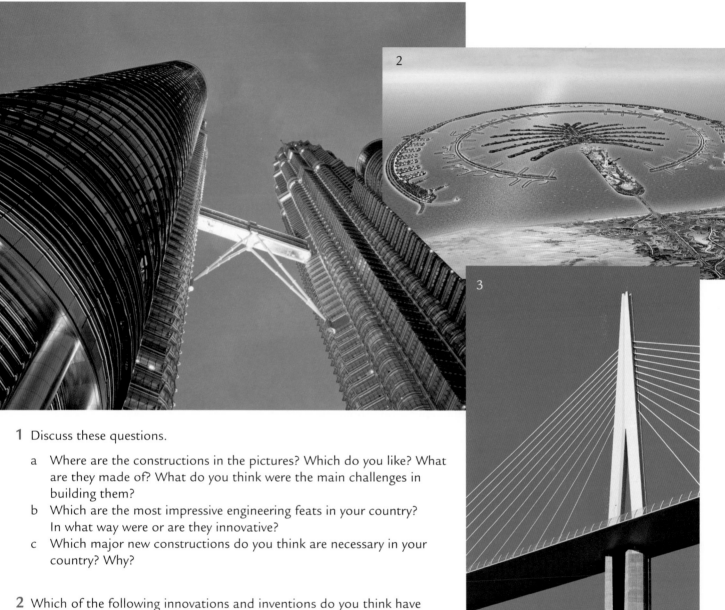

1 Discuss these questions.

a Where are the constructions in the pictures? Which do you like? What are they made of? What do you think were the main challenges in building them?

b Which are the most impressive engineering feats in your country? In what way were or are they innovative?

c Which major new constructions do you think are necessary in your country? Why?

2 Which of the following innovations and inventions do you think have improved people's lives? Which have had a negative effect? Give reasons in each case.

concrete	steel	light bulb
bicycle	aerosol	petrol/diesel engine
telephone	jet engine	air conditioning
gunpowder	nuclear power	sound amplifier
fibre optics	clock/watch	television

3 Discuss these questions.

a What do you think is the most important thing ever invented?

b What do you wish had never been invented?

c Why do some innovations such as texting catch on, while others like the wrist TV do not?

d What do you think will need to be invented in the future?

Reading

Orientation

1 Discuss these questions about the pictures.

    a   Do the pictures represent art, biology, or engineering?

    b   What shapes do the two pictures have in common?

2 Quickly read the text to check your answers.

Text organization

note
Divide the text into groups of paragraphs, then decide in which group you will probably find the answer to each question.

3 Which paragraphs relate to these areas?

works of art   biology research   engineering and architecture

4 Look at Questions 1–3 below. In which of your groups of paragraphs in 3 do you think you will find each answer?

IELTS practice

Questions 1–3: Classification

According to the information in the Reading Passage, when were the following made?

    A   the 18th century

    B   the first half of the 20th century

    C   the second half of the 20th century

    D   the 21st century

Write the correct letter A, B, C, or D next to questions 1–3.

    1   an advance in biology based on tensegrity principles

    2   a work of art based on tensegrity principles

    3   a building based on tensegrity principles

Tower OF strength

A   **Of all the stories of art** influencing science, tensegrity is one of the most far-reaching. On one level, tensegrity is a system of creating architecture or sculptures involving rods in compression and wires in tension. It was invented by sculptor
5   Kenneth Snelson at Black Mountain College, the hotbed of international modernism, in 1948. At the time, Snelson was taking part in a summer school with the engineer Buckminster Fuller, who pioneered the idea of applying geometric forms to architectural and engineering innovation.

B   Using an abstract sculpture as a starting point, Snelson then added tension wires to the free-floating members. Fuller encouraged him and when they met up again in 1949, Snelson had perfected a concept in which stiff rods can be supported without touching by a network of wires. Although
15   'tensegrity' (from 'tensional integrity') was coined by Fuller, the idea was entirely Snelson's, and he went on to make many more tensegrity sculptures, the most famous of which is the sixty-foot high Needle Tower (1968), now at the Hirshhorn Museum and Sculpture Garden, Washington DC.

C   Basic tensegrity structures can be made from three drinking straws, six paper clips, and nine rubber bands. When the structure is wired up, you can see that none of the rods actually touch: they're held in equilibrium by the rubber bands. Even this simplest model has very interesting
25   properties. Although drinking straws are weak, with a tendency to buckle, the tension bands hold them in such a way that the compressive force is always directed straight down the tube and buckling doesn't happen. The first thing you notice if you make one is that it is immensely fiddly to
30   assemble – pieces keep falling apart – but once the last band is secured, you can fling the object around, squash it, and it seems indestructible. The structure isn't symmetrical in its properties. In one direction, it squashes flat and bounces back. In the other direction, it resists the pressure. If you
35   wanted to create versatile 3D structures out of nothing much, tensegrity would take some beating.

D   It is strange that architects and engineers didn't discover the principle before 1948, since the benefits of structures held in tension over traditional building techniques had been known
40   since the invention of the suspension bridge in 1796. And the great maverick biologist D'Arcy Thompson in *On Growth and Form* (1917) had extensively analysed the principles of tension and compression both in nature and engineering.

Kenneth Snelson believed that tensegrity was a pure art and
45   that it would never be really useful architecturally. It took some time to prove him wrong, but in the 1980s, tensegrity architecture began to appear. The key protagonist was David Geiger and the first important structure was his Gymnastics Hall at the Korean Olympics in 1988.

E   Five years later, its significance in quite a different field became apparent when scientists described the tensegrity model of cell structure, and this is where the principle is now making waves. What is it that prevents living things from collapsing to a blob of jelly on the floor?
55   Unsurprisingly, it is likely to be tensegrity. For a long time, biologists ignored the mechanical properties of cells: they were just 'elastic bags' full of interesting chemicals. But there has to be an architecture: tissue is tough, resilient stuff that keeps its shape.

F   The human body is certainly a tensegrity structure: it consists of 206 bones – tensegrity rods – that do not touch, held together by tendons and muscles. And the tension of living cells seems to be maintained by tensegrity structures within the cell: microfilaments play the role of the rubber
65   bands and stiff microtubules are the rods. Donald Ingber, at the Harvard Medical School, researches how cells move and stick to each other, and he believes that tensegrity offers 'the most unified model of cell mechanics'. It explains some basic properties of cells very well.

G   If cells are placed on a microscope slide, they flatten under gravity. When cells are surrounded by other cells, proteins called integrins attach one cell to another at specific locations. These act as tensegrity wires, pulling the cells taut in all directions. When the integrin network is disrupted, the cells
75   sag. Whether or not the cell is a tensegrity structure is still controversial, but in a series of recent papers, Ingber and his team have been gradually picking off the objections with detailed studies of cell structure. For the lay observer, pictures of a cell showing triangular structures resembling a geodesic
80   dome are highly suggestive of tensegrity.

H   It has been a long road since Black Mountain College in 1948, but it all comes back to Kenneth Snelson and his sculpture. Once asked what he would save from a fire in his office, Donald Ingber replied: 'The tensegrity model made
85   by Kenneth Snelson, a gift from the artist himself.' ●

Questions 4–10: Locating information

The Reading Passage has eight paragraphs, A–H.
Which paragraph contains the following information?
NB You may use any letter more than once.

4　an error made by the inventor of tensegrity
5　the branch of science on which tensegrity is currently having the greatest impact
6　the writer's surprise that tensegrity remained unknown in engineering
7　an account of how a sculpture was made
8　an unresolved issue concerning the nature of individual cell structure
9　an explanation of why a basic tensegrity structure keeps its shape
10　an analogy between components of a tensegrity model and a skeleton

Questions 11–14: Short-answer questions

Answer the questions with words from the Reading Passage. Write NO MORE THAN THREE WORDS for each answer.

11　Who first used the word 'tensegrity'?

....

12　Which parts of the tensegrity model prevent the straws losing their shape?

....

13　Which parts of a cell hold its microtubules in place?

....

14　What substances join cells to each other?

....

Exploration　**5** Find words in the text with the following meanings.

a　being squeezed (paragraph A)
b　being stretched (paragraph A)
c　not bending (paragraph B)
d　weaken and bend under pressure (paragraph C)
e　having two halves which are exactly the same (paragraph C)
f　falling inwards (paragraph E)
g　having moving parts (paragraph E)
h　tightly stretched (paragraph G)

6 Find the phrasal verbs in the text and match them with meanings 1–7.

    a   take part (paragraph A)
    b   go on to (paragraph B)
    c   wire up (paragraph C)
    d   fall apart (paragraph C)
    e   fling around (paragraph C)
    f   bounce back (paragraph C)
    g   pick off (paragraph G)

    1   break into its component parts
    2   return to its normal state
    3   do something after you finish doing something else
    4   throw in many different directions
    5   do something together with other people
    6   destroy one after another
    7   connect one thing to another

7 Complete the sentences with the correct forms of the phrasal verbs in 6.

    a   Instead of trying to fight all our opponents at the same time, we prefer to

        .... them .... one by one.

    b   To avoid the model aeroplane .... , the wings and tail are held on with superglue.

    c   If more people want to .... in a particular activity, increased space can be made available.

    d   Once they have completed the fourth stage, they .... to finish the process.

    e   When all the houses have been .... , everyone will be able to watch cable TV.

    f   Engineering output fell sharply for two years, but it has now .... to its previous level.

    g   Children can .... this toy .... as much as they like, but it still won't break.

8 Discuss these questions with other students.

    a   Do you prefer modern or traditional styles of archictecture? Why?
    b   Is there a traditional style of architecture in your country? What are its main features?
    c   How can the design of a building affect the people who use it?
    d   Are there any natural forms we could imitate to create new designs in buildings?

Listening

Section 4

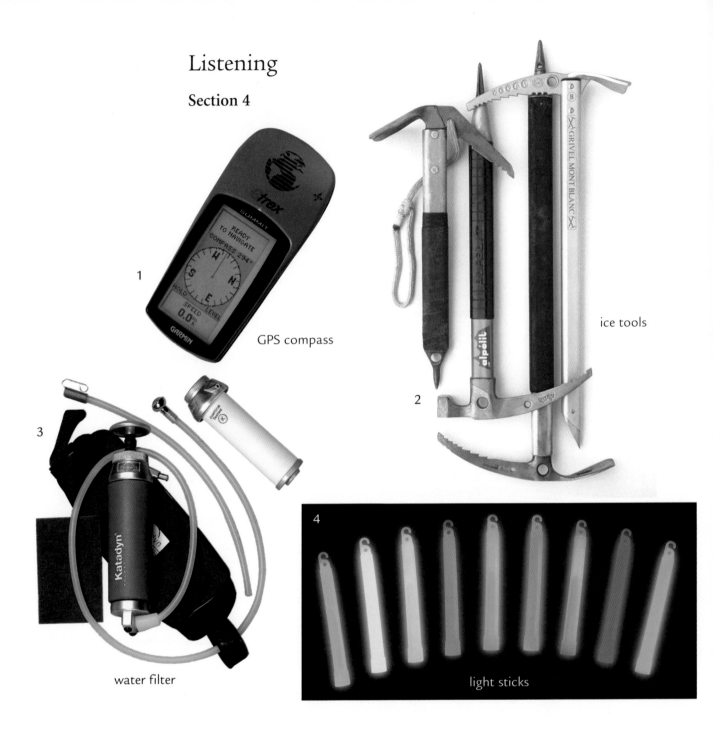

GPS compass

ice tools

water filter

light sticks

Orientation   **1** Answer these questions with another student.

    a   What do you think the items are used for? How do they work?
    b   On what kind of journey or expedition would each one be most useful?
    c   What did people use before these were invented?
    d   What other items would you want to have with you on an expedition? Explain why you think these items are essential.

Thinking ahead   **2** What do you think the survival item in the diagram on page 147 is used for? How do you think it works?

           3 Study IELTS questions 1–6 below. What kind of information – for example, weight – do you need to answer each one?

IELTS practice

Questions 1–6: Short-answer questions

🎧 Answer the questions below. Write NO MORE THAN THREE WORDS AND/OR A NUMBER for each answer.

note

When answers require numbers, you may also have to listen for units such as kilos, dollars or miles.

1 How much was the watch used by Fossett sold for?

....

2 Where were the two men near when the accident happened?

....

3 How long can the watch continue transmitting an emergency signal?

....

4 What is the maximum range of the watch at sea?

....

5 How much does the watch weigh?

....

6 When was the self-winding watch invented?

....

Questions 7–10: Labelling a diagram

Label the watch. Write NO MORE THAN THREE WORDS for each answer.

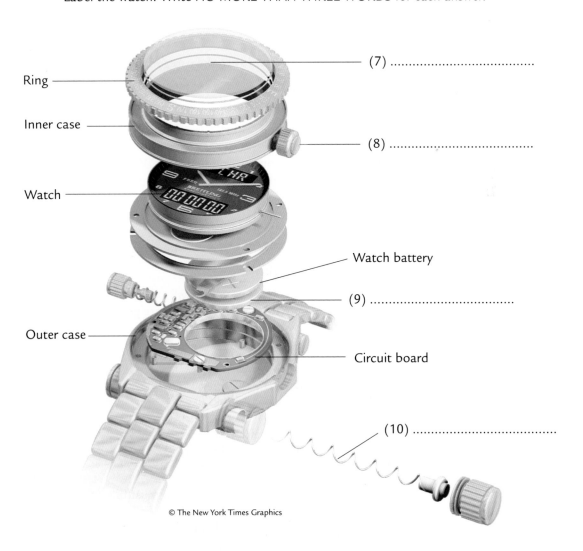

Ring

Inner case

Watch

Outer case

(7) ....

(8) ....

Watch battery

(9) ....

Circuit board

(10) ....

© The New York Times Graphics

Speaking

Describing objects

This innovative **vertical mouse** is held by the computer user in an upright handle, greatly reducing the strain on the wrist and arm. Made of smooth black plastic, this elegant piece of electronic equipment has a sky-blue button for the thumb to click left or right.

1 Work with another student. Read the catalogue description of an item below. Which of the items in the photos does it describe?

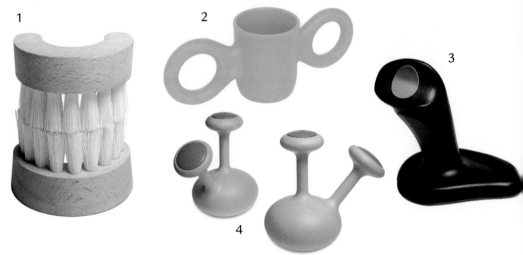

2 Which words does the description above use in each of the following categories?

SHAPE   TEXTURE   MATERIAL   COLOUR
HOW IT WORKS   IMPRESSION IT GIVES

3 Match these other words to the categories above.

rounded   metal   manual   rough
flat   intriguing   reddish   mechanical
bluey-green   soft   wooden   cute

4 Look at the other objects in the photos. What are they for? How do they differ from similar objects that you've seen? Use language from 3 above and the phrases below.

Describing objects

It's for ... *-ing*   It's designed to ...   It's made of ...   It looks a bit like ...

IELTS practice

Part 2: Extended speaking

5 In Speaking Part 2, the examiner will give you a topic verbally and on a card. You then have one minute to prepare what you are going to say. Think about the task below and make a few notes.

note

Before you choose a particular object to talk about, be sure you know how it is used and what the English words for its main features are.

> Describe an object that you particularly like.
>
> You should say:
>   what it is and what it looks like
>   what it is made of
>   what it is for
> and explain why it is special to you.

6 Work in pairs. In Speaking Part 2, you must talk for one or two minutes. Take it in turns to talk about your chosen object. Follow the instructions on the card, using any notes you have made and adding more details. You can start with an expression such as 'My favourite object is ..., which ...', or 'I've decided to talk about ..., which ...'

Language for writing

Expressing purpose

1 Choose the correct alternative from the phrases in brackets.

a You move the mouse *in order to/so that* the cursor points to an icon.

b Flaps extend *to/for* increase the area of the aircraft wing.

c The oil passes through a filter *in order that/in order to* it does not become dirty.

d Big helicopters have two rotors *for/to* greater lift capacity.

e They have redesigned the space vehicle *in order to/so that* reduce the risks.

f Digital cameras are in place *to/for* viewing the exterior.

g Ensure a free flow of air *not to/in order not to* overheat the machine.

2 Complete the rules below based on the correct answers to 1.

a Use .... or .... before a subject and verb.

b Use .... or .... before an infinitive.

c Use .... before an *-ing* form.

3 Combine the sentences using expressions from 1. In some cases, more than one answer is possible.

a This radio uses an external aerial. The aerial picks up local stations.

b We are building smaller apartments. We hope they will be more popular.

c Solar panels don't always need bright sunshine. They can generate electricity.

d They use synthetic materials. Less weight is essential.

e Close down the computer properly. You mustn't damage it.

Cause and effect

4 What object is explained in each of these texts?

> A It is used in many applications owing to its small size. A chemical reaction inside it leads to the generation of energy. However, since the reaction is only triggered when the positive and negative ends are connected, it can last a long time when not in use.

> B This everyday item enables the user to control the flow of water with little effort because of its simple but effective design. Turning the handle clockwise results in the twisting of a screw, which in turn drives a small flat rubber ring into the water flow. Consequently, the water stops. Turning the handle anticlockwise lets it flow again.

> C Changes in temperature make things expand or contract. A rise of ten degrees, for instance, causes twice the expansion created by a five-degree increase. When, therefore, the liquid in this item gets hotter, it is forced up a thin tube to a precisely calculated point on a scale, thus allowing the current temperature to be measured.

5 Note down the words used in the texts for causes and reasons, e.g. *leads to*, *since*.

6 Rewrite the following sentences using the words given.

a The construction is stronger because of the use of steel.

The use of steel ....

b The mechanism does not overheat because this fan rotates.

This fan rotates. ....

c Fatal car accidents have decreased owing to the development of effective airbags.

The development ....

d The dial is luminous, enabling it to be read at night.

Since ....

e Brakes are applied in order to slow the machine down.

Applying ....

f A valve closes. Therefore, the correct pressure is maintained.

Owing ....

7 Write a sentence explaining each of these newspaper headlines using expressions from 5.

a **ELECTRONIC ITEMS COULD GET EVEN SMALLER**

b **Airlines under pressure to develop cleaner planes**

c POOR HANDWRITING A GROWING PROBLEM

d **Kick this year's football further than last year's**

e **New solutions to traffic chaos essential**

f More students doing part-time jobs

Writing

1 2 3

Orientation

1 Discuss these questions with another student.

a What vehicles are shown in the three pictures?
b Can you explain in general terms how each of these vehicles works?
c Which of these vehicles is the easiest and most difficult to describe?

Organizing a description

2 Imagine you have to describe a–c below. Briefly say how you would organize each description.

Example
an electric bell and how it works
Describe what happens in a sequence following the direction of the electrical current, starting with the button being pressed and ending with the hammer striking the bell.

a how solar panel systems work at day and night
b a bicycle and how it works
c how televisions have changed over time

note

Remember that you're not expected to have technical knowledge. If you don't know the precise expression for part of the object or the way it works, say it in different words.

3 Work with another student. Discuss what the diagrams below show and describe in your own words how the object works.

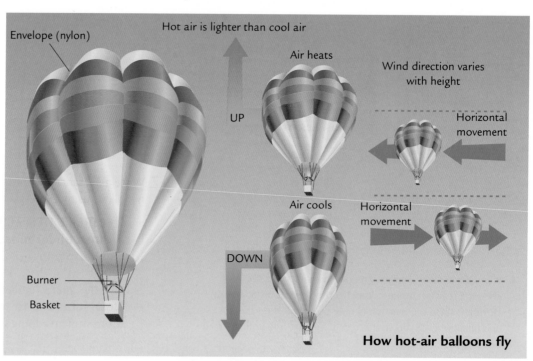

How hot-air balloons fly

4 Read the description below of the diagram.

    a How is the text organized?
    b What examples of purpose links are used?
    c What examples of cause and effect links are used?
    d What information from the diagram has been omitted? Add a paragraph which includes this information, using purpose and cause and effect links.

> The pictures show a hot-air balloon and the basic principles that enable it to be flown. The balloon has three main parts: the envelope, which is made of nylon, a burner to produce a flame, and a basket to carry the people.
>
> The pilot has to be able to control the upward and downward movement of the balloon so that it can fly. In order to make the balloon go up, the pilot uses the flame from the burner to heat the air inside the envelope. As the hotter air inside is lighter than the air outside, this causes the balloon to rise.
>
> The direction in which the balloon moves horizontally depends on the direction of the wind. Nevertheless, since the wind direction may vary at different heights, moving up or down allows the pilot to steer the balloon.

5 Write a few sentences to describe one of the vehicles you discussed in 1.

Think, plan, write   6 Read the Writing Task 1 below and answer the questions.

    a In what order are the three objects?
    b What design features do the three have in common?
    c Which features distinguish each object from the one before? What is the purpose of each of these differences?
    d What is the practical effect of each difference? What trends do you notice?

> The diagrams below show stages in the development of the aeroplane since the first powered flight in 1903.
> Summarize the information by selecting and reporting the main features, and make comparisons where relevant.

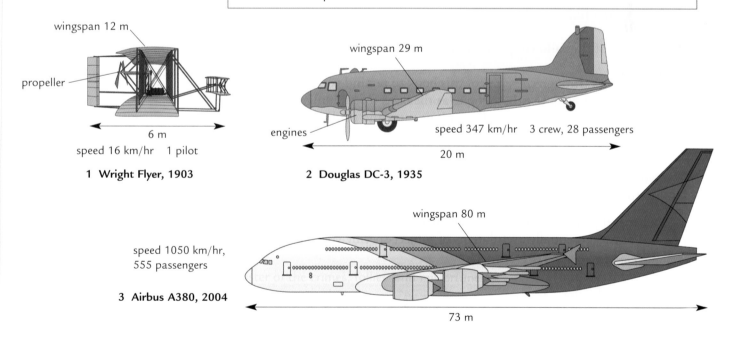

wingspan 12 m

propeller

6 m

speed 16 km/hr   1 pilot

1 Wright Flyer, 1903

wingspan 29 m

engines

speed 347 km/hr   3 crew, 28 passengers

20 m

2 Douglas DC-3, 1935

speed 1050 km/hr, 555 passengers

3 Airbus A380, 2004

wingspan 80 m

73 m

7 Write your answer in 150 words. Group information and organize the text effectively, using cause and effect links where appropriate.

Speaking

Changes over time

1 Answer the questions about each picture.

   a What is shown? What did people have to do in the past?
   b When and in which country do you think the photo was taken? What clues are there?
   c What would people there probably use today?

2 With another student, put these expressions into two groups.

Describing the past	Describing the present	
Nowadays …	These days, …	In those days, …
They no longer have to …	It was common to see …	People are becoming …
Until quite recently, …	Once, …	They used to …
Things are getting …	Since then, …	Back in …, they would …

3 Work with another student. Use the expressions in 2 to contrast your answers to 1a and 1c.

   Example
   People used to have to light a candle and make sure it didn't go out, but nowadays they just switch on an electric light, or a torch.

4 Read these quotes with your partner. Which do you agree or disagree with? Give reasons, using expressions from 2.

   a 'Entertainment is far better and more varied than it was in the past.'
   b 'People felt much happier and more secure when everyone lived together in big families.'
   c 'Life's more stressful today than it's ever been before.'
   d 'Young people – especially women – have far more opportunities than their parents' or grandparents' generations had.'
   e 'Compared with thirty years ago, life is much more dangerous now, particularly in the cities.'
   f 'In general, most people are in better health today than at any time in history.'

IELTS practice

Part 3: Topic discussion

5 In Speaking Part 3, the examiner will ask you about more abstract aspects of a topic. Work in pairs. Take it in turns to ask questions a–c below.

   a How has life changed for young people in your country since your parents' time?
   b In which other period of history would you like to have lived? Why?
   c What do you think future historians will say about the way we live now?

Language for writing

Conditionals

1 For each sentence, underline the verbs. What verb tenses are used? What do we use this kind of conditional for?

    a   You will understand this point if you read Barr's *Society in 1750*.
    b   If the documents had survived, we would know more about those events.
    c   Such material loses strength if it bends.
    d   If they had built the city on the coast, it would have become a major port.
    e   If tourists used photography, the colours of the cave paintings would fade.

2 Underline the expressions used instead of *if*. Which can mean *if not*?

    a   There is no danger provided that the safety mechanism works correctly.
    b   Supposing you found some gold coins, would you keep them?
    c   But for the support of the nobles, Philip would not have become King.
    d   Providing the vase is genuine, it will be exhibited in the museum.
    e   Tourists will be allowed to visit the ruins on condition that nothing is removed.
    f   You can't go to the burial site unless you promise to keep the location secret.
    g   The jewels can go on public display as long as there is maximum security.
    h   Without the map, Jones would never have found his way out of the caves.

3 Rewrite the sentences.

    a   This museum is not rich, so it can't buy valuable objects.
        If this ....

    b   By digging deep enough, we may find a complete building.
        Providing ....

    c   There is freedom in this country today because there was a revolution.
        If there ....

    d   You will only be able to excavate here with official permission.
        Unless ....

    e   Communications improved, which enabled industrialization to take place.
        If communications ....

    f   To learn more about your ancestors, you need to know their address in 1851.
        As long ....

    g   It was only possible to find the pharaoh's tomb with the aid of modern technology.
        Without ....

4 Use your imagination to complete these ideas.

    a   If the wheel had never been invented ...
    b   Supposing Columbus had not sailed to America in 1492 ...
    c   Provided we learn lessons from history ...
    d   Without the invention of gunpowder ...
    e   Unless rich countries do more to help poorer countries ...
    f   But for the discovery in 1928 of penicillin ...
    g   As long as there isn't another world economic crisis ...
    h   If the Industrial Revolution had begun in the East, not the West, ...

Writing

1 With another student, look at the Writing Task below and briefly discuss these questions.

    a Which part of the statement is fact and which is opinion?

    b Do you agree with this opinion?

> Museums often contain objects of great value from ancient civilizations around the world. Some people say these items should be returned to their countries of origin. To what extent do you agree or disagree with this opinion?

Argument and hypothesis

2 Read the sample answer below. Some sentences have been removed from the essay. Fill each gap with the correct sentence from the list below. There is one sentence you don't need.

Large national museums in major cities often contain ancient objects from other countries. (1) … However, as I shall argue, there may now be very good reasons for sending them back.

It is certainly true that some ancient treasures have been preserved by major museums. (2) … Ancient monuments were often not cared for on their original site, or were even used as building materials.

Furthermore, in the world-famous collections, experts have been able to use the best techniques to preserve these items. (3) …

Nevertheless, the previous point only really relates to the past. Today, modern technology and techniques can be found almost everywhere. (4) …

In addition, the significance of ancient treasures is more easily appreciated by people who know the historical context behind them. (5) … Ancient treasures are essential too in creating a sense of a national heritage.

To conclude, many objects have been saved for future generations by experienced insitutions, but there may now be a strong case for returning most of them to where they originally came from.

    a Unless the countries of origin reject responsibility, the objects should be returned.

    b If the objects were returned, facilities could be created over time to make sure that they were correctly conserved.

    c These facilities would not have been available until recently in their original countries.

    d Left in their original locations, objects would have disappeared or been destroyed.

    e Some people claim that leaving them in their original location would have had negative consequences.

    f The local people would have a greater understanding of their significance since the objects form part of their culture.

3 Answer the following questions about the sentences which fit the gaps in 2.

    a Which verb forms occur often in the sentences?
    b Which types of conditional are these typical of?
    c Why do you think this structure is particularly appropriate for expressing arguments?

4 In an essay it may be appropriate to suggest solutions and use conditional stuctures to imagine consequences. The following statements propose solutions to the situation expressed in the task. Do you think they are good or bad solutions? What would the consequences of each one be?

    a Museum collections can be lent to museums around the world.
    b Technology now allows museums to make replica copies.

5 Write a short paragraph for each of the statements in 4.

    a State whether you agree or not that it is a good idea.
    b Support your argument with a conditional sentence.

Think, plan, write

6 Read the Writing Task 2 below and answer the questions.

    a Do you agree with this opinion?
    b What arguments can you think of, for and against?
    c What would be the most logical order to write these points?
    d For each argument, what hypothesis could you put forward?
    e What solutions are possible? What would be the consequence(s) of each?

> Many modern films and television programmes about past events and people contain a mixture of fact and fiction. Some people say this distorts the public's view of history and should therefore be discouraged. What are your views?
> Give reasons for your answer and include any relevant examples from your own knowledge or experience.

7 Write your answer in at least 250 words, using conditional forms to discuss arguments and solutions.

Help yourself

Pronunciation: individual sounds

1 🎧 Listen and repeat each pair of words, making clear the difference between them.

Vowel sounds
far/fur
bin/bean
pull/pool
heart/hut
barn/ban
port/pot
stays/stairs
toy/tour
air/ear
tell/tale
coat/caught
liar/layer

Consonant sounds
live/life
tick/thick
owl/howl
rice/rise
light/right
sip/ship
head/hedge
bat/vat
sin/sing
hide/height
vet/wet
jaw/your

2 Think about the words in each list and answer these questions.

a Which did you find hard to pronounce?
b For each of the words you found difficult, think of at least two more words with the same vowel sound or consonant sound.
c Practise saying your words aloud.

3 🎧 Try saying each of these 'tongue-twisters' at normal speed, then listen to the recording. Which do you find difficult? Why?

a 'world wide web'

b 'today's the third Thursday this term'

c 'eleven benevolent elephants'

d 'three free throws'

e 'red lorry, yellow lorry, red lorry, yellow lorry'

f 'the sixth sick sheik's sixth sheep's sick'

IELTS to do list

Choose one of the following to do outside class.

☐ Listen carefully to spoken English and practise repeating it to yourself. Using recorded language, e.g. audio books, enables you to check anything you find difficult.

☐ Identify the sounds that you find most difficult and find ways of practising these. For example, start by saying just the sound, then repeat it in a word, and finally say it in a phrase or sentence.

☐ On your Internet search engine, key in 'pronunciation: sounds', or 'English tongue-twisters'. This will help you find websites that give examples in written, spoken and sometimes visual form. Practise saying these aloud.

Where to look

ⓔ www.oup.com/elt/ielts

14 Language

1 Discuss these questions with other students.

  a What do the photographs suggest about language in the modern world?

  b How much English language do you see in public places in your country?

  c How important a part of someone's identity is their first language?

  d Is the use of a foreign language in any way damaging to this identity?

2 Look at the newspaper headline, then discuss questions a–d below.

  a This English headline uses four words borrowed from other languages known as 'loan words'. Which words are they and do you know which languages they are originally from?

  b Why do languages borrow words in this way?

  c What English loan words are in common use in your country?

  d Do most people in your country like using loan words, or do they prefer to use equivalent words in their own language? How about you?

> Café owner to sue
> paparazzi after
> ketchup fiasco

Reading

Orientation

1 Read the title and first paragraph of the article below. Answer these questions.

  a If 'polyglot' means a person who speaks several different languages, what do you think 'hyperpolyglot' means?
  b What does Dick Hudson want to know?
  c What do you think is the world record for the number of languages a person can speak? Have a rough guess.
  d Which of your friends and acquaintances knows the greatest number of languages?

Scanning

2 Scan the whole article and answer these questions.

  a Which of the following people mentioned in the article are academics?

CJ	Lomb Kato	Stephen Krashen
Dick Hudson	Loraine Obler	Steven Pinker
Giuseppe Mezzofanti	Philip Herdina	Suzanne Flynn

  b Who or what are the other people?
  c Which of the academics express specific opinions about hyperpolyglottism?

3 Which paragraphs of the article include information about 'N' and his family?

Hyperpolyglots –

a case of brain power or hard work?

IN 1996, DICK HUDSON, a professor of linguistics at University College London posted an email to a listserve for language scientists asking if anyone knew
5 who held the world record for the number of languages they could speak. Replies listed the names of well-known polyglots, such as Giuseppe Mezzofanti, an eighteenth-century Italian cardinal.

10 Then, in 2003, Hudson received an unexpected reply to his email from someone who had belatedly come across his question. The writer, 'N', described how his grandfather, who was Sicilian and had never gone to school, could learn
15 languages with such remarkable ease that by the end of his life he could speak seventy, and read and write fifty-six. N's grandfather was twenty when he moved
20 to New York in the early 1900s. There he worked on the railways, which brought him into contact with travellers speaking many languages. When N was ten, he accompanied his grandfather on a cruise
25 which took them to over twenty countries, from Venezuela to Hong Kong and Japan. N claimed that whatever port they visited, his grandfather knew the local language.

WHEN HUDSON READ N's note, he immediately recognized the potential significance of the claims and posted them on the Internet. In his posting, he coined the term 'hyperpolyglot', which he defined as someone who speaks six languages or more.

Language is known to be part of humans' unique cognitive endowment, and scientists have long studied how language abilities can be impaired by disease or trauma. It is less clear, however, what upper limits this endowment has. After a long silence on this topic, linguists and psychologists are now looking to hyperpolyglots for answers. Do these people possess extraordinary brains, or are they ordinary folk with ordinary brains who do something extraordinary through motivation and effort?

Until recently, there was little scientific information about hyperpolyglots. Mezzofanti, for example, was supposed to have known seventy-two languages, and to have spoken thirty-nine fluently, but nowadays such tales are often greeted with scepticism. In the discussion that followed Hudson's publication of N's claims, a reader disputed the Mezzofanti story, saying he found it absolutely preposterous, and pointing out how long it would take to learn seventy-two languages. Assuming that each language has 20,000 words and that Mezzofanti could remember a word after encountering it once, he would have to learn one word a minute, twelve hours a day for five-and-a-half years! Professional linguists, too, are divided on this question. Philip Herdina, at the University of Innsbruck in Austria, is a sceptic. He doubts whether anyone has the capacity to speak seventy-two languages, arguing that maintaining this ability would take resources from other activities.

But others see no reason why people should not be able to learn a huge number of languages. 'There is no limit to the human capacity for language except for things like having time to get enough exposure to the language,' says Suzanne Flynn, a psycholinguist at Massachusetts Institute of Technology. Harvard University psycholinguist Steven Pinker agrees. Asked if there was any reason someone couldn't learn dozens of languages, he replied: 'No theoretical reason I can think of, except, eventually, interference; similar kinds of knowledge can interfere with one another.'

But if Flynn and Pinker are correct, and an ability to learn many languages is the norm, why are so few people able to exploit it? Stephen Krashen, from the University of California, maintains that exceptional language learners simply work harder, and have a better understanding of how they learn. Krashen cites the case of Lomb Kato, an eighty-six-year-old Hungarian interpreter who could speak sixteen languages. Lomb apparently felt she had no special talent for languages: she had taken classes in Chinese and Polish, but the others she taught herself. According to Krashen, Lomb was an ordinary person with no special qualities, apart from a desire to learn languages and an effective way of achieving this aim.

Other researchers say that exceptional brains play a more significant role. In the 1980s, neurolinguist Loraine Obler of the City University of New York found a talented language learner she called 'CJ', who could speak five languages. CJ had learned to read late, had an average IQ, and had always been a mediocre student. However, on the Modern Language Aptitude Test, he scored extremely high. His verbal memory was very good, he could remember lists of words for weeks, but he quickly forgot images and numbers, and had problems reading maps. All of this seemed to indicate that CJ's language talent was inborn and not related to a higher level of general intellectual ability.

Some researchers also believe that there is a genetic component to hyperpolyglottism, and evidence suggests that the trait runs in families. Unfortunately, however, it is difficult to get families to agree to subject themselves to a genetic study. Neither 'N' nor his family were prepared to grant an interview on the subject. What makes this particularly frustrating for linguists trying to study hyperpolyglottism is that, in his original message, N mentioned another member of his family, a seven-year-old girl, who could count to 100 in three languages and could pick out words spoken in other languages and say what they meant.

N and his hyperpolyglot family may have retreated from public view for now, but they could yet provide more fascinating insights into our language abilities.

Questions 1–5: Matching

Look at the following list of statements (1–5) relating to hyperpolyglottism. Match each statement with the correct person A–E.

1 Successful language learning requires motivation, application, and a learning strategy.
2 Speaking many languages would adversely affect other abilities.
3 Effective learning requires sufficient close contact with a language.
4 Language aptitude is probably inherited, not a facet of intelligence.
5 As someone learns more languages, they may get them confused.

> A Loraine Obler
> B Philip Herdina
> C Stephen Krashen
> D Steven Pinker
> E Suzanne Flynn

Questions 6–12: Summary completion

Complete the summary. Choose NO MORE THAN TWO WORDS AND/OR A NUMBER from the article for each answer.

> N came from a family which was partly of (6) .... origin. The
>
> evidence of unusual linguistic ability came from two relatives. The first was N's
>
> (7) .... , who was said to speak (8) ....
> languages. N witnessed this ability during a tour of more than
>
> (9) ....
>
> The second relative, a young girl, could count well in (10) ....
>
> Research came to an end since N's family would not agree to
>
> (11) .... If true, N's story supports the idea that
>
> hyperpolyglottism (12) ....

Questions 13–14: Multiple-answer question

Which TWO of statements A–E reflect linguists' knowledge of hyperpolyglottism?

A They do not know how many languages humans are capable of learning.
B They know that people become hyperpolyglots because of a need to know many languages.
C They know how hyperpolyglottism is passed on from one generation to the next.
D They know that hyperpolyglots have above-average intelligence.
E They know that humans are capable of learning many languages.

Exploration

4 These verbs are used to report information that could originally have been spoken or written. Complete extracts a–e from the article with one of the verbs, then check your answers in the article.

arguing	claimed	described
disputed	doubts	maintains
pointing out	saying	

a N .... how his grandfather could learn languages ...
b N .... that whatever port they visited, his grandfather knew the local language.

c   A reader .... the Mezzofanti story, ... he found it

absolutely preposterous, and .... how long it would take to learn

seventy-two languages.

d   Philip Herdina .... whether anyone has the capacity to speak 72

languages, ... that maintaining this ability would take resources from

other activities.

e   Stephen Krashen .... that exceptional language learners simply work

harder.

5 Now answer these related questions.

a   How might the ideas in 4a–e have appeared originally in direct speech?
b   Complete the extracts again, this time using the appropriate form of these
alternative reporting verbs. In some cases more than one answer is possible.

challenge	contend	insist
question	remark (that)	report
show	state	

6 Complete these sentences using appropriate reporting verbs.

a   A study in the USA has (1) .... that men gossip more than women
rather than the other way round. The authors of the study, reacting to the surprise
which their findings caused, (2) .... that the two sexes gossip in
quite different ways.

b   A recent study (3) .... that anthropologists now understand the
reasons why humans developed complex language systems. They
(4) .... that there is a universal language of motherhood, which they
have called 'motherese'.

c   The world famous linguist Noam Chomsky (5) .... that humans
have an inborn capacity to apply rules of grammar and to speak. A previous 18th
century theory (6) .... that speech developed naturally through a
process by which humans associated objects, actions and ideas with particular
sounds.

7 Discuss these questions with other students.

a   What, in your experience, makes some people better language learners than others?
b   How important do you think motivation is in the language learning process? What
different motivations do people have? What is your main motivation for learning
English?
c   In your experience, who would you say gossips more, men or women?
d   What do you understand by 'motherese'?
e   What everyday evidence is there that humans have an inborn capacity to apply
rules of grammar?

Listening

Section 4

In Section 4 , you will hear a talk or a lecture on a topic of general interest.

Orientation

1 Look at the photo and discuss these questions.

    a How do children learn their first language? What part do mothers play in this process?

    b In addition to words, what other sounds do adults make when they are talking to babies?

    c How do animals communicate with their young?

IELTS practice

Questions 1–5: Sentence completion

🎧 Listen and complete sentences 1–5 below. Write no more than three words for each answer.

    1 When talking to babies adults .... several times.

    2 'Motherese' provides a .... which allows language to develop in children.

    3 In comparison with a .... , a human baby is relatively helpless.

    4 Human mothers used their voices to .... their young.

    5 Language began as sounds became standardized into ....

Questions 6–9: Multiple-answer questions

Choose two letters A–E

6-7   Why might mothers have put their babies in slings?

    A to transport them
    B to protect them
    C to control them
    D to keep them warm
    E to communicate with them

Choose two letters A–E.

8-9   Linguists say a comprehensive theory would not explain

    A how grammar developed
    B how language is learnt
    C how sounds got meanings
    D how sounds are produced
    E how speech developed

Question 10: Multiple-choice question

Choose the correct letter A, B, C, or D.

    10 What is the speaker's main purpose?
        A to describe how mothers talk to their babies
        B to compare how humans and animals look after their young
        C to explain a new theory of origin of human language
        D to contrast the views of linguists and anthropologists

Exploration

2 Discuss these ideas with other students.

    a What different areas of study are anthropologists and linguists interested in?

    b How might the views of anthropologists and linguists differ on the subject of the development of human language? What might be the reasons for any differences of opinion?

    c Why do you think the speaker makes no specific reference to fathers in her talk?

Speaking

Part 1: Familiar discussion

1 In Speaking Part 1, you will be asked questions about everyday subjects. Discuss these questions with other students.

    a Which of the following do you enjoy reading in your language?

novels	poetry
plays	strip cartoons
newspapers	magazines
biographies	popular science books
sports books	

    b What kinds of things do you enjoy reading in English?

    c Are you someone who can read anywhere, or do you have a favourite place?

    d Do you need peace and quiet to be able to read, or can you concentrate even in noisy situations?

Part 2: Extended speaking

2 In Speaking Part 2, you have to speak continuously for one to two minutes about a topic you are given. Choose one of the task cards below and spend one minute preparing what to say. Make a few written notes to remind yourself of points to include.

Task card 1

Describe a book you have enjoyed reading.

You should say:
what the book was and who it was written by
what it was about
when and where you read it and explain what you liked about it.

Task card 2

Describe a newspaper or magazine you enjoy reading.

You should say:
what kind of newspaper / magazine it is
which parts of it you read regularly
when and where you read it
and explain why you enjoy reading it.

---

3 Take turns to speak about your subject for one to two minutes. Refer to any notes you have made. After your partner has finished, ask them one of these follow-up questions.

Do you know other people who enjoyed / enjoy reading this book / newspaper / magazine?
Is there anything you dislike about this book / newspaper / magazine?
How would you describe the language in this book / newspaper / magazine?

Part 3: Topic discussion

4 In Speaking Part 3, the examiner will ask you about more abstract aspects of the topic in Part 2. Work with another student. Take it in turns to ask each other the questions below, allowing time for a full answer to each question.

The importance of reading
How important is it for young children to learn to read?
What disadvantages are there for adults who cannot read?

Reading for enjoyment
How can children be encouraged to read for enjoyment?
How is reading books different from watching television or playing computer games?

The future of reading
Do you think that reading will become a more or a less important ability in the future?
Do you think a time will come when people get all factual information from the Internet?

Language for Writing

Sentence focus

1 For each of sentences (a) and (b) below, there are two follow-on sentences i and ii. How are these follow-on sentences different in structure? Which do you find clearer to understand?

a One simple idea of language suggests that children learn by associating words with objects.
i This theory does not explain how children learn prepositions or adjectives.
ii How children learn prepositions or adjectives is not explained by this theory.

b Experiments have taken place to find out whether apes can learn simple languages.
i These experiments showed some limited communication using signs and symbols.
ii Some limited communication using signs and symbols was shown by these experiments.

2 Re-order the information in the sentences that make up the paragraph below. Do not change the first sentence.

> A competition took place recently to find the most popular words in the English language. The British Council carried out the survey. Over 35,000 people sent suggestions in response. 'Mother' was the most popular word, according to the results. 'Smile', 'love', and 'destiny' were other words included in the top ten.

Placing emphasis

3 Sentences beginning with 'it' or 'what' are called cleft sentences and can be used to emphasize new or particular important points in a sentence. Sentences (a) and (b) below are rewordings of the first sentence. What information is emphasized in each case?

William Jones was first to recognize that many European and Asian languages are related.

a It was William Jones who was first to recognize that many European and Asian languages are related.
b What William Jones recognized was that many European and Asian languages are related.

4 Rewrite each of these sentences so that the emphasis is placed on the information in italic. Some words are given to help in the first two cases. There may be more than one possible answer in the others.

Example
The time and effort required put me off learning a foreign language.
It was the time and effort required that put me off learning a foreign language.
What put me off learning a foreign language was the time and effort required.

a *Regular overseas travel* can really help you gain confidence in your language ability.
  What can ......
b *By adopting many words* from other languages, English developed a huge vocabulary.
  It was ......
c Most people learn English *for practical purposes such as business or study*.
d Many people are fascinated by *the complex system of tones in Chinese*.
e The artificial language Esperanto was created *in the late nineteenth century*.
f People have difficulty understanding *how the spelling rules of English work*.

5 Rewrite the sentences below to emphasize the new information. This is marked in italic.

a One simple idea of language suggests that children learn *by associating words with objects*. The theory does not explain *how children learn prepositions or adjectives*.
b Experiments have taken place to find out whether apes can learn simple languages. The experiments showed *some limited communication using signs and symbols*.

Writing

Orientation **1** Work with another student to answer the questions below.

a The total number of native speakers of English is approximately

    100 million   300 million   600 million

b Name at least three countries in each of these continents where English is the first or second language.

South America and the Caribbean

Africa

Asia

Australasia

c Do you think the use of English will continue to increase?

d Do you think there are any dangers or problems associated with the spread of English?

Useful language **2** The extract below was taken from a student essay on the subject of English as an international language. Fill the gaps with an appropriate expression from the list below.

> (1) … , having a strong international language is useful for diplomacy and trade. (2) … some language fulfilled this function, international relations would be set back considerably. (3) … , there would be more conflict and less wealth.
>
> (4) … , that language does not have to be English. (5) … the transition may take a long time, an artificial language such as Esperanto or an alternative natural language may be preferable for historical and cultural reasons. (6) … , an artificial language, (7) … it was carefully chosen, could be considerably easier to learn.

firstly (organizing)

unless (hypothesis)

as a result (cause and effect)

on the other hand (organizing)

although (concession)

furthermore (organizing)

provided (hypothesis)

3 What other phrases make up the categories given? Complete the lists below with as many as you can think of.

Organizing
Concession
Cause and effect
Hypothesis

Think, plan, write

4 Read the Writing Task 2 below and answer the questions.

    a Which part of the statement are you being asked to agree or disagree with?

    b Do you have a strong opinion on this subject? Or can you see both sides of the argument?

> A second language is regarded as essential to success in the modern world. It should be compulsory for all children to study a second language as soon as they start school.
>
> To what extent do you agree or disagree with this opinion?
>
> Give reasons for your answer and include any relevant examples from your own knowledge or experience.

5 Think of the main arguments which you would include to support your opinion. Write them in the left-hand column of the table below. Complete the right-hand column with examples, reasons, and consequences to support these arguments.

Main arguments	Supporting ideas
Example Need languages to travel	Travel essential in modern world

6 Apart from the introduction and conclusion, how many main paragraphs will you need to make your points? What order will you make your points in?

7 Write your own answer to the Writing Task given in 4 in at least 250 words. Remember to include an appropriate introduction and conclusion.

Help yourself

Pronunciation: word stress

1 Say these words aloud, stressing the syllables in red.

pres**ident** (first syllable stressed)
uni**ver**sity (second syllable stressed)
enter**tain** (third syllable stressed)

2 Choose the correct alternatives to complete the paragraph.

When you stress a syllable, it is usually both
(1) *quieter / louder* and (2) *longer / shorter* than the other
syllables in the same word. You also say it (3) *more / less*
clearly than unstressed ones, and the pitch is normally
(4) *lower / higher* than that of any syllables which come
before and after it. You may also notice that your face
makes (5) *bigger / smaller* movements when you
pronounce stressed syllables.

3 🎧 There are some word stress patterns which can
help you. Listen to the words in each set a–c. Say each
word aloud.

a easy
   context
   social
   lecture

b record (verb)   record (noun)
   object (verb)   object (noun)
   export (verb)   export (noun)
   contrast (verb)   contrast (noun)

c compete   competition
   photograph   photography
   educate   education
   economy   economic
   China   Chinese
   voluntary   volunteer
   active   activity
   luxury   luxurious

4 🎧 Listen again and highlight the stress on each word,
for example, 'easy'. When you have finished, what
patterns can you recognize? Think of more words
stressed in the same way.

IELTS to do list

Choose one of the following to do outside class.

☐ Mark the stress on the words in your vocabulary notebook, and
on new words as you add them.

☐ Write a few sentences about yourself, your home and what you do.
Mark the stress on all the words of more than one syllable,
checking any you are unsure of in your dictionary. Then practise
reading your sentences aloud.

Where to look

🅔 www.oup.com/elt/ielts

Answers

Unit 1. Page 14. Exercise 1

a   1 Poland   2 United States
    3 Hong Kong, China   4 Dutch island of Aruba

Unit 2. Page 22. Exercise 3

1 b 6.2 billion   2 a 2.5 people per second
3 a 0–25   4 c 2.1

Unit 3. Page 40. Exercise 3

1   False. Frozen fruit and vegetables can be just as nutritious as fresh.
2   b Potatoes are a vegetable, but nutritionally they are more like starchy foods such as rice and bread and so they do not count towards the recommended five portions of fruit and vegetables a day.
3   b, d, e, Some biscuits are high in fat and sugar, and pastry and chips are also high in fat. Too much sugar and fat can contribute to weight gain, and these may need to be reduced when trying to lose weight.
4   False. The calcium in milk is contained in the non-fat part of the milk, and so removing fat from milk does not reduce the calcium content.
5   a, d, f
6   False. The starchy foods that we eat, such as bread, rice, pasta and potatoes, provide us with an excellent source of energy, as well as many nutrients, so there is no need for us to take extra sugar in our diet.

> **Six out of six?**
> Well done! You have an excellent knowledge of nutrition. Thought about taking up dietetics as a career?
>
> **Three to five out of six?**
> Your knowledge is quite good, but there's room for improvement.
>
> **Less than three?**
> Oh dear! You need to see a dietician!

Unit 6. Page 80. Exercise 2.

The man had put sugar in the original cup of coffee. Because his replacement coffee was sweet, he knew that it wasn't a completely fresh cup.

Unit 7. Page 81. Exercise 1.

a   *False* The Olympus Mons on Mars, at 24 km in height, is three times as tall as Everest.

b   *True* Carbon dioxide is heavier than air, so it stays on top of the burning material, thus preventing oxygen reaching it.
c   *True* The water, unlike air, will completely absorb the heat of the flame.
d   *False* They are filled with nitrogen, an inert gas which does not corrode the metal used in aeroplane tyres. It runs cooler than other gases and is virtually non-combustible.
e   *False* The heat exchanger at the back of the fridge will heat up the room more than it cools the inside of the fridge, as it takes more energy to cool something down than warm it up.
f   *True* There is generally more life in cold, moving waters, partly because cold water has a higher oxygen content.
g   *False* Each whole number on the Richter Scale represents a 32-fold increase in energy, so an 8 is 32 X 32 times stronger than a 6. The correct answer is therefore 1024 times stronger.
h   *True* Light travelling at very high speed towards the eye is perceived by the brain as being blue. Conversely, if it is moving away very fast it will appear to be red. This is one example of the 'Doppler Effect'.

Unit 10. Page 122. Exercise 3

Area: 1510 sq km
Altitude: 1500–2180 m
Rainfall: 83 mm per month
Temperature range: 12–30°C
Species: 80 mammals, 450 birds

Unit 11. Page 133. Exercise 8

Fading dot You may not be aware of it, but your eye constantly makes rapid movements. Each time it moves, your eye receives new information and sends it to your brain. You need this constant new information to see images. Although the dot fades, everything else in your field of vision remains clear. That's because everything else you see has distinct edges.

Bird in cage The birds you see here are 'afterimages', images that remain after you have stopped looking at something. Your eye is lined with cells, called cones, which are sensitive to certain colours of light. When you stare at the red bird, your red-sensitive cones lose their sensitivity, so that when you look at the white bird cage, you see white, minus red, where the red-sensitive cones have adapted. White light minus red light is blue-green light. This is why the afterimage you see is blue-green. When you stare at the green bird, the green-sensitive cones adapt. White light minus green light is magenta light, so you see a magenta afterimage.

Tapescripts

Unit 1. Page 9. Exercise 2.

Narrator: The people in the photographs live on different continents. How much can you guess about their lives? Photograph 1 shows somebody living in the mountains of Nepal. If you lived here, what would you be unlikely to eat for dinner? Would it be, A: Anchar, a kind of spicy pickle, B: Cheese, C: Beef, or D: Salad.

OK. Now, photograph 2 shows a villager from the Alaskan island of Shishmaref. What modern convenience would be unavailable if you lived here? Would it be, A: electricity, B: running water, C: the telephone, or D: television?

In photograph 3 you can see a Quechua Indian from the Peruvian Andes. If you lived here, which of these animals would you be likely to tend for a living? Would it be, A: goats, B: cows C: llamas, or D: chickens?

Finally, photograph 4 shows the Sami people in the North of Scandinavia. A popular game is played with animal hoof bones. What do you think it's called? Is it A: the bone game, B: reindeer roundup C: throwing bones, or D: wishbone pull?

Unit 1. Page 9. Exercise 3.

Narrator: So, let's see how well you did. Here are the answers to the four questions. The answer to Question 1 is C, beef. In Nepal the cow is considered a sacred animal and legally protected from slaughter.

Question 2. The answer is B. Most people in Shishmaref do not have running water in their houses. They collect rain or gather ice blocks to melt for drinking water.

Question 3. The answer to this question is C, llamas. The Quechua people of the Andes depend on the llama because it can carry loads at any altitude while providing people with wool, leather, meat and dung fuel.

Question 4. The answer to the last question is B. The bones are used to represent the people herding their animals and the reindeer on which their livelihood depends.

Unit 1. Page 15. Listening. IELTS practice. Questions 1– 6.

Adviser: Hello, Admissions Guidance, how can I help?

Student: Hello, I'd like some information about studying at your university. Can you help me?

Adviser: Yes, of course. What course are you interested in applying for?

Student: International Business. I already have a first degree from a university in my country.

Adviser: Fine, so you'd want to do a Master's level course?

Student: Yes, that's right.

Adviser: OK, we offer an MIB course – that's a twelve-month full-time course. I can send you details of that course or you can download a pdf file from our website.

Student: Could you put it in the post, please – I don't have access to the Internet at the moment. Could you tell me what qualifications I need for that course?

Adviser: Yes, for the MIB, you need a first degree. The minimum qualification is a 'two one' or a 'first'.

Student: OK.

Adviser: And in English language you need a score of 7 or above in IELTS.

Student: That's not a problem. I have a 9.

Adviser: That's fine.

Student: Could you tell me the course hours and the semester dates, please?

Adviser: Yes, there's a total of ten hours of lectures, seminars, and tutorials a week, and there's an extended stay abroad at the beginning of the second semester. That involves spending a month at the national head office of a multinational corporation.

Student: OK.

Adviser: And the semester dates are, just a moment, OK – the first semester starts on the twenty-seventh of September and ends on the twenty-second of January, and the second semester runs from the seventh of February to the twenty-seventh of May.

Student: Can you tell me a bit more about the actual course content?

Adviser: Well, I don't know much about the course personally – I'm an admissions officer, but I can read the course description for you if you like. If you need to know more about the academic side, you'll need to speak to the course tutor.

Student: Thanks – I'd be very grateful if you could tell me as much as possible now.

Adviser: I'll just read the main points: 'it involves the advanced study of international organizations, their management and their changing external context. Students develop their ability to apply knowledge and understanding of international business to complex issues, both systematically and creatively, to improve business practice.'

Student: Thank you very much.

Adviser: You're welcome. Now, if you could give me your name and address, I'll have full details of postgraduate courses sent to you.

Student: OK, my name is ...(fade out)

Unit 1. Page 15. Listening.
IELTS practice. Questions 7–10.

Student: OK, my name is Javed Iqbal. That's J- A- V- E- D … I- Q- B- A- L.

Adviser: Thank you. And your home address Mr Iqbal?

Student: It's Aga Khan Road, Shalimar 5, Islamabad, Pakistan.

Adviser: Thank you, and could I ask you one or two more questions for our records?

Student: Yes, of course.

Adviser: What was your first degree in?

Student: I did Economics. I got a first class degree.

Adviser: And where did you study?

Student: At the university here in Islamabad.

Adviser: OK. Now, you said you had an IELTS level 9. Could I ask what your first language is?

Student: Actually, I'm bilingual in Urdu and English.

Adviser: Thank you very much. I'll put full details in the post today.

Student: Thank you – and thanks for all the information.

Adviser: Not at all, Mr Iqbal. Thank you for calling.

Unit 1. Page 16. Speaking. Exercise 2.

Speaker 1: My home town is a medium-sized market town. It's about a hundred kilometres from the capital city. It's on a river and quite near the mountains. About ten thousand people live there. A lot of people from the town work in a sugar factory.

Speaker 2: What I really like most about my village is the people. They're so friendly. Everyone knows everyone else and that makes you feel very safe and comfortable.

Speaker 3: The main thing I dislike is the traffic – it's getting worse every year. It's almost impossible to cross the road in the town centre during the day. And the parking is terrible. There aren't enough car parks and people park all over the place.

Speaker 4: I think they'd find its old buildings very interesting. There's an ancient church with beautiful paintings on the walls inside. Visitors come from quite long distances to see those. Also the town hall is very impressive – it's over four hundred years old and they still use it everyday.

Speaker 5: The main improvement would be more sports and entertainment facilities. There's not much for young people to do, which means they have to catch the train to the nearest town if they want a good night out. We've got an old cinema and a couple of football pitches at the moment– that's all.

Unit 2. Page 21. Exercise 3.

Presenter: Next up on Northeast news, a story which involves complex issues and conflicting interests. The decision about whether or not to allow the dismantling of hazardous ships to go ahead in the area will not be an easy one for the authorities to reach. We'll start by hearing from the organization Green Earth, which has strong views on the subject:

Speaker 1: As environmentalists, we are very concerned about the environmental and health risks posed by the breaking up of these ghost ships in Britain. The vessels are carrying a number of highly toxic substances including oil and asbestos. It's been reported that more than half the ships are already leaking or have a high risk of leaking in the future.

Presenter: The director of a local employment agency has equally strong views.

Speaker 2: I'm fed up of all this negative publicity, like the views we've just heard. We really ought to be celebrating the fact that one of our region's companies has got the world-class recycling facilities necessary to undertake this important work. In the past most contracts of this kind have gone to companies in the Far East.

Presenter: A manager of the company which won the contract in the face of stiff international competition points out that what is good for his company and its shareholders is also good for the town.

Speaker 3: This contract, the first of many we hope, will create two hundred permanent jobs in the town. That's 200 new jobs that will breathe life back into our dying industry. We've got the experience and we've got the expertise. We should seize the opportunity with both hands and bring an injection of much-needed cash into the town.

Presenter: We'll finish with the perhaps more balanced views of a local resident, who is incidentally also a town councillor.

Speaker 4: I've lived in this town all my life and I detest the scourge of unemployment we've had to live with for the last thirty years. We desperately need these jobs, everyone knows we do, but not at any cost. In the end the safety of our workers and our environment must be our priority. In the end, we need to think of future generations, not just ourselves.

Unit 2. Page 27. Listening.
IELTS practice. Questions 1–5.

Presenter: … For more practical details, I'll pass you over to Jon Ward, from the London Tourist Agency

Jon Ward: Thanks. So, that was a brief introduction to the congestion charging scheme, but if you're actually going to be driving your car in London on weekdays, there are a few more details you will need to know. Firstly, you don't need to worry about paying all the time. The charge applies between seven in the morning and half past six in the evening, Monday to Friday. You'll be pleased to hear however that, because the scheme is intended to reduce traffic during busy working hours, evenings and weekends are free. If you enter the zone during the charging times, you'll be eligible to pay the standard charge of eight pounds, which you can pay until ten o'clock on that day. After ten o'clock this charge rises to ten pounds. But be warned, if you fail to pay before midnight, you will have to pay an automatic penalty charge. In other words, there's no escape. Let's move on to paying. The charge, as I've said, is eight pounds a day, and the authorities have set up a number of systems to make it easy for you to pay, or rather to ensure that nobody has a good excuse for not paying. So, using your credit card, you can pay by phone, by text message, or on the Internet. The other option is to go to one of the 200 Pay Points inside the zone or the 9500 Pay Points elsewhere in the country. If you know you're going to be driving in and out of London on a regular basis, you can buy weekly, monthly or annual passes, rather like a railway season ticket.

Unit 2. Page 27. Listening.
IELTS practice. Questions 6–10.

Jon Ward: OK, on to the area itself. The congestion charging zone is everywhere inside London's inner ring road. For those of you not familiar with London's road system, this includes the City of London, that's the main financial district, and the West End, the commercial and entertainment centre. If you're still not sure, there are very clear signs on all roads which indicate when you are entering the area. These are round and have a white letter 'C' on a red background. The scheme is policed by cameras which photograph all cars entering the area and send them to a computer which can recognize all British and European car registration plates. If you pay the eight pound charge, you'll find London a little easier to drive round than it was before the charge was introduced. But if it's all too much trouble, and you decide to leave your car at home, then you are left with public transport: that's trains, buses, taxis or the underground. Some of the money from the congestion charging scheme is being used to upgrade public transport, so you should see improvements there. And because of reductions in the number of private vehicles on London's roads brought about by congestion charging, buses and taxis are providing a quicker, more efficient service than they did in the past. OK, I've covered the main details that you need to know.

Unit 3. Page 39. Listening.
IELTS practice. Questions 1–6.

Adam: Before we go on to look at specific sports, let's think for a moment about the non-sports facilities we really need here. Things like better changing rooms and showers.

Emma: Yes, if this really is going to be a state-of-the-art building it'll need to have hi-tech amenities but also places for people to chill out after all the exercise they've been doing. Somewhere they can meet up for a drink or whatever afterwards is essential in a place like this, but what else?

Adam: How about a sauna? Those who use them say it's the perfect way to relax after you've trained.

Emma: The trouble is, though, that there's a debate going on about how safe they are. Some say it's risky to be exposed to all that heat before or after strenuous exercise – which of course is exactly when people in sports centres want to use them. There have also been problems with people overusing them to sweat off weight. So to avoid any possible dangers I don't think I'd include them on my list.

Adam: Talking of dangers, I wonder whether we ought to have some sort of facility where minor injuries like cuts and bruises and sprains can be treated?

Emma: Maybe. It would seem to make sense with all the mishaps that are bound to occur when you have so many people running and jumping about and so on. Ah. Hold on though: isn't the new medical centre going to be built right opposite?

Adam: Yes, it is. It should be finished by the end of next year.

Emma: Then there's no point, is there? Anyone who gets hurt can go over there, where there'll be much better treatment than anything we could offer on-site.

Adam: Yes, I can see that.

Emma: What we should provide, though, is a facility with full-time physiotherapists, for everybody on the campus that is. As well as treating people, they could work on prevention of things like muscle tears and strains.

Adam: Right.

Emma: And something else the new place ought to have, also as a way of preventing injuries, is somewhere to test just how fit people are before they start lifting weights or running long distances and so on.

Adam: Yes, I was going to suggest that. When I was at the Newport centre they put me on a static bike to check out my cardiovascular system, then they worked out how much body fat I had … all of it valuable information, telling you exactly what shape you're in.

Emma: Another thing I've heard some universities do, especially some of the newer ones, is provide rooms and equipment for lectures to take place actually inside their sports centres. How do you feel about that?

Adam: Well as it happens I've got first-hand experience of that too. We used to have some of our Sports Science lectures right next to the main sports hall, and I think it made what we were hearing about seem much more relevant to the real world. So in that respect I definitely think it's a good idea, yes.

Emma: Hmm. I can see that, though my own feeling is that we need to have more concrete reasons. The problem is that we won't have unlimited space, and somehow I don't think providing more lecture halls is going to be one of our priorities. So I'd be against that one, I'm afraid. Anything else?

Adam: Well just that I agree about the need to have a place where people can go for a chat and maybe have a coffee or a bite to eat together. That was something I always thought was one of the strong points of the centre in London. It was a great place to find out about new activities from the people who actually did them.

Unit 3. Page 39. Listening.
IELTS practice. Questions 7–10.

Adam: So what about the main sports facilities themselves? What do we need?

Emma: Well we don't need a rugby pitch because there's already one on the campus. The same's true of table tennis, really – most of the halls of residence for students have their own tables, so there's no point in using precious space here for any more.

Adam: Agreed. Something none of them have, though, is any sort of pool. A lot of students have complained about this, saying they have to take a bus downtown if they want to go for a swim.

Emma: Yes, that's definitely one for this place. Perhaps a Jacuzzi, too. That would be nice, wouldn't it?

Adam: It would. Perhaps next to the squash courts, just down there to the right. They're very popular, by the way. I think we should have a couple more here, don't you?

Emma: Absolutely. And another sport that's been growing in popularity is volleyball, especially since we did so well at the last Olympics.

Adam: Don't you mean basketball?

Emma: Yes, I do, sorry. Anyway, the point is that there is a court in the old gym next to the Students Union building, but it always seems to be fully booked up, even though it's not very good. And there's nowhere else on campus to play.

Adam: OK, let's have one of those, too. How much space have we got left, by the way?

Unit 4. Page 51. Listening.
IELTS practice. Questions 1–10.

Lecturer: The trumpet is quite a remarkable instrument. Take the B-flat type for instance, the kind of trumpet most people use today. If we stretched one out in a straight line, it would measure nearly 140 centimetres in length. What we see in the diagram, then, is a very long brass tube wrapped around itself in order to save space. To produce its characteristic sound, the musician blows continuously into the small metal cup on the left called the mouthpiece, which is shaped to fit the lips. The air travels along the lead pipe and round the tuning slide, which can be moved in or out to change the instrument's pitch. The air then reaches the feature that distinguishes the trumpet from, for instance, a bugle: the three valves that extend from above the top to below the bottom of the instrument. Each valve can send the air flow one of two ways: either along the main pipe, the shortest route, or else into an extra length of tube, thus lowering the pitch of the sound being played. The musician does this by pressing one of the finger buttons at the top, diverting the air into the first tube if the first is pressed, into the second – and shortest – by using the second, or into the longest one – the third – by pressing number three. The air then continues its way round the

bend in the lead pipe and along to the end at the widest part of the body, known as the bell, which projects the powerful sound forwards. Incidentally, all this breath forced through the metal of the instrument does of course contain water vapour, and this will start to condense and form droplets after a certain amount of playing. The result is a 'gurgling' sound from the trumpet, so to avoid this there is a device on the tuning slide called the water key, which, when pressed, lets the water drip out.

The trumpet, in one form or another, has been around for a long time. The earliest type we have actual proof of was a short, straight instrument used with marching soldiers by the ancient Egyptians' eighteenth Dynasty, which makes it three thousand five hundred years old, although other cultures in China and Peru certainly had something similar very early on. This use of the trumpet in military contexts, as well as at ceremonial occasions, was to continue through the times of the ancient Greeks and Romans, but it wasn't until the seventeenth century that it became a genuinely popular instrument, at least in the West. At the beginning of the eighteenth century it was finally accepted as part of the typical orchestra, and the addition of valves in the nineteenth century, making it much more versatile, consolidated its position as a major orchestral instrument. Nowadays the sound of the trumpet, which is of course both loud and clear, means that for many pieces it is used to lead the brass section of the orchestra. This sound, and its versatility, have helped extend its use to other forms of music such as jazz and pop, but there is another, very practical, reason for its widespread popularity. In comparison with many others such as the tuba, the cello, or even the trombone, it is a fairly small instrument that can easily be transported and played just about anywhere. The downside of all this popularity, though, is that as everyone wants to be a trumpeter it can be difficult for the young musician looking for work to find a vacancy. As a result, it's often the case that quite a few of the French horn players in a modern orchestra actually began their musical careers as trumpet players.

Unit 4. Page 52. Speaking. Exercise 1.

Speaker 1: I've decided to talk about *Billy Elliot*, which I saw at the Victoria Palace Theatre a while ago. The musical, that is, not the film, which I still haven't seen. Anyway, it's about a boy who wants to be a ballet dancer, but everything and everyone – except his teacher – seems to be against him. It's a good story, and the dancing and singing are brilliant.

Speaker 2: There are a lot that I've enjoyed, but the best one was last year's Cambridge Folk Festival. There were musicians from all over the world and all sorts of music, like gospel and salsa. The atmosphere was great too, and there was a real mix of people. My own particular favourite was a Celtic band, who did some traditional stuff but with a modern beat.

Speaker 3: My favourite was an outdoor performance of Shakespeare's *Macbeth*, which I saw at Wenlock Priory in July. It's such a dark play, with witches and ghosts and murder. It was the perfect setting. The best thing of all was the way the evening gradually got darker as the end of the play approached, with the ruins of the church towering over the stage. Perfect for an ending like that.

Speaker 4: I remember one film which was perhaps the best I've seen: *The Lord of the Rings*. I'd read the book and I thought nobody could ever make a movie of it, but Peter Jackson, the director, did a fantastic job. OK, some parts of the book, and a few characters, have been left out, but there's so much attention to detail that you hardly notice, even in a film that lasts three hours.

Unit 5. Page 62. Listening.
IELTS practice. Questions 1–5.

Ellen: Hello, Top Job Employment Agency. Ellen Sykes speaking. How can I help you?

Steve: Good morning, my name's Steve Collins and I'm calling about the call centre job advertised in today's paper.

Ellen: For an operative handling credit card enquiries?

Steve: Yes, that's right. The wages and working conditions are all in the ad, so what I'd like to know now is what the work actually consists of. I should explain that I'm a student looking for a summer job, not long-term employment.

Ellen: That's OK. The people at InterCard say they've always found students to be honest, which of course is essential in this line of work, and they have the basic IT skills needed there. Apparently there have been a few who didn't find it easy to get there on time in the morning, but in most cases their punctuality is as good as anybody else's! Anyway, about the work, and I know a bit about this because as it happens I've worked there myself.

Steve: Really?

Ellen: Yes, for about a year. You'd find that most callers would be people wanting to check the balance on their cards, query payments made and so on.

Steve: And from those who've had their cards stolen?

Ellen: No, they ring another number for that: an emergency line. People also call that number if they lose their cards.

Steve: And what are most callers like? I mean, what kind of people are they?

Ellen: All sorts, really. All ages, every kind of background. Though one definite trend is the change in the number of women. Nowadays they make up around 55% of the total, whereas years ago there used to be a majority of men calling. At one time, I heard, as many as three-quarters of all credit cards were actually held by men, but that must have been long before I was there.

Steve: It's certainly different now. So to do this job, what sort of experience do I need?

Ellen: None really. Have you got a credit card yourself?

Steve: Yes, I have.

Ellen: Then you probably know quite a bit about them already, and as a student you're obviously intelligent, which of course you need to be for the job. So after a day or so working with an experienced operative I'm sure you'll have picked up enough to deal with routine enquiries, which of course most of them are.

Steve: But there are bound to be questions I can't deal with, at least at first. What happens then?

Ellen: In that case you can ask a supervisor. They're very helpful to new staff.

Steve: I think I like the sound of this. What do I do next?

Unit 5. Page 63. Listening.
IELTS practice. Questions 6–10.

Ellen: Can you get over there for 9.45 on Monday morning, for an interview?

Steve: Definitely, yes. Whereabouts are they?

Ellen: In Riverside Business Park. Do you know it?

Steve: Yes, I've been there once.

Ellen: How do you usually travel?

Steve: By bus.

Ellen: Right. So you take either the 136 or 137 to the bus station, and when you come out of there you turn right.

Steve: Along Orchard Road, that is? The road from the railway station?

Ellen: Yes, that's right. You go past the petrol station next to the car dealers, then carry on down the road.

Steve: Do I take the first left? At the main car park?

Ellen: Well you could do that, and walk up Newfield Avenue alongside the shopping centre, but it's a long way round. I'd suggest continuing along Orchard Road, with the water company and then the insurance offices on your right. They used to be local government offices, by the way.

Steve: Yes, I remember those.

Ellen: And you keep going until you reach the advertising agency. Now facing that is a small road called Cherry Lane. There's a newspaper office on the corner and opposite that is a big hotel, so you can't miss it.

Steve: And how far down that road is it?

Ellen: Well they aren't actually in Cherry Lane. You walk as far as the next junction and turn right into Almond Drive, at the mail centre. InterCard is in the third building on the right, between the airline offices and the shipping company.

Steve: Fine. I'll be there on Monday. Thanks very much. Bye.

Ellen: Good luck. Bye.

Unit 5. Page 64. Speaking. Exercise 2

Speaker A: My name's Mark Davies and my job is to find out what's going on and report it. The best thing about it is the excitement. I never know what story I'll be covering next, and no two days are ever the same. The only thing I don't like about it are the unsocial hours: if a major story breaks,

I have to be there at any time of day or night. My ambition is to be a foreign correspondent with one of the big radio networks.

Speaker B: I'm Jennifer Symons. I did an MBA at university and nowadays I'm in charge of twelve people selling mainly to manufacturing companies in the area. I particularly enjoy the responsibility and the good salary, but one drawback of working here is that there are limited prospects for further promotion. In the medium or long term my aim is to work for a larger organization, possibly in a different industry.

Speaker C: My name's Chris Dean and for five months I've been working in the coastal waters off Antarctica, studying a species of algae. What makes the job so fascinating is that every day we're building knowledge, knowledge about how the entire world's ecosystems work. To me the downside to it is not the cold, I'm used to that, but the darkness in the winter months. When this job ends I'll be looking for a permanent position in a marine biology department.

Unit 6. Page 75. Listening. IELTS practice. Questions 1–6.

Presenter: Hi and welcome to the Students' Union. You've all been here a week now, and hopefully, you're finding your feet. You might be wondering what there is to do on campus apart from going to lectures, doing essays, going out with friends and having late nights. Tonight you're going to hear about some of the societies, clubs, and associations that you can join as a new student, as well as the cultural events going on that might interest you. Richard Hillman, from Student Services has come along this evening to tell you more.

Richard: Good evening – it's good to be here and to see you all. Let me say straightaway that, as students of the university, you are entitled to join, free of charge over a hundred societies on the official list. OK, let's begin. I'd be prepared to bet that whatever your interests, you're almost sure to find a club or society here for you. Not surprisingly, there are the long-established clubs that you can find at any university, like the Football Club or the Drama Society, along with a whole range of less usual clubs, for example the Rock Society. We do have a Rock Climbing Club here, but the Rock Society has nothing to do with outdoor activities – it's a music club. That takes me neatly on to the Mountaineering Club. Now it might surprise you that a university in one of the flattest parts of the country has a thriving group of mountaineers. They meet twice a week: on Tuesdays from five in the afternoon until ten o'clock in the evening, and on Thursday afternoons from one o'clock until five. At their regular meetings they use the climbing wall, but they also organize trips to real mountains both here and abroad during the vacation. Another rather out-of-the-ordinary society you might like to try is the Dance Club. They meet regularly every Friday. This term they're running salsa classes, next term it's tango and in the summer it'll be Scottish dancing – quite a selection. They also put on special events twice a term – either performances by visiting groups, or actual dances. Their next event is next Saturday when

they're putting on a Latin evening. Go along and try out your samba. At the moment the Dance Club is trying to attract new members who may have new ideas for future classes and events. If you're an overseas student you may find there's a society for students from your country putting on events that'll make you feel more at home. The Mexican Society, for example is putting on a special Christmas celebration with traditional Mexican food and drink. And every four weeks, the Hellenic Society has a film evening. There are also national societies for Malaysian, Turkish and Chinese students. And don't forget these societies are open to everyone – whether you're from that country or not.

Unit 6. Page 75. Listening. IELTS practice. Questions 7–10.

Richard: Finally, I'd like to say something about the flourishing arts scene here. This is centred mainly on the Lakeside Theatre and includes a full programme of music, theatre and visual arts. As far as visual arts are concerned, the University Gallery has exhibitions throughout the year. The work of local, national, and international artists is regularly on display as well as exhibitions featuring contemporary architects and designers. The University also has a permanent collection of Modern Eastern European art on display. As well as the conventional theatre productions, put on by visiting professional companies and student groups, there is a Workshop Studio which stages more experimental drama. And finally music. Concerts catering for a variety of musical tastes include performances by visiting groups as well as home-grown talent: the university has its own jazz band and choir. As with the other groups I referred to earlier, you are eligible to join these, but of course you will be required to go for an audition. So there you have it. Obviously, I haven't covered everything in this short introduction, but I hope I've given you a flavour of what's on offer here.

Unit 6. Page 78. Writing. Exercise 2.

Speaker 1: As far as I'm concerned going to university is a two-edged sword. Sure, it's interesting and enjoyable – I've made loads of new friends and hopefully I'll get a useful qualification and a good job at the end of it. On the other hand I'll have a huge debt to pay back. I've heard people say it can take years for fees and loans to be repaid. So, I'm really enjoying my course, but I must admit I'm a bit worried about what happens afterwards.

Speaker 2: If we want to compete with other countries, we really do need to have at least 50% of our young people in higher education. Especially in areas like technology, science and business, we need young people who are educated to a world class standard. The only way for this to happen is for us to increase access to higher education; this means we have to provide more places at more institutions and therefore extra funding, massive extra funding if we are serious about enabling half or more of our young people to go to university.

Speaker 3: Of course we want what's best for them. When I was that age only about 10% of 18-year-olds went on to higher education. You were special if you went to university in those days – a sort of elite. Now, anyone can go – and I suppose that's a good thing, as long as the universities aren't lowering their standards. Our main worry is money. We think university education should be free for everyone who's good enough to get in. As it is, our son will be paying off his debts for at least ten years. That doesn't seem fair, given that his having a degree will help the country.

Speaker 4: We're all in favour of opening up higher education to as many young people as possible. But of course this costs money – not just in the education itself, staffing and so on, but in additional administrative costs, extra student accommodation. And of course the money's got to come from somewhere. If the government's not prepared to fund us, then we have to depend on other sources. At the moment, our main source of income is home student fees, but in the future we expect to recruit more overseas students who pay higher fees.

Unit 7. Page 82. Reading. Exercise 1.

Speaker: The simplest reflecting telescope, developed by Newton in the 17th century, consists of a wide tube pointing at the sky with a large, concave mirror at the bottom. Light rays from space travel down the tube and strike this primary mirror. The light is reflected upwards to a much smaller 'secondary mirror' in the centre of the tube. The secondary mirror is set at an angle of 45^0, so the light is then reflected out to the left-hand side where it can be viewed through a round eyepiece lens at 90^0 to the tube.

Unit 7. Page 87. Listening. IELTS practice. Questions 1 and 2.

Carol: In the nineteenth century, scientific discoveries took a long time to produce any actual applications, and scientists might have had a case for giving little thought to the social or environmental impact of their work. That all changed in the twentieth century, with the huge advances first in physics and then in biology. Science started to play a much more important role in our lives, and the relationship between scientists and society became much closer. Many scientists became increasingly concerned about the ethics of what they were doing as they quickly saw the consequences: the benefits such as vastly improved crop yields and the eradication of diseases like bubonic plague, but also terrible damage in the form of pollution and chemical weapons.

Matt: Yes but some scientists still claim, even today, that their only duty is to make public the findings of their research. They need to do that of course, but I think the key points are that they ought to stop making any distinction between pure science and applied science because in practical terms it no longer exists, and also they must accept full responsibility for the consequences of their work.

Unit 7. Page 87. Listening. IELTS practice. Questions 3–10.

Carol: Let's explore that last point a little further. How can scientists put that responsibility into practice?

Matt: By educating the public, particularly through the media and at the workplace.

Jan: Another thing they must do is advise on what might one day go wrong as a result of what they're coming up with now.

Matt: That seems essential. And just as importantly, if and when things do go wrong, they need to sort them out, especially where the fault lies with the original research.

Carol: How do you feel about the international role of scientists, given that their work crosses frontiers so readily?

Jan: I think it gives them, or at least should give them, a global view. In this respect some of them are better placed than many politicians to see how new discoveries are likely to affect particular parts of the world.

Matt: But will the politicians listen?

Jan: Probably not, but I'm not suggesting getting involved with politics or politicians. Much better to raise the public's awareness of scientific issues, so they can put the pressure on at election time.

Matt: There's a problem here, though, isn't there, with the way the public sees scientists: they're all either mad or bad.

Jan: That's something they need to work on, definitely. To regain public trust they'll have to show they're accountable, and that science is about improving people's lives.

Carol: That may not be so easy. What do you think are the areas in science that really worry people these days?

Matt: Science in agriculture, above all. There's been all this media hysteria about 'Frankenstein Foods' but there is a genuine issue here: whether adding specific genes to plants is a valid way of increasing food production, or whether it risks the appearance of new diseases, of super-weeds and pests.

Jan: Which links it to another controversy: using chemicals to control pests. And that's something else that was at first thought to be harmless, but we now know that the careless spraying of crops has led to all kinds of health problems for people. Plus a devastating loss of biodiversity, with huge numbers of insects, birds and mammals simply disappearing from the countryside, fish dying in poisoned rivers, and so on.

Matt: And of course if we're talking about death on a massive scale, then we have to mention the role of science in enabling the military to wage chemical and biological and nuclear warfare, which has destroyed life in so many parts of the world.

Carol: OK, I think we've identified some major topics there.

Matt: There's something I'd like to add, if I may. Sure, it's important for scientists and future scientists to talk about major issues like these, but we might also want to look at what we can do or not do in our everyday lives, particularly as many of us will be earning more money than we actually need for basic necessities. I'm thinking here of things like burning fossil fuels by driving everywhere. What do you think?

Carol: Well something that scientists seem to do rather too often is take planes to distant places, which is highly damaging environmentally.

Matt: For instance to attend conferences on subjects like the disappearing ozone layer …

Jan: When nowadays they could probably stay at work and use a video conferencing link anyway …

Carol: Which may in fact be an example of how progress in computer science can impact positively on the environment.

Matt: But going back to harmful things. What else can be done?

Carol: Again on the air transport theme, there are the huge distances a lot of consumer goods travel before they actually reach the shops in this country. This seems another extreme waste of energy, especially if much of what is being produced and carried is packaging. Perhaps it's worth shopping for more locally-produced items?

Unit 7. Page 92. Help yourself. Exercise 2.

1 ageing
2 excellent
3 controversial
4 independent
5 necessary
6 beneficial
7 category
8 knowledgeable
9 significance
10 commitment
11 controlled
12 exaggerate
13 successful
14 maintenance
15 attendance
16 opportunity
17 recommend
18 analyse (NB: US English – analyze)
19 embarrass
20 fulfil (NB: US English – fulfill)

Unit 8. Page 99. Listening. IELTS practice. Questions 1–10.

Jenny: Good afternoon. I'm Jenny Ironbridge and today I'm going be continuing my series of talks on information technology, by looking at an innovative information source available on the Internet. I'm sure you're all familiar with the strengths and weaknesses of the popular search engines like Google or Yahoo. Sometimes you can find what you're looking for instantly. At other times searching for something which may or may not exist can be a frustrating and time-consuming experience. So, where can you go to get the information you want? The information source I want to talk about is called Wikipedia. As its name suggests it's a

form of encyclopedia. It's already the largest information source in history both in terms of its breadth and its depth. But what makes Wikipedia really unique is that it's a democratic project. The content is completely free to access, and it's written entirely by unpaid volunteers. Changes and additions are being made all the time to articles which exist already, but it's also possible to contribute whole new articles. And basically, anyone can contribute, once they've grasped the basics of editing the pages.

Let's look at how someone goes about editing Wikipedia articles. It's a very straightforward procedure which has been made deliberately easy so that people who have contributions to make are not discouraged from participating because of their limited understanding of information technology. Let's start by imagining that we are reading an article and we come across information that we consider to be incorrect or incomplete on a page of Wikipedia. First of all, we decide we'd like to change it. To do this, we click on the Edit button at the top of the page. This takes us to another page with a text box containing all the editable text on that page. It's at this point that we can input our changes in exactly the same way as we would if we were writing or editing a document we had created on our own computer. In other words, we can type, cut and paste, delete and use all the normal word-processing functions. When this has been done and we've finished editing, we are then asked to summarize the changes we have made. This doesn't go into the main text box but into a separate area below it. That's the main part of the process over with, but we need to make sure that the changes we've made are going to appear as we want them. A last check, if you like. In order to do this we select the preview option. If we're still not satisfied, we have the option of returning to the edit stage and working through the same procedure again. Finally, if we're satisfied with the result, we simply click on save, and our changes will take immediate effect.

A question that might already be forming in your mind if you are not familiar with Wikipedia is this: 'How can I tell whether information is accurate?' This particular point has led to criticism from some people, especially academics and professionals. The short answer is that you can't tell, but, if you think about it, how can you check the accuracy of information you read in a conventional encyclopedia, or in a newspaper or on other Internet websites. Besides, it's possible for contributors to Wikipedia to register with the organization, and, as named contributors gradually build up a reputation for themselves as reliable sources of information. The other point to be aware of is that there are administrators who monitor contributions that are added by anonymous sources and check for biased, out of date, or incorrect information. One of the problems that arises from the openness of Wikipedia is that vandals have gone into the site to change and damage pages of information, so the administrators have a role in policing this too. Lastly, Wikipedia encourages editors to stick to certain rules, which help ensure the quality of entries. For example, contributors are expected to maintain a neutral tone in their writing, although perhaps it's impossible to be completely neutral. Also, entries are not allowed to include original research, which is intended to prevent contributors from simply submitting their own views. It's unlikely that the more conventional information sources will ever be completely replaced by Wikipedia or similar projects which may be developed in the future, but this is an ambitious experiment to democratize information, using modern technology to enable anyone and everyone to contribute to and access a common body of knowledge. And because it's free, it doesn't restrict access to those with the ability to pay.

Unit 8. Page 100. Speaking. Exercise 2.

Speaker 1: Hmm, that's a big question. Obviously modern technology makes our lives easier in many ways, and gives us more leisure time than we've ever had, but there are more things to worry about than there were in the past and stress levels are higher than they used to be. I think this can only get worse. In fact, I'd say it's fairly unlikely that technology itself will make us happier. It may make people expect more out of life and then feel disappointed because the reality doesn't live up to their expectations.

Speaker 2: I think it's quite likely that many more people will work from home in the future. To some extent this is already happening. I suppose this will probably mean that there'll be less need for large offices in the centre of cities, as more and more employees access their computers from their homes.

Speaker 3: As I see it, it all depends on individuals. I don't think that the technology itself will change our behaviour or somehow stop us wanting to spend time with our friends and other people. On the other hand, a lot of people seem to want to shut the world out by spending a lot of time listening to music through headphones or playing computer games. If this continues, it could result in more people feeling lonely and isolated.

Unit 9. Page 110. Listening. IELTS practice. Questions 1–5.

Assistant: Hello, Volunteers Worldwide, how can I help you?

Ben: Hello, I'm ringing to find out about opportunities for doing volunteer work. Could you give me some information, please?

Assistant: Yes, certainly – but before I do, I need to ask you for a few personal details – that's just because the opportunities open to you are dependent on your age and on what qualifications and skills you have.

Ben: That's fine.

Assistant: So, if you could just start by telling me your name and age.

Ben: OK, my name's Ben Oppermann and I'm twenty-two years old.

Assistant: OK. And what qualifications do you have, Ben?

Ben: I've got a BA degree in Social Studies, that was from the University of Kent. And I'm a qualified teacher. I've just completed my PGCE, my post-graduate certificate in Primary Education.

Assistant: And you're interested in doing unpaid voluntary work rather than a full-time job with our organization?

Ben: Yes, that's right. I'd like to do voluntary work before I start looking for a more permanent job.

Assistant: How long were you hoping to work for us for?

Ben: I was thinking of two years at most.

Assistant: OK, well for people in your age group, we have two programmes: Global Youth Contact and Youth for Action on Development. GYC – Global Youth Contact – is a six-month exchange programme which provides opportunities for young people from different countries to work together in local communities.

Ben: I see, but that's only a six-month programme?

Assistant: That's right, but our other programme – Youth for Action on Development – requires people to volunteer for a year at least. On this programme most of the placements are for 12 or 18 months.

Ben: That'd be the programme I'd go for.

Assistant: OK. Now, do you have any other skills or special interests that might be useful for the kind of work we do?

Ben: Well, I've done a lot of conservation work in the area where I live.

Assistant: Good, that's useful to know.

Ben: And I belong to a wildlife protection group.

Assistant: Right, that could be very helpful.

Unit 9. Page 111. Listening. IELTS practice. Questions 6–10.

Assistant: Do you have any questions you'd like to ask me?

Ben: Yes, could you tell me what sort of placements are available?

Assistant: Well, all our placements are related to the four main areas that we work in, that's: Education, Health, Social participation, and Employment.

Ben: Education sounds like the obvious choice for me. And if I wanted to go ahead and apply to work on a programme like this, what do I have to do?

Assistant: OK, well our selection procedure is quite a lengthy process, I'm afraid. It can take up to nine months. We get many more applicants than we have placements for, so we need to make sure that we get the best people for the kind of work we do. It's very important to realize that voluntary work like this is not an easy option. Although you'll have a brilliant experience with us, you are expected to work hard and make a real contribution – it is not just sitting around enjoying a different culture.

Ben: Of course, I understand that.

Assistant: OK, so, if you're interested, I can send you an application pack. You complete the forms and send them back to us. If you are short-listed, we invite you to come for an interview – that's normally in January. Assuming you are successful, we then start looking for a suitable placement. While we are doing this, we ask you to raise some funds of your own, so that you end up contributing about two-thirds of the cost of your training and travel.

Ben: OK fair enough. I suppose people get sponsorship do they?

Assistant: Yes, lots of volunteers do that. Then, in June, we ask you to come to our headquarters for a week's training. This starts with general training which is applicable to all volunteers. It includes topics like: how to fit into new cultures; looking after yourself, mentally and physically; and how to go about relating to the kinds of people you'll be working with. And then you'll have sessions related specifically to your placement. We'll tell you about the country and the area you'll be going to, about the problems and difficulties to expect, and about the kind of responsibilities you'll have once you're there.

Ben: And when does the work start?

Assistant: It depends, but generally speaking, placements start in September and run for up to eighteen months.

Ben: Sounds brilliant. Could you send me an application pack please?

Assistant: Yes, certainly. If you'd like to give me your address.

Ben: OK. It's ...

Unit 9. Page 116. Help yourself. Exercise 2.

Talk one

Speaker: Today I shall be looking at what we mean by the term 'community' and the importance of the concept of community from a sociological point of view. In everyday life, the term community has a wide range of meanings. It can be applied to places, for example the village community, to social groups like the student community, to religious or racial groups, like the Bhuddist community. Even among sociologists, there is little agreement about a precise definition, although there is a degree of acceptance for Newby's broad ideas. Newby defined 'community' in three main ways: firstly as a social system, that is a set of social relationships; secondly as a fixed locality, in other words a geographical location; and thirdly a quality of relationship, by which he meant a spirit of community. Some sociologists, regard these three aspects of community as interlinked, but Newby insists that they are distinct. Newby illustrates his point by pointing out that we cannot guarantee that living in the same locality automatically promotes a warm spirit of community.

Talk two

Speaker: Today we'll be looking at what we mean by the term 'community', and I'd like to start by asking you to tell the student sitting next to you what different communities you belong to. When you've done that, go on to think of a definition of 'community'. I'll give you a couple of minutes for that.

OK, let's find out what you came up with. How many of you said a community was essentially a geographical location, maybe somewhere people live - a village, for example?

OK, thank you. And how many preferred to describe a community as a group of people with similar ideas - like a political party for example?

Thank you. And, finally, how many thought of community as something less tangible, a feeling of belonging, perhaps, an emotional location, if you like?
OK. Well that's very interesting ...

Unit 10. Page 122. Listening. Exercise 2.

33 mg	thirty-three milligrams
the 90s	the Nineties
850 cc	eight hundred and fifty cc
3,634 sq km	three thousand six hundred and thirty-four square kilometres
455 BC	four hundred and fifty-five BC
8,850 m	eight thousand eight hundred and fifty metres
£1500	fifteen hundred pounds
3.141	three point one four one
5 ft 10 in	five foot ten inches
100 mph	a hundred miles per hour
2/3	two thirds
7 cm/day	seven centimetres per day
37°	thirty-seven degrees Centigrade
25²	twenty-five squared

Unit 10. Page 123. Listening. IELTS practice. Questions 1–8.

Presenter: Today I have with me Moira Mackenzie, the author of several books in a well-known series of travel guides, and she'll be talking about what is probably the most fascinating wildlife area in Europe: the Scottish Highlands. Moira.

Moira: Yes, that's right, and it's a wonderful place to visit with lots to do in an area that makes up over half of Scotland. Including the seven hundred and ninety islands that lie scattered around the coast, it covers thirty-nine thousand square kilometres. Getting there is easy. From here in Glasgow a good starting point is Fort William on the west coast, with regular bus and rail services linking the two. I'd recommend the train, which takes four hours to get there. Alternatively, you can take the Highland Line which takes the more easterly route up to Inverness. That in fact is a bit quicker, taking around three and a half hours to cover the two hundred and eighty kilometres from here. There are also two main options by road. You can take either the A9 up through Stirling and Perth and then on to Inverness, or else on the west there's the A82, which runs up to Fort William and then, if you want, on to Inverness. Now a lot of people associate the Highlands with bitterly cold weather, but in fact the region has a generally mild climate as a result of being surrounded on three sides by sea, particularly the warm waters of the Atlantic. At sea level in the west, for instance, the temperature ranges on average from a minimum of one degree Centigrade in January up to eighteen in July, and you can actually see palm trees growing there. Obviously, though, the temperatures will be lower inland and on higher ground. You can expect it to rain a lot, too, particularly in the west where annually as much as two thousand millimetres regularly falls, though this helps account for the rich variety of vegetation and wildlife. When you get there, you'll find there are plenty of reasonably-priced places to stay. In Fort William, for instance, you can find a room for the night in a small hotel or a bed and breakfast for just twenty-five pounds, or for twenty-eight to thirty pounds in Inverness. It's probably a good idea to book ahead, though, especially in the summer months. With all the leisure, sports and cultural activities on offer, the towns are becoming increasingly popular with visitors. For example, accommodation in Inverness won't be at all easy to find this year around the twenty-third of July, as that's when the local Highland Games will take place. So if your aim is to see the countryside, it may be best to stay in a small village.

Unit 10. Page 123. Listening. IELTS practice. Questions 9 and 10.

Moira: As I mentioned, there's a huge range of wildlife in the Highlands, but for those visiting the area there are some basic ground rules that are essential if we are to protect it. Firstly, you should make every effort not to disturb birds and animals, and one way of doing this is to blend in with your surroundings, for instance by avoiding brightly-coloured garments such as orange anoraks. To see wildlife clearly, it's best to use binoculars, keeping your distance. This is particularly important during the breeding season. Wherever possible, use a hide so that they are less likely to detect your presence. Surprising though it may seem, visitors are advised to use their cars where no purpose-built hides are available, as people are apparently less likely to startle animals if they stay inside their vehicles. You may even find that creatures come up close to where you're parked, in which case wait until they've gone before you move off. It should really go without saying that it's essential to be as quiet as possible, though sadly some people need reminding of this. Oh, and one other thing: wild animals and pets don't mix, so please leave your dog at home, or at least somewhere he or she can't chase the wildlife or damage their habitat.

Unit 11. Page 135. Listening. IELTS practice. Questions 1–10.

Lecturer: Hello. My name is Alexandra Blaby and today I'll be talking about one of the ways in which personality can be assessed: 'psychometric testing'. Psychometric literally means 'measuring the mind', and there are many carefully constructed tests which attempt to carry out this process. Probably the most common use for these tests is to help people find out the careers that most suit their personality. Many employers ask new job applicants to take a psychometric or personality test as part of their selection procedure. One of the features of this type of test is that there are no right or wrong answers to the questions. For this reason, it would be more accurate to call them assessments rather than tests. There are four main types of personality test currently in use. These are questionnaires, ratings tests, projective tests, and objective tests. Let's start by considering questionnaires, as these are by far the most common method. Here subjects are asked between fifty and a hundred questions about themselves. A typical question might be 'Do you enjoy spending time alone?' There are two advantages to questionnaires: firstly, they are easy to administer, and secondly, the questions are answered by the person who knows the subject best – themselves. By contrast, a ratings test is done by someone who knows the subject well, rather than the subjects themselves. A rater might be asked, for example, to agree or disagree with a statement about the subject. A typical statement might be: 'He laughs a lot.' The effectiveness of ratings tests depends on how well the rater knows the subject. Projective tests ask the subject to make sense of information which is unclear in some way. In the famous 'inkblot test', for example, subjects have to say what a patch of ink on a piece of paper looks like to them. Finally, objective tests. In these tests the subject has to engage in a physical activity. How they do it will tell the tester something about their personality. For example, the subject might be asked to blow up a balloon until it bursts. From observing how the subject does this, the tester will be able to say how timid or brave he or she is.

Perhaps at this stage, we should clarify what exactly we learn about people from psychometric tests. The overall purpose of the tests is to identify personality leanings or inclinations rather than fixed qualities or, as some people fear, character weaknesses. This explains why tests often include several similar questions. How consistently the subject answers these will enable the tester to reach an accurate assessment. Incidentally, the assessment procedure may be carried out by a psychologist or another trained individual, but is most frequently done automatically by a computer. The effectiveness of any method which asks questions, of course, is heavily dependent on the individual's willingness to answer a set of standard questions. One of the most well-respected psychometric tests is the Myers-Briggs test, which asks subjects about their preferences in four main areas. Firstly the test asks people where they direct their energy: to the outer world of activity or the inner world of thoughts and emotions.

Secondly, people are asked how they prefer to process information: in the form of known facts or in the form of possibilities. The third area is decision making: do people make decisions on the basis of logic or of personal values. Lastly Myers-Briggs tests ask people how they prefer to organize their lives – in a structured or a flexible way. Although there are those who disapprove of personality testing, there is no doubt that it is here to stay. Human beings have always been curious to find out about themselves and others: psychometric testing gives them an objective, scientific means of doing this. Well, that's all for today. Tomorrow I'll be examining ways of measuring intelligence …

Unit 11. Page 136. Speaking. Exercise 2.

Speaker 1: I do various things in my free time, but my passion is collecting Coke cans. I've got nearly 800 different ones, from all over the world. I belong to a soft drinks container collecting group which has members in 47 different countries. Apart from the language printed on cans from different countries, it's amazing how different the designs are. There are the normal everyday cans, but there are also special commemorative cans they produce for big events like the Olympic games. I've made loads of new friends through my hobby and even visited a couple of them – and it's a real change from the work I do as a supermarket manager.

Speaker 2: I spend nearly all my free time playing with a jazz quartet – I play the drums. We started off as a school band, and just kept going. We play for private parties and in bars – about twice a week. We even get paid for some of the bookings – not that any of us do it for the money. For me, it's just good fun – a chance to be with my mates and relax doing something different.

Speaker 3: I'm into restoring antique furniture in a big way. It all started when I mended an old chair for my grandparents. It took me ages to do, but it was quite interesting. To do it properly you have to find out about different kinds of wood, as well as learning a whole range of techniques like carving, planing and polishing. There's more to it than people think. Since that first chair I've repaired tables, cupboards, all sorts of things – even clocks for friends, and friends of friends. It's actually quite a lucrative hobby probably because there aren't that many people around who can do it properly – I'm even thinking of turning it into my full-time job.

Unit 12. Page 147. Listening. IELTS practice. Questions 1–10.

Sandy: Good afternoon. I'm Sandy Raymond and I'm going to be talking about a remarkable timepiece called the Breitling Emergency Watch. Some of you may remember it as the watch that Richard Branson auctioned off on eBay, raising £20,000 for charity, after he'd lent it to Steve Fossett for his non-stop round the world flight. Perhaps more significantly, though, it was the kind of watch being worn last year by two British pilots whose helicopter crashed into the sea just off Antarctica. Finding themselves in a lifeboat with no other means of communication, they activated the transmitters inside their watches. The signals were picked up by a Chilean aircraft, which homed in on them and then organized a rescue that saved the men's lives. And these are just the people the watch was designed for: aviators and air crew who suddenly find themselves on the ground or in the water after a forced landing. The watch has a built-in microtransmitter which can broadcast a signal for up to 48 hours on 121.5 megahertz, the aircraft emergency frequency. It's water resistant, too. Even with the transmitter operating, it can be used at depths of up to 30 metres. The operating range depends to a great extent on whether there are any obstacles between the transmitter and the rescue aircraft. On flat terrain with few trees, for instance, the signal can be picked up at up to 160 kilometres away, and it's the same on water as long as the seas are calm, while from the top of a mountain it has a range of up to 400 kilometres. It's not a particularly bulky or heavy item to wear, though: at 16 millimetres thick and measuring 43 in diameter, it's just 85 grams, which is about the normal weight for this kind of wrist watch. So, what makes this watch tick, as it were? The answer to that is two separate mechanisms: one quartz electronic with an LCD digital display, and the other a self-winding mechanical system that turns the hands. This is driven by an oscillating weight that swings in time with the movements of the wrist, thus creating the energy to rewind the watch automatically. I should point out here that this is hardly a new invention, as it dates back to 1770 when the Frenchman Abraham-Louis Perrelet first made a watch of this kind. Incidentally, an example of his work is still keeping good time today, over two hundred years later.

Let's take a look inside an Emergency Watch. Possibly the first thing you notice at the top is the gold ring indicating compass points and degrees. This surrounds the crystal, which looks like glass but is in fact made of a scratch-proof synthetic material. On a scale of one to ten, with ten as diamond hardness, this scores nine. So the crystal fits onto a protective case made of titanium, a hard but light antimagnetic metal that is also used in the manufacture of high-performance aircraft. On the right-hand side of the inner case is the crown, used for setting the time and the date. This rounded knob has a locking device to prevent moisture or dust getting into the watch. The watch itself, with the two independent timing systems I mentioned before, is kept separate from the other components. This means that even if the timekeeping functions are damaged in a crash, the emergency signal can still keep going out. For this reason there are two batteries, an upper one for the watch and a transmitter battery below which fits neatly into the circuit board. All the above are housed in the outer case, which in the case of the version shown is made of gold alloy. On the right of this case you'll notice a rounded cap, which looks like a winding knob, but isn't. This is the real 007 bit: if you twist the cap anticlockwise and then pull to its full extent, the cap comes off and you have a 43-centimetre antenna, which immediately starts transmitting on 121.5 megahertz. Incidentally, on the other side of the case there's a secondary antenna which can also be extended, thereby increasing the range of the transmitter.

Unit 13. Page 158. Listening. IELTS practice. Questions 1–4.

Presenter: Welcome to the 'Museums UK' audio series, a collection of downloadable audio files introducing the best of British museums. My name's Sam Cooper and in this file I'll be introducing the Ashmolean Museum of Art and Archaeology in Oxford, with its fabulous collections of Eastern and Western Art, Antiquities, Casts and Coins. It's one of the oldest public museums in the world and it's actually part of Oxford University, though it's free to go in, whether you're a student or not. You'll find the main museum in Beaumont Street near the centre of Oxford, close to both the railway station and the bus station. Opening hours for visitors are from ten o'clock in the morning till five in the evening on Tuesdays to Saturdays, twelve to five on Sundays, and ten to seven on Thursdays in the summer months. It usually closes for three days over Christmas, a couple of days at New Year and three days for the St Giles Fair in early September. You can take photos in the galleries, but only with hand-held cameras and not using flash or lights, which can do serious harm to exhibits. Also, as long you follow all the copyright regulations and you get permission from the staff on duty, you can ask for Antiquities documents of less than 100 years in age to be photocopied, at a cost of 5p per A4 sheet.

Unit 13. Page 159. Listening. IELTS practice. Questions 5–10.

Presenter: Perhaps not surprisingly given its links with the University, the Ashmolean has an Education Service for schools and the general public. Activities include guided group visits, which for adults last sixty minutes and cost four pounds each. This makes the minimum price per group twenty-eight pounds, as group sizes vary from seven to fifteen people. Visits by groups of young people take the same amount of time as the adult tours, but cost just two pounds for university students. So with at least seven to a group the lowest price is fourteen pounds, though please note that there's an upper limit of fourteen group members rather than the fifteen for adults. For schools, there are visits to suit all age groups, and for the most popular ones – such as those to see the Greek and Egyptian collections – it's best to book a term in advance. Tours last fifty minutes, starting at ten-fifteen, eleven-thirty and a quarter past one, with a maximum of thirteen children per group. Now if you're free in the middle of the day, why not go along to one of the 45-minute lunchtime talks? There's a really wide range of topics. On the 19th, for example, the subject is 'Greek Mythology', and on the 20th there's 'Celebration of India'. Both begin at one-fifteen, the usual time for these talks, and they're held every Tuesday, Wednesday and

Friday. Another regular feature, on Saturday mornings through to the afternoons, are the workshops. If you're interested in developing your own illustrative and artistic skills, these are for you. They're aimed at artists of varying levels of experience, and are always led by practising artists. Running for six hours from ten o'clock, this is wonderful value at just five pounds, including basic materials – and also a decent cup of coffee.

Unit 13. Page 164. Help yourself. Exercise 1.

Vowel sounds

far/fur
bin/bean
pull/pool
heart/hut
barn/ban
port/pot
stays/stairs
toy/tour
air/ear
tell/tale
coat/caught
liar/layer

Consonant sounds

live/life
tick/thick
owl/howl
rice/rise
light/right
sip/ship
head/hedge
bat/vat
sin/sing
hide/height
vet/wet
jaw/your

Unit 13. Page 164. Help yourself. Exercise 3.

a   world wide web

b   today's the third Thursday this term

c   eleven benevolent elephants

d   three free throws

e   red lorry, yellow lorry, red lorry, yellow lorry

f   the sixth sick sheik's sixth sheep's sick

Unit 14. Page 170. Listening. IELTS practice. Questions 1–10.

Emma: Hi, I'm Emma Bailey, and today I'm going to be talking 'baby-talk'. Hopefully, you'll find the subject interesting rather than infantile. I'd like to start by getting you to imagine a scenario. You're in an office or at a family gathering when a mother comes in with her young baby.

Like everyone else, you want to see the mother and baby and you probably want to talk to the baby. How do you do this? What kind of language do you use? Recent research has shown that adults all talk to babies in similar ways: they repeat phrases over and over again in a high-pitched 'sing-song' voice with long vowel sounds. And if they ask questions they exaggerate their intonation. Researchers have discovered that this kind of language, which they have called 'motherese', is used by adults all over the world when they talk to babies. And according to a new theory, 'motherese' forms a kind of framework for the development of language in children. This 'baby talk', so the theory goes, itself originated as a response to another aspect of human evolution: walking upright. In contrast to other primates, humans give birth to babies that are relatively undeveloped. So, whereas a baby chimpanzee can hold on to its four-legged mother and ride along on her back shortly after birth, helpless human babies have to be held and carried everywhere by their upright mothers. Having to hold on to an infant constantly would have made it more difficult for the mother to gather food. In this situation, researchers suggest, human mothers began putting their babies down beside them while gathering food. To pacify an infant distressed by this separation, the mother would 'talk' to her offspring and continue her search for food. This remote communication system could have marked the start of 'motherese'. As mothers increasingly relied on their voices to control the emotions of their babies, and, later, the actions of their mobile juveniles, words emerged from the jumble of sounds and became conventionalized across human communities, ultimately producing language.

Not all anthropologists, however, accept the assumption that early human mothers put their children down when they were looking for food. They point out that even modern parents do not do this. Instead, they prefer to hold their babies in their arms or carry them around in slings. They suggest that early mothers probably made slings of some kind both for ease of transportation and to keep their babies warm by holding them close to their bodies. If this was the case, they would not have needed to develop a way of comforting or controlling their babies from a distance. It is not only anthropologists, but also linguists who challenge this explanation for how language developed. They say that although the 'motherese' theory may account for the development of speech, it does not explain the development of grammar. Nor, they say, does it explain, how the sounds that mothers made acquired their meaning. Most experts believe that language is a relatively modern invention that appeared in the last 100,000 years or so. But if the latest theory is right, baby talk – and perhaps fully evolved language – was spoken much earlier than that. We know that humans were walking upright one and half million years ago. This means that mothers may have been putting their babies down at this time, and communicating with them in 'motherese'. We can be sure that this is not the end of the story, as anthropologists and linguists will continue to investigate the origins of this most human of abilities – language.

Unit 14. Page 176. Help yourself. Exercise 3.

a) easy
    context
    social
    lecture

b) record (v)   record (n)
    object (v)   object (n)
    export (v)   export (n)
    contrast (v)   contrast (n)

c) compete   competition
    photograph   photography
    educate   education
    economy   economic
    China   Chinese
    voluntary   volunteer
    active   activity
    luxury   luxurious

ACKNOWLEDGEMENTS

*The authors and publisher are grateful to those who have given permission to reproduce the
following extracts and adaptations of copyright material:* p10 Extract from
'The Pursuit of Happiness' by Michael Bond, *New Scientist*, vol 180, issue 2415,
4 October 2003. Reproduced by permission of *New Scientist*. p23 Extract from
'The other population crisis' by Robin McKie, *The Observer*, Sunday September 26,
2004. Copyright Guardian Newspapers Limited 2004. Reproduced by permission of
Guardian Newspapers Limited. p34 Extract from 'The Power of Nothing'
by Geoff Watts, *New Scientist*, vol 170, issue 2292, 26 May 2001. Reproduced by
permission of *New Scientist*. p40 Extract from 'Fat & Food Quiz What Do You
Really Know About Fat?' from http://www.extra.rdg.ac.uk/eating/eatmainpage2.
htm. © The University of Reading. Reproduced by permission. p45 Extract from
'How to... appreciate art' by Guy Browning, The Guardian, Saturday November
24, 2001. Reproduced by permission of *Guy Browning*. p47 Extract from 'When
is a room not a room' by Stuart Jeffries, *The Guardian*, Saturday November 24,
2001. Copyright Guardian Newspapers Limited 2001. Reproduced by permission
of Guardian Newspapers Limited. p57 Extract from 'Going it alone' by Adeline
Iziren, *The Guardian*, Thursday May 20, 2004 © Adeline Iziren. Reproduced by
permission of Adeline Iziren. p58 Extract from 'The great work myth' by Richard
Reeves, *The Guardian*, Friday May 18, 2001. Reproduced by permission of Richard
Reeves. p70 Extract from 'Boys continue to struggle with reading and writing' by
Jen Horsey from http://www.singlesexschools.org/links-boysreadwrite.htm.
Reproduced by permission of The Canadian Press. p76 Extract from 'Peter
Honey & Alan Mumford, The Learning Styles Questionnaire, 80-item version,
Peter Honey Publications, 2000, ISBN 1-902899007-5', as presented on the
Campaign for Learning website at http://www.campaign-for-learning.org.
uk/aboutyour learning/whatlearning.htm. Copyright 2000, Honey & Mumford.
p77 Extract from *Psychology, an integrated approach*, page 69 Chapter 3 'Learning
and conditioning' by Helena Matute edited by Michael Eysenck published by
Pearson, Prentice Hall 1998. Reproduced by permission of Pearson Education.
p83 Extract from 'Stars in their eyes' by Robin McKie, *The Observer*, Sunday

November 18, 2001. Copyright Guardian Newspapers Limited 2001. Reproduced
by permission of Guardian Newspapers Limited. p88 Extract from 'Fair Trade
Coffee' from www.globalexchange.org/campaigns/ fairtrade/coffee. Reproduced
by permission. p107 Extract taken from an article which first appeared in the
New Statesman 'Friendship is the invisible thread running through society' by
Richard Reeves. Reproduced by permission of New Statesman. p119 Extract from
'Armed and dangerous' by Graham Lawton, New Scientist, vol 180, issue 2420, 8
November 2003. Reproduced by permission of New Scientist. p130 'The Phantom
Hand' by Vilayanur S Ramachandran and Diane Rogers-Ramachandran,
Scientific American Mind, Volume 14, Number 5, December 2004. Adapted with
permission. Copyright © 2004 by Scientific American, Inc. All rights reserved.
p134 Sample psychometric test from www.peoplemaps.com. Reproduced by
permission of PeopleMaps Ltd. p143 Extract from 'Tower of Strength' by Peter
Forbes, The Guardian, September 5, 2002. Peter Forbes is the author of The Gecko's
Foot: Bio-inspiration – Engineered from Nature (Fourth Estate 2005). Reproduced by
permission of Peter Forbes. p154 Extract from 'The Lost Civilisation of Peru. The
rise and fall of the 'Greeks of the Andes' from http://www.bbc.co.uk/sn/tvradio/
programmes/horizon/peruprogsummary.shtml. Reproduced by permission of
the BBC. p166 Extract from 'The Gift of the Gab' by Michael Erard, New Scientist,
8 January 2005. Reproduced by permission of Michael Erard and Pom Inc.

Sources: p9 http://www.nationalgeographic.com/channel/worldsapart/quiz.html
p18 Statistics from National Statistics www.statistics.gov.uk
p19 Statistics from National Statistics www.statistics.gov.uk
p54 Statistics from Australia Bureau of Statistics www.dcita.gov.au
p55 Statistics from National Statistics www.statistics.gov.uk
p55 http://www.liswa.wa.gov.au
p65 The 100 Top Brands from Business Week August 1, 2005
p66 U.S. Advertising Markets from http://yahoo.businessweek.com
p126 Statistics taken from 'The Disappearing Tiger' The Independent, Saturday
4 June 2005.
p159 http://www.ashmol.ox.ac.uk

Although every effort has been made to trace and contact copyright holders
before publication, this has not been possible in some cases. We apologize for
any apparent infringement of copyright and if notified, the publisher will be
pleased to rectify any errors or omissions at the earliest opportunity.

*The author and publisher would like to thank the following for their kind permission to
reproduce photographs and other artwork copyright material:* AKG - Images pp45tr
(Erich Lessing), 158br (Erich Lessing); Alamy pp9br (Bryan and Cherry Alexander/
Bryan & Cherry Alexander Photography), 29 (Renee Morris), 42cl (Malcolm
Case-Green), 50l (Peter Usbeck), 57tl (Anthony Oliver), 69l (Lyndon Beddoe),
74br (Gianni Muratore), 74l (Richard Cooke), 78 (Andrew Fox), 86bl (David
Gregs), 86t (David R. Frazier Photolibrary, Inc.), 117tr (Carol Buchanan), 129tr
(Eugene Breaux/ OnRequest Images, Inc.), 141br (Mark Zylber), 141l (Jon Arnold
Images), 146tl (John James), 150c (mediacolor's), 150l (Buzz Pictures), 157 (Sue
Cunningham Photographic), 158l (M Crame/Worldwide Picture Library), 160r
(Popperfoto), 165tl (David Crausby); Ardea pp117tl (D. Parer & E. Parer-Cook), 118
(Ron+Valerie Taylor); Ashmolean Museum p159; Corbis UK Ltd. pp9bl (Danny
Lehman), 9tl (WildCountry), 10 (Fine Art Photographic Library), 11 (Fine Art
Photographic Library), 14bl (Yang Liu), 14br (Buddy Mays), 16 (Michael Keller),
21bl, 21tl (Louie Psihoyos), 26l (B. Mathur/Reuters), 26r (Kristi J. Black), 28l
(Edifice), 28r (Keren Su), 33bl (Bryan F. Peterson), 33br (Thierry Orban/Sygma),
33tl (Kelly-Mooney Photography), 33tr (Cathrine Wessel), 34l (Walter Hodges),
34r (Gareth Brown), 35 (Ariel Skelley), 38l (David Madison), 38tc (Roy Morsch),
38tr (Patrik Giardino), 42cr (Pat Doyle), 42l (Layne Kennedy), 45bl (Gerrit Greve),
45br (John Slater), 45tl (Hubert Stadler), 49 (artist/Photodisc), 50r (Christian
Maury/Sygma), 52bc, 52l (Richard Hamilton Smith), 57bc (Paul Barton), 57bl (Rob
Lewine), 57br (Pete Saloutos), 57tr (SIE Productions), 69br (Jennie Woodcock/
Reflections Photolibrary), 69tr (Louise Gubb/Saba), 74tr (Roy Morsch), 83
(Ludovic Maisant), 105bc (David Turnley), 105l, 105r (Jose Luis Pelaez, Inc.), 105tc
(Richard Berenholtz), 110l (Wolfgang Kaehler), 117bl (CDC/PHIL), 122c (Louise
Gubb/Saba), 122l (Paul A. Souders), 122r (Joe McDonald), 123 (Jason Hawkes),
124bl, 124tl (Reuters), 126 (tiger/Digital Stock), 136c (Tom & Dee Ann McCarthy),
136l (Rick Maiman/Sygma), 136r (George D. Lepp), 139 (roses/Photodisc), 142l
(150r (Jeff Curtes), 142r (Bildarchiv Monheim GmbH/Alamy), 153bl (Bettmann),
153br (NASA), 153tl (Robert Maass), 153tr (Hulton-Deutsch Collection), 155b
(Gianni Dagli Orti), 155t (Gianni Dagli Orti), 158c (Asian Art & Archaeology, Inc.),
158tr (Werner Forman), 160c (Bettmann), 160l (Hulton-Deutsch Collection),
163 (Robert Holmes), 165bl (Macduff Everton), 165br (Jeremy Horner), 165tr
(YBSHY); Die Imaginare Manufaktur p148l; Ecoscene p42r (Melanie Peters);
Empics pp21br (Owen Humphreys/PA), 21tr (Tim Ockenden/PA), 46 (Markus
Stueklin/AP), 141tr (Abaca); Field & Trek p146bl; Freund Factory p121 (Jürgen
Freund/www.freundfactory.com); Getty Images pp38bc (Eric Pearle/Taxi), 38br
(Doug Pensinger/Allsport Concepts); John Cleare Mountain Camera p146tr;
Keytools Limited, www.keytools.com p148r; Magis p148bc (Carlo Lavatori); NASA
p174; Oceanwide Images p119 (Gary Bell); Omniglow Corporation p146br; Panos
Pictures p9tr (Karen Robinson); Photolibrary.com pp14tr (Workbookstock.Com
Co/Op Service), 57tc (Foodpix), 117br (Tobias Bernhard), 117tc (Howard Hall),
124r; 129br (Mauritius Die Bildagentur Gmbh), 129l (Index Stock Imagery);
Photostage p52tc; Rex Features pp14tl (Henryk T. Kaiser), 110r (Gary Roberts),
142r; Richard Hutten Collection p148tc; Ronald Grant Archive p52r (New Line
Cinema); Science Photo Library p117bc (Mark Smith); Still Pictures p86br.

Commissioned photography by: Chris King pp22, 54, 62, 70, 93, 98, 101, 170, 171
Illustrations by: Julian Baker pp50, 51, 63 (map), 82, 84, 90, 91,112, 122, 131, 133,
150, 151,154; Phil Disley p102; Melvyn Evans p24; Oliver Gaiger pp23, 107, 166;
Neil Leslie/Debut Art pp30, 81; The New York Times Graphics p147; Chris Nurse/
Debut Art p88; Gary Sawyer/Eastwing p94; Alex Williamson/Debut Art pp58, 114

What is on the Student's MultiROM?

The MultiROM in this Student's Pack has two parts.

- You can listen to the audio material that accompanies the workbook by playing the MultiROM in an audio CD player, or in a media player on your computer.

- You can also access one practice test online with the MultiROM. Read the next page to find out about test features. To find out how to access it, read this page.

How do I use my MultiROM?

You will find your practice test on a website called oxfordenglishtesting.com. The website contains many different practice tests, including the one that you have access to. Because the practice test is on the internet you will need:
- to be connected to the internet when you use the test
- to have an email address (so that you can register).

When you're ready to try out your practice test for the first time follow these steps:
1 Turn on your computer.
2 Connect to the internet. (If you have a broadband connection you will probably already be online.)

3 Put the MultiROM into the CD drive of your computer.
4 A screen will appear giving you two options. Click to access your test.

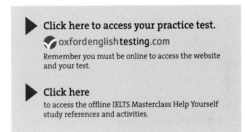

▶ **Click here to access your practice test.**
  ✔oxfordenglish**testing**.com
  Remember you must be online to access the website and your test.

▶ **Click here**
  to access the offline IELTS Masterclass Help Yourself study references and activities.

What do I do when I get to the website?

After a few moments your internet browser will open and take you directly to the website and you will see this screen. Follow steps 1–4. If the screen does not appear follow step 5.

If you have any problems or questions, click the **Support** tab. This is where you will find a list of **Frequently Asked Questions** (FAQs), a Flash demo on how to use the test, and details of how to contact us.

4 After filling in the registration form click on **Register**. Your registration will be confirmed. Click on **My tests** and you will see the **My tests** page. You are now ready to start your practice test. You have three months to use the practice test before you have to submit it for final marking.

1 Choose a language from the drop-down list and click **Go**. All pages, apart from the actual practice test, will be in the language you choose.

2 Click on the **System Requirements** link to find out how your computer needs to be set up in order to do the practice test. It is important to do this before you try to use the test.

3 Click on the **Register now** button and fill in the details on the registration form. You will need to give an email address and make up a password. You will need your email address and password every time you log into the system.

5 The website knows which practice test you have access to because it reads a code on your MultiROM. If the above page does not appear, go to www.oxfordenglishtesting.com/unlock You will be asked to click **Register now** if you are a new user. You will then be asked to fill in a registration form and to enter an unlock code. You can find the unlock code printed on your MultiROM. It will look like this 9219e6-9471d9-cf7c79-a5143b Each code is unique.

Once you have registered, you can access your test in future by going to oxfordenglishtesting.com and logging in. Remember you will need your email and password to log in. You must also be online to do your practice test.

What are the features of the test?

Exam tips	You can see a tip on how to answer every question.
Dictionary look-up	You can look up the meaning of any word in the practice test. Just double click it and a definition will pop up. You need to have pop-up windows enabled.
Instant marking and feedback	When you've answered a question, you can mark it straight away to see whether you got it right. If your answer was wrong, you can get feedback to find out why it was wrong.
Change your answer or try again	You can then go back and have another go as many times as you like. Understanding why you answered a question incorrectly helps you think more clearly about a similar question next time.
Save and come back later	You don't have to complete a Paper in one go. When you log out it saves what you've done. You can come back to it at any time. You have 90 days before you have to submit the practice test for final marking. The **My tests** page tells you how many days you have left to access the test.
Mark individual answers, a part, a paper or the whole test	However much you've done of the practice test, you can mark it and see how well you're doing.
Audio scripts	These are available for all parts of the Listening test. Reading the audio script will help you understand any areas you didn't understand when you were listening to them.
Sample answers for essay questions in the Writing paper	You can see *sample answers* after you've written your own. They've been written by real students, and will give you a good idea of what's expected. The essay you write will not be marked automatically. If you would like your teacher to mark it, you can print it off to give to them or email it to them. When they've marked it, you can enter the mark on your **Results** page. It does not matter if you do not enter a mark for the essay. The final marks will be adjusted to take that into account.
Useful phrases for the Speaking paper	You get sample Speaking papers and *Useful language* to help you practise offline. You can print the Speaking paper from the **My Tests** page, and ask your teacher to do the Speaking paper with you. As with the Writing paper, you can enter the mark your teacher gives you. However, even if you don't, your final marks will be adjusted to take that into account.
Results page	Remember this is a practice test not the real exam. You will see your score by paper and part and as a percentage. You will only get an indication as to whether your score is equivalent to a pass or not.
Try a sample test first	You can try out a short version of a practice test before you do a real one. This lets you find out how to use a test before you start.
Buy more practice tests	To get even more practice, you can buy more tests on oxfordenglishtesting.com